Leach Library

276 Mammoth Road

Londonderry, NH 03053

Adult Services 603-432-1132

Children's Services 603-432-1127

THE 100 GREATEST AMERICAN ATHLETES

THE 100 GREATEST AMERICAN ATHLETES

Martin Gitlin

ROWMAN & LITTLEFIELD
Lanham • Boulder • New York • London

Published by Rowman & Littlefield
An imprint of The Rowman & Littlefield Publishing Group, Inc.
4501 Forbes Boulevard, Suite 200, Lanham, Maryland 20706
www.rowman.com

Unit A, Whitacre Mews, 26-34 Stannary Street, London SE11 4AB

British Library Cataloguing in Publication Information Available

Library of Congress Cataloging-in-Publication Data

Names: Gitlin, Marty, author.
Title: The 100 greatest American athletes / Martin Gitlin.
Other titles: One hundred greatest American athletes
Description: Lanham, Maryland : Rowman & Littlefield, [2018] | Includes
   bibliographical references and index.
Identifiers: LCCN 2018013101 (print) | LCCN 2018019838 (ebook) | ISBN
   9781538110270 (ebook) | ISBN 9781538110263 (cloth : alk. paper)
Subjects: LCSH: Athletes—United States—Biography. | Athletes—Rating of. |
   Sports—United States—Anecdotes. | Sports—United States—History.
Classification: LCC GV697.A1 (ebook) | LCC GV697.A1 G494 2018 (print) |
   DDC 796.0922 [B] —dc23
LC record available at https://lccn.loc.gov/2018013101

CONTENTS

INTRODUCTION

The debates have raged around the living rooms and water coolers and bars across the United States. They are mostly friendly, sometimes heated. The opinions are generally subjective, with tinges of objectivity. The arguments revolve around the following question: Who are the greatest athletes in American history?

Discussions on this topic have been played out for generations but have intensified in more recent years as a greater number of worthy athletes have added fuel to the fire and the proliferation of televised sports has brought more awareness of their talents to a larger number of people. Average fans are no longer experts only on players from their hometown teams. Where once only the Game of the Week and postseason battles on national television provided opportunities to witness performances from athletes on other teams, now the internet offers previously unavailable information about athletic performances and achievements, and specialized networks allow viewers to watch the best of the best in sports such as tennis and golf. Such media attention provides an opportunity for fans to become more knowledgeable about athletes than ever before, and they can debate about who are the greatest with a higher level of expertise.

Some might claim that familiarity merely serves to muddy the waters. One can argue that the abundance of statistical ammunition used in the debate about the greatest American athletes of all time blurs their comparative credentials more than it separates them. After all, how do you compare an NBA player who shot 47 percent from the field in the 1990s with a baseball player who managed a plus-118 lifetime Wins Above Replacement (WAR) in the 1970s with a sprinter who ran a 10.3 in the 100 meters in the 1930s?

I get the whole apples and oranges thing. How do you compare a skier to a cornerback, a pitcher to a discus thrower, or a point guard to a tennis player? How do you contrast an athlete from the 1920s with one of today? How do you eliminate subjectivity in favor of objectivity?

The answer: very carefully and as scientifically as possible. The point system utilized in this book—albeit imperfect—works to remove the barriers between both eras and endeavors. It is weighted to benefit the most accomplished and rewards those deemed the finest pure athletes, but it also heavily weights the sport in which they participated. One simply cannot give golfers—in the most extreme example—the same consideration as basketball players. The athletic requirements of the former do not sit in the same ballpark as those of the latter. Those who rail against the ranking here of Jack Nicklaus, for instance, must understand that although he was a fine athlete, he was not required to utilize some of the specific athletic skills he possessed as he competed in his sport.

Several factors entered into these rankings. The first and most basic was that no athlete was eligible without having been tremendously accomplished. One might run like Jesse Owens and boast the leaping ability of Bob Beamon and the strength of Al Oerter, but could not be honored with inclusion in this book without having achieved greatness in his or her athletic endeavor. Great athletes must prove themselves on the field or on the court or on the slopes or in the pool. Multisport athletes received the highest consideration. Decathletes and versatile professional sports standouts such as Jim Thorpe, Deion Sanders, and Bo Jackson are ranked well here because of the athleticism and durability required of them. And only American-born athletes are included in this book, a requirement that certainly limited the number of hockey players. Opening up the rankings, for instance, to Chinese-born ping-pong players or Russian-born weightlifters would have made the task impossible. Even athletes who hold US citizenship but were born elsewhere, such as Martina Navratilova and Brett Hull, are not represented on these pages.

It also must be pointed out that every athlete in this book has been judged within the era in which he or she competed. One cannot compare the speed of Jesse Owens to that of Carl Lewis or the home run totals of Ty Cobb to those of Hank Aaron. The athletes included here have been ranked based on their dominance at the time of relevance.

Here is the point system (with a combined total of 100) used to rank the premier American athletes of all time and an explanation of each. Please keep in mind that each was judged more individually than how he or she contributed to team success. Athletes could be neither positively nor negatively affected by the strengths or weaknesses of their teammates or opponents, though some credit or debit was given to those who either contributed to or prevented each accomplishment.

- **Achievements: 35 possible points.** This was largely based on statistical data or factors such as medal counts and records established.
- **Athleticism: 25 possible points.** Many athletic attributes were considered here, including speed, quickness, upper and lower body strength, leaping ability, power, hand-eye coordination, conditioning, balance, durability, endurance, acceleration, coordination, and agility.
- **Athletic Requirements of the Sport and Position/Event/Division: 20 possible points.** This measures the number and level of athletic talents and skills necessary to thrive in the athlete's particular sport.
- **Clutch Factor/Mental and Emotional Toughness/Intangibles: 15 possible points.** How well did this athlete perform with games and championships on the line? Was he or she a good teammate? Did he or she perform with a high level of passion and intensity? Did off-the-field issues negatively affect his or her performance? These are questions that are answered and judged in this category.
- **Versatility: 5 possible points.** Athletes who participated in other sports at a competitive level or were athletically versatile within their own sports get bonus points here. Those who played at the major college or—especially—professional level in more than one sport receive a strong score here.

This is not a flawless system. The rankings in this book are destined to spur debate, and that is certainly welcome. I will receive some criticism for my methods and the resulting rankings. But it does take a bit of courage to go where no other author has gone. I will keep that in mind when the inevitable insults are being hurled in my direction. And I know one thing for sure: There are 100 incredible athletes listed in this book.

Oh, and one of them is a horse. Deal with it.

JIM THORPE: THE SPORTS CONQUEROR

Decathlon, Football, Baseball

Jim Thorpe. *Library of Congress*

The athletes of today run faster than Jim Thorpe. They jump higher. They gain more yards or hit the ball farther. But these rankings compare competitors to others from the same era. And no one in American history has ever achieved greater dominance as an all-around competitor than Jim Thorpe.

Thorpe is simply the most accomplished multisport athlete to ever grace a track or gridiron or diamond. Who, after all, could have claimed Olympic gold medal triumphs in the decathlon and pentathlon, a brilliant professional football career, *and* seven years in major-league baseball. Bo Jackson, eat your heart out. King Gustav V of Sweden once declared to Thorpe, "Sir, you are the greatest athlete in the world." In a historical sense, he's still right.[1]

James Francis Thorpe was born in a one-room cabin near Prague, Oklahoma, on May 28, 1887. His farmer dad had nothing in terms of notoriety on his mother, Charlotte Vieux, who was a Pottawatomi and a descendant of Chief Black Hawk, a prominent warrior and athlete. Thorpe was given the Pottawatomi name Wa-Tho-Huk, which is translated into English as "Bright Path." He quickly set out on one that others could only follow, but not match.

Thorpe was a student at the Carlisle Industrial Indian School in Pennsylvania. Though the institution was criticized for Americanizing

and proselytizing the Native Americans, it did provide practical training and allowed Thorpe to explore his athleticism and launch his career.
He thrived in track and football, earning first-team All-American status
in 1909 and 1910 on the gridiron under the tutelage of legendary coach
Glenn "Pop" Warner. Thorpe would soon become an international star.

His coming-out party was held in Stockholm, Sweden, site of the 1912
Summer Olympics. He trained aboard the ship that sailed to that European city, where he dominated the competition in both the decathlon
and pentathlon. His records would stand for decades. Never mind that
his gold medals were stripped when it was learned he had been paid for
playing two years of semipro baseball (later restored in 1982 by the International Olympic Committee); that he combined the two endeavors simply
strengthened his historical claim on the "greatest athlete of all time" status
later confirmed by his continued brilliance and versatility.[2]

More remarkable than his performance on the football field and baseball diamond was that he played both sports during the same period of his
life. Thorpe played for the New York Giants, the Cincinnati Reds, and the
Boston Braves from 1913 to 1919, batting a hefty .327 in his final season.
Meanwhile, he was a star with the football Canton Bulldogs from 1915 to
1920, helping to launch the National Football League in the process, and
remained a professional in that sport through 1928. He even earned a spot
on the All-Pro team in 1923 as a member of the Oorang Indians, a team of
Native Americans that he organized and coached.[3]

POINT TOTAL EXPLANATION

Achievements: 35/35

One can argue that Thorpe's accomplishments in baseball and football
were comparatively modest, though his numbers in the latter can be taken
with many grains of salt given that few statistics were kept during the
infancy of the NFL and his totals remain unknown. Suffice it to say he is
considered the finest football player to lace up a pair of sneakers before
World War I. His participation in other athletic endeavors minimized his
impact on the baseball field. His perfect score in this category is based
more on his Olympic dominance. Remarkably, he won four of the five
pentathlon events, taking third in the javelin, to easily snag the gold. He
nearly medaled in the high jump the next day. He then began a three-day

They Said It

He was the greatest athlete who ever lived. . . . What he had was natural ability. There wasn't anything he couldn't do. All he had to see is someone doin' something and he tried it . . . and he'd do it better.
—1912 Olympic silver medalist Abel Kiviat

Heartache does something to a man. . . . [M]any of the things I did would have been done differently . . . but I didn't know what I know now. No one ever told me . . . no one ever guided me . . . I just did things form day to day . . . hour to hour. . . . Sometimes I didn't know I was doing them.—Jim Thorpe

rampage in the decathlon, setting records that would have remained until 1926 had they not been struck from the books. He won the shot put, high jump, 110-meter hurdles, and 1500-meter run. He placed among the top five in every event in a display of versatility unmatched in Olympic history. His final total of 8412.955 was nearly 700 points more than what silver medalist and Swedish hero Hugo Wieslander earned.[4]

Athleticism: 25/25

Thorpe's Olympic feats, as well as his early feats on the football field, scream out perfect score here. Imagine an athlete so gifted and well-rounded that he could defeat all others in events that require such a variety of skills and talents. Thorpe proved his speed and leaping ability in the high jump and hurdles, his strength and agility in the shot put, and endurance in the 1500 meters—attributes he had already displayed on the gridiron as a running back. Though his achievements in football at Carlisle, where he peaked in that sport, remain a bit sketchy, those who watched him perform marveled at his dominance at many positions. That he added many years as a credible major-league baseball player merely adds a cherry atop the sundae.

Athletic Requirements of the Sport and Position: 20/20

Thorpe won gold medals in the decathlon and pentathlon, both of which test one's talents in arguably the most grueling competition known to the world of sports. Thriving in such events requires speed, quickness, strength, leaping ability, and endurance. And running back is perhaps the most physically challenging position on the football field. Thorpe earns all the points here as well.

Clutch Factor/Mental and Emotional Toughness/ Intangibles: 14/15

Though one can only speculate on the extent to which Thorpe's mental and emotional toughness contributed to his monumental athletic achievements, an athlete does not dominate both the Olympic decathlon and pentathlon without heaping portions of both. That he emerged from rather poor circumstances adds to his credentials in this category.

Versatility: 5/5

He blew everyone away in the Olympic decathlon and pentathlon, was ranked seventeenth by *Football Digest* among the hundred greatest players in the twentieth century, and played six seasons of major-league baseball. If Thorpe did not get five points here, nobody would.

TOTAL POINTS: 99

MICHAEL JORDAN: HIS AIRNESS

Basketball

Stroll into the room of a dozen sports-minded high school kids in America in the 1990s and you were likely to spot the same poster. It featured Michael Jordan defying the laws of gravity, sailing through the air, still several feet from the basket, en route to a thunderous dunk. The image encapsulated the difference between Jordan and every other athlete of his generation. His athleticism surpassed all others.

But it was not only his remarkable skills on the basketball court that made Jordan the greatest athlete in the modern era. His brilliance extended beyond the soars skyward, the ball fakes that resulted in downright silly reverse layups, and the footwork that stifled hapless opponents on the defensive end. Jordan also boasted supreme confidence, a justified cockiness that played perhaps the most significant role in his Chicago Bulls' six NBA championships. Jordan simply willed his team to victory.

He was simply on another level, particularly as a scorer and defender. Jordan led the league in scoring in ten consecutive full seasons from 1986 to 1998. The fourteen-time first-team all-star earned a spot on the All-Defensive team nine times. His player efficiency rating of 27.9 ranks number one in NBA history. Jordan is second in career points and fourth in steals. Few argue that he is the greatest basketball player to ever lace up a pair of sneakers.[1]

Jordan was born, but not bred, in Brooklyn. The youngest son of James and Delores, he was particularly close to the former and to his older hoop-standout brother Larry, whose lack of height doomed his basketball dreams. It is hard to imagine that the man eventually deemed basketball royalty with his nickname of "His Airness" was actually cut from his high

They Said It

I play to win, whether during practice or a real game. And I will not let anything get in the way of me and my competitive enthusiasm to win.
—Michael Jordan

I think he's God disguised as Michael Jordan.—Fellow NBA superstar Larry Bird

Once Michael gets up there, he says, "Well, maybe I'll just hang up here in the air for a while, just sit back." Then, all of a sudden, he says, "Well, maybe I'll 360. No, I changed my mind. I'll go up on the other side." He's just incredible.—Lakers Hall of Famer Magic Johnson

school team as a skinny 5-foot-11 sophomore. But a growth spurt, tireless work ethic, and athletic gifts combined to launch him to superstardom. He averaged nearly 27 points a game his senior season at Laney High School in Wilmington, North Carolina, to earn a scholarship to play for Dean Smith and the North Carolina Tar Heels.

Jordan established his penchant for heroics as a mere freshman. Despite playing alongside such future NBA stars as James Worthy and Sam Perkins, it was Jordan that nailed the 16-foot game-winner in the NCAA Finals. Jordan earned College Player of the Year honors as a sophomore and junior, yet was passed over by Houston and Portland in the first two picks of the 1984 NBA draft. The Rockets could be excused—they snagged future Hall of Famer Hakeem Olajuwon with the first overall pick—but the Blazers would be kicking themselves for years to come after taking fellow center Sam Bowie over Jordan.[2]

The rest is history. Jordan not only led the league in points scored as a rookie, he emerged by this third season as the finest player in the game. It took Jordan and the Bulls several years to raise themselves up to a championship level, but once they did, he proved himself to be easily the greatest clutch player ever.

He saved his best for last. His top-of-the-key jumper with five seconds remaining against host Utah in Game 6 of the 1998 NBA Finals clinched his sixth title. That Jordan won every title round in which he competed and was named the Most Valuable Player of each one bespeaks his brilliance.[3]

POINT TOTAL EXPLANATION

Achievements: 35/35

That the Bulls would have wallowed in mediocrity if not for Jordan is a given. The team featured a Robin to his Batman in Scottie Pippen, but no other premier talent. Simply put, Jordan was responsible for six NBA championships, not to mention his individual accomplishments such as annual scoring championships and even a Defensive Player of the Year award.[4]

Athleticism: 25/25

The athletic gifts and skills gained through practice and determination were unmatched among players from his generation—and arguably in the modern history of American sports. Jordan even boasted the hand-eye coordination to compete in Double-A baseball for a short time before returning to lead the Bulls to another title. Jordan not only boasted speed, quickness, and an awe-inspiring vertical leap, but his ability to contort his body to create space for open shots frustrated defenders and played a huge role in his offensive dominance.

Athletic Requirements of the Sport and Position: 18/20

Excellence in basketball requires greater athleticism than the other two major American sports, particularly due to the necessary endurance and constant movement, and there are no more taxing positions on the court than off-guard and small forward. That Jordan controlled the ball so often at those spots is a testament to his athleticism.

Clutch Factor/Mental and Emotional Toughness/ Intangibles: 15/15

Jordan's icy resolve and ability to raise the level of his performance when needed the most is legendary. His Airness delivered the dagger time and again, particularly in the postseason. If Jordan did not earn 15 points in this category, nobody should.

Versatility: 5/5

Jordan played baseball well enough to excel at the high school level, took a decade off, then became a viable minor-league player with virtually no practice time. He also played football in high school.[5]

TOTAL POINTS: 98

BOB MATHIAS: THE MANCHILD

Decathlon

Bob Mathias was anemic as a child. The problem became so acute that a doctor prescribed liver and iron pills, as well as a daily nap. One could hardly have imagined then that he would grow into arguably the greatest decathlete of all time.

Mathias became the youngest Olympic track-and-field champion ever when he beat the competition at age seventeen in the 1948 London Games. Not bad for a onetime anemic who had never even heard of the decathlon three months earlier. Though Mathias tossed the shot put and discus in high school, his coach—who was quite aware of the young man's all-around athleticism—suggested he compete in a decathlon meet in Los Angeles. Mathias won that to qualify for the national championships, where he upset three-time champion Irving Mondschein in that event to earn a spot on the US Olympic Team.[1]

At the Olympic Games, Mathias displayed his athletic brilliance and versatility by winning the discus and placing second in the pole vault, third in the 100 meters, and second in the 1500 meters. Most impressive was his performance in severely adverse conditions: These feats were achieved in heavy winds and on slippery surfaces. Mathias wrapped himself in a blanket during the second day of the decathlon to keep warm and dry. It became so dark for the javelin throw that cars were driven into Wembley Stadium so that their headlights could be used to allow officials and athletes to see the foul lines.

When he arrived home, the teen, who won the Sullivan Award as the nation's finest amateur athlete, was welcomed by President Harry Truman and received more than two hundred marriage proposals. The whirlwind of activity motivated Mathias to vow that he would not again compete in

> ### *They Said It*
>
> *He is not only the greatest athlete in the world, but he's also the greatest competitor.*—University of California track coach Brutus Hamilton
>
> *I have always believed that everyone has the potential to do something extraordinary if they're guided and helped along the way.*—Bob Mathias

the Olympics "in a million years," but he went back on his word. He proved even more dominant and wide-ranging in the 1952 Helsinki Games, taking first in the shot put, 400 meters, discus, and javelin while placing second in the 100 meters and third in the high jump.[2]

Mathias was raised in a California farming community in the San Joaquin Valley. The prescribed treatments for anemia certainly helped—he grew into a strapping 6-foot-2, 190 pounds in high school, where he averaged 18 points a game for the basketball team and a whopping 9 yards per carry as a football running back. His achievements in those sports paled in comparison to his accomplishments in track and field, where he won state championships in both the shot put and discus.

By age twenty-two, Mathias had retired with nine victories in nine competitions, three world records, four US championships, and two Olympic gold medals. He had become so legendary that a movie was made about his life even though he was just twenty-three years old. The leading role was played by none other than Bob Mathias, who would later serve four terms in Congress.[3]

POINT TOTAL EXPLANATION

Achievements: 34/35

Mathias packed a lifetime's worth of athletic achievements into far less than a decade, but those accomplishments are certainly worthy of nearly every point available in this category. He was the first of two Olympians to twice win the decathlon (Daley Thompson of Britain would achieve this in 1980 and 1984). He was among the greatest three-sport stars in California prep history and proved remarkably versatile in his Olympic efforts. His dedication and athletic talent allowed him to thrive in events with which was previously unfamiliar.

Athleticism: 25/25

No two-time decathlon champion who performed so well in the speed and field events can be denied a point here. Mathias displayed the speed, balance, and leg strength to thrive in the sprints and hurdles, as well as the power and agility to prove himself as one of the greatest field event athletes of all time. He even placed near the top in the pole vault, which requires wide-ranging athletic skills usually gained through years of practice, but which Mathias mastered in comparatively little time.

Athletic Requirements of the Sport: 20/20

Decathletes must be well-rounded to qualify for the Olympics, but their athletic gifts need to go beyond that to win gold. Some events require speed and quickness. Others require agility and leg strength. Others require endurance. Still others require sheer power. Mathias needed all of these athletic traits to win two gold medals in the decathlon.

Clutch Factor/Mental and Emotional Toughness/ Intangibles: 14/15

Mathias's work ethic and training were legendary. He simply outworked his competition, developing skills in events with which he had no previous experience at a painfully young age. The mental and emotional toughness required to go from a young man who had never even heard of the decathlon to one who earned Olympic gold in the event just a few months later cannot be underappreciated.[4]

Versatility: 5/5

The career of Bob Mathias was all about versatility—and greatness. He starred in basketball and football as well as track and field, and his athletic versatility was on display every time he won another decathlon championship or gold medal.

TOTAL POINTS: 98

4

JIM BROWN:
THE INDESTRUCTIBLE

Football

The hapless defenders who tried—most often in vain—to tackle Jim Brown solo felt like they had been hit by a Mack truck. They recall even in their old age the scenario surrounding most Brown efforts during his NFL career from 1957 to 1965. He would drag one or two defenders along. They would merely slow him down until more help arrived, as gang tackling was the only way to bring him to the ground. Brown would then rise slowly, methodically, and with great effort. He would shuffle back to the huddle, line up, take the handoff as if shot out of a cannon, and wreak havoc all over again.

Every defensive player knew Brown was going to get the ball. They keyed in on him. No running back in the history of football has received that level of attention and focus. But it didn't matter. Down the road at Ohio State, legendary Buckeyes coach Woody Hayes touted his "three yards and a cloud of dust" philosophy. With Jim Brown, it was at least five yards and a lot of bruised tacklers. Brown has been historically defined as a power back, but—like fellow Cleveland superstar LeBron James, who would hit the scene about a half century later—Brown boasted a combination of speed and strength that made him easily the best player of his generation and arguably of all time.

James Nathaniel Brown was born on February 17, 1936, in St. Simons, Georgia, but made his athletic mark at the high school level in Manhasset, New York, where he averaged an absurd 15 yards per carry in his junior and senior seasons combined, despite opposing linebackers and safeties tracking his every move. He then landed a scholarship at Syracuse University, where he averaged 5.9 yards per carry as a sophomore and earned

All-America status after rushing for 986 yards and thirteen touchdowns as a senior.[1]

The Cleveland Browns snagged Brown with the sixth pick in the 1957 draft. Brown, however, had grown into far more than just a football player. He embraced the civil rights and burgeoning black pride movements of the era and stated his belief that NFL owners preferred "nice guy blacks, humble blacks, just-glad-to-be-there blacks"[2] rather than strong-willed African American athletes. Brown did not allow his feelings to deter him from making an immediate impact as easily the finest running back in NFL history. Only in the early 1960s did friction with his coach begin to negatively affect his performance.

In 1957 he led the NFL with 942 yards and nine touchdowns, earning Rookie of the Year and Most Valuable Player honors. He had transformed a Cleveland team that was coming off its first losing season into one that landed in the NFL championship game. But Brown was merely scratching the surface. He exploded for 1,527 yards in 1958, shattering the NFL record by a ridiculous 400 yards, and was again named MVP. He scored fourteen touchdowns the next season, including five against the defending league champion Baltimore Colts.[3]

Contract disputes and a deteriorating relationship with his coach did not prevent Brown from maintaining his status as the most destructive offensive player in football. He tied an NFL record with a 237-yard performance against Philadelphia in the 1960 season, during which he led the league in rushing yards for the fourth straight time. Brown led a revolt that got coach Paul Brown fired after the 1962 season; he was replaced with the well-liked Blanton Collier. A happy and motivated Brown ran wild in 1963, breaking his own marks with 1,863 yards on the ground and setting a new one with 6.4 yards per carry while earning his third MVP award.[4]

Brown led Cleveland to the NFL championship in 1964 and paced the league in rushing for the eighth time in nine years in 1965. He finished his career with 12,312 yards and would have broken records that might have still stood today had he not cut his career short while still in its prime to pursue an acting career.

Those who sought to defend Brown maintain their conviction that he was not merely the greatest running back ever, but the best by far. Others have broken his career marks, but none has earned a reputation as a force anywhere close to that of Jim Brown.

> ### *They Said It*
>
> *Jim Brown really represented achievement for the black community. And he was so good that it didn't matter what color they were; they had to acknowledge him as the best in his field. And that meant a lot to black Americans in the 60s, when everything that any black person achieved was questioned as to whether it was significant.*—Basketball superstar Kareem Abdul-Jabbar
>
> *Jim Brown was a combination of speed and power like nobody who has ever played this game. You just didn't know if you were going to get a big collision or be grabbing at his shoelaces.*—NFL cornerback and coach Dick LeBeau

POINT TOTAL EXPLANATION

Achievements: 34/35

Brown not only led the NFL in rushing eight out of nine years, but he was considered quite possibly the greatest lacrosse player of his generation while at Syracuse University. He nearly doubled the career rushing yardage leader in NFL history by the time he retired. The only potential minor drawback is that Brown only helped his team win one league crown, but that must be taken with many grains of salt given that any team requires contributions from twenty-one other starting players and some reserves. Running backs are greatly dependent on blockers opening holes. No football player is a one-man team.

Athleticism: 25/25

The athleticism Brown possessed was unheard of in the NFL of his generation. His combination of power, speed, and quickness had never been encountered by defenders. He would elude speedy defensive backs on one play, then drag a lineman and two linebackers into the end zone on the next. Brown was particularly deadly on the sweep, where he could gather a head of steam, read the defense, then utilize his strength to overwhelm potential tacklers, quickness to evade them, or speed to simply outrun them. Brown was even adept at catching passes out of the backfield, though he was not called upon as often as many premier backs today. If so utilized, given his open-field skills, he would have been devastating.

Athletic Requirements of the Sport and Position: 18/20

No position on the football field is more athletically challenging than running back. Brown often rushed twenty-five to thirty times per game and was called upon to block and sometimes catch passes. Backs are involved in every play, and Brown rarely left the field. The position requires physical attributes not a necessity to those playing other spots, such as linemen, quarterbacks, and even wide receivers. It can be argued that the only comparable position in requiring such wide-ranging athleticism to thrive is linebacker.

Clutch Factor/Mental and Emotional Toughness/ Intangibles: 14/15

Brown's mental and emotional strength cannot be denied, considering he was the focus of defensive attention on nearly every play. He performed well from the first to the last game of his brilliant career, but no better or worse on the biggest stages, which accounts for his score in this category.

Versatility: 5/5

Brown was not only a tremendous lacrosse player, but he starred in track and baseball as well in high school. He threw two no-hitters to attract the attention of the New York Yankees but rejected a minor-league offer. He took up golf one year, practiced tirelessly, and soon shot a 77. Everything Brown touched turned to gold.[5]

POINT TOTAL: 96

5

MICHAEL PHELPS: THE BALTIMORE BULLET

Swimming

Michael Phelps. © Rob Schumacher—USA TODAY Sports

Few people who watched the Summer Olympics after the turn of the new millennium wondered, when the gun sounded, if Michael Phelps was about to win a gold medal; they only conjectured how much sooner he would complete the race than the second-place finisher and whether the silver medalist would be in the same picture on the television screen when Phelps touched the side of the pool to signal yet another triumph.

Phelps spent more time on the top step of the victory stand than any other athlete in history. The most decorated Olympian ever won twenty-eight medals, including a mind-boggling twenty-three gold. It mattered not if it was the butterfly, individual medleys, or the 100- and 200-meter freestyle. Phelps destroyed the competition in all of them. He also anchored the American relay teams, the most dominant quartets in the history of the sport.[1]

This story of greatness began when Phelps was born on June 30, 1985, in Towson, Maryland. It hit an early crossroads when Phelps expressed fear of putting his face in the water. He also struggled with attention deficit hyperactivity disorder (ADHD) in school, but he eventually overcame both issues. His ADHD was least evident when he swam, and his talents quickly rose to the surface. Phelps became so accomplished that he earned a spot on the US Olympic Team at age fifteen, placing fifth in the 200-meter butterfly at the 2000 Summer Games in Australia. He shattered the world record in that event at age sixteen the next year in the World Championship Trials. Phelps broke it again later in 2001 at the World Championships in Japan.

The rest is history. Though Phelps dominated off-year competitions such as the 2007, 2009, and 2011 International Swimming Federation championships, such events did not capture the attention of the world as the Olympics did. Phelps saved his best efforts for the Olympic Games, overshadowing such American greats of the past as Mark Spitz as well as contemporaries such as Ian Thorpe and Ryan Lochte.

Phelps began his blitz at the 2004 Summer Olympics in Greece focusing on his shorter-distance specialties. He won four individual gold medals— two in the butterfly and two medleys. He also helped American relay teams earn two other first-place finishes.

He reached his peak in 2008 in Beijing, China, capturing nothing but gold in every individual and team event. He won the 200-meter freestyle after managing only a bronze in 2004. He again won both butterfly and individual medley races, touching in more than two seconds ahead of second-place finisher Laszlo Cseh of Hungary in both the individual medley events.

Phelps hit his goal of becoming the most medaled Olympian of all time in 2012. He planned to make the London Games his last. After losing to Lochte in the 400 individual medley, he earned six more gold medals: two in the relays and four more in butterfly and shorter individual medleys. He left England with twenty-two career Olympic medals, three more than Russian gymnast Larissa Latynina. Phelps then retired with six long-course world records.

His retirement lasted less than two years. Phelps finished a close second to Lochte in his first race back, the 100-meter butterfly at the Arena Grand Prix in Arizona. He eventually set his sights on the 2016 Summer Olympics in Rio de Janeiro. Phelps participated in only three individual events, winning the gold in the 200-meter butterfly and 200-meter individual medley, but helped the Americans top the field in three relays.[2]

Phelps announced his second retirement two days later on the morning talk show *Today*: "This time I mean it," he said. His swimming competition around the world certainly hoped so.[3]

They Said It

I feel most at home in the water. I disappear. That's where I belong.
—Michael Phelps

It doesn't matter if he's got one, 19 or 23 gold medals, he doesn't think like that. He thinks like he's trying to win his first medal. He has a competitive switch you only see in very few people. Michael Jordan had it . . . that killer instinct.—Swimming writer John Lohn

POINT TOTAL EXPLANATION

Achievements: 35/35

Phelps reached the pinnacle of success not only as a swimmer, but as an Olympic athlete. Winning more gold medals in the history of the ultimate international competition, which spans well over a century, represents one of the greatest athletic accomplishments ever. That he participated in five Summer Games, earned a spot on the US team at age fifteen, and continued dominating and winning gold medals after an announced retirement simply adds to his legend. There is one Olympic athlete here that deserves all 35 points in this category, and that is Michael Phelps.

Athleticism: 25/25

It takes tremendous timing, strength, coordination, and endurance to win any gold medal in swimming. To win twenty-three requires incredible athleticism. The high level of dedication and amount of practice required of Phelps to reach and maintain gold medal dominance should not be underestimated. Phelps thrived in not just one event but several, including the butterfly, freestyle, and individual medley. He participated in the maximum number of events allowed of Olympians, including relays that resulted in American gold greatly because of him.

Athletic Requirements of the Sport and Events: 18/20

Swimming is not a daily competition; Phelps participated in a limited number of events leading up to the World Championships, Olympic Trials, and Olympic Games. But it is a daily grind. The butterfly is particularly grueling and exhausting, particularly the 200 meter. It can be argued that short-distance swimmers are better athletes than sprinters. They both go full tilt in short bursts, but swimmers must maximize the use of every body part for longer periods of time against water resistance.

Clutch Factor/Mental and Emotional Toughness/ Intangibles: 15/15

There is no more pressure-packed event in sports than the Olympics. The fate of the American swim team and the eyes of the world were on Phelps every time he leaned over the side of the pool to mentally, emotionally, and physically prepare for a race. Winning an Olympic record twenty-three gold and twenty-eight total medals under those circumstances warrants a full point total here.

Versatility: 3/5

In this case, versatility is judged not by how many other sports Phelps participated in during his lifetime, but rather the array of events in which he thrived. Most gold medal swimmers excel to that level in one event, but Phelps dominated in both the butterfly and individual medley while turning possible silver or bronze medals into gold for the relay teams. He was also adept at longer distances, but Olympic event limits prevented him from displaying those talents.

TOTAL POINTS: 96

6

DEION SANDERS: PRIME TIME

Football, Baseball

Deion Sanders promoted himself with a cockiness and braggadocio that annoyed both peers and fans. Many who have exhibited such brashness throughout sports history could not back up their words with deeds. Sanders wasn't among them.

Some consider Sanders the greatest cornerback in NFL history. None other than Jerry Rice once admitted that he lost sleep knowing a matchup against Sanders was on the horizon. But his brilliance was not limited to sticking to receivers like glue. His brilliance was not even limited to football. The only factor that prevented Sanders from starring in major-league baseball was scheduling; he could not appear on the gridiron and the diamond simultaneously, so he waited until the football season ended to turn doubles into triples with his sprinter speed.

Sanders spent time with the Atlanta Falcons, San Francisco 49ers, Dallas Cowboys, Washington Redskins, and Baltimore Ravens. He became the first player to ever score a touchdown in every way possible. He specialized in taking interceptions to the house for pick-sixes, and he also scored on punt and kickoff returns, fumble recoveries, receptions, and rushes. But his specialty was covering and frustrating receivers.[1]

The six-time All-Pro, eight-time Pro Bowler, and 1994 NFL Defensive Player of the Year landed in the Pro Football Hall of Fame in 2011. He recorded 53 career interceptions despite playing time limited by his baseball career. Sanders was also among the most feared kick returns in the history of the sport and often doubled as a wide receiver nearly a half century after the utilization of two-way players had been swept into the dustbin of football history.

They Said It

They don't pay nobody to be humble. Some people will come out to see me do well. Some people will come out to see me get run over. But love me or hate me, they're going to come out.—Deion Sanders

Deion gets up to the line and runs his first 40 and everyone has him at 4.3. We figured he was done. He gets up and runs another one, and he runs even faster. Some people had him at 4.25. And the funniest damn thing about it was he finishes the 40, continues to run, waves to everybody, goes right through the tunnel and we don't see him again. We all got up and gave him a standing ovation.—Buffalo Bills scout Dave Gettleman on Sanders's performance at the NFL combine

You can't jump around and get excited and go crazy in baseball. Nobody ever masters that game.—Deion Sanders

Then there was baseball. Sanders played for the New York Yankees, Atlanta Braves, Cincinnati Reds, and San Francisco Giants. His time on the football field prevented him from recording more than 465 at-bats in any season, but he certainly made his mark. He led the National League in triples, with 14 in 1992 despite playing in just 97 games. He batted between .268 and .304 each year from 1992 to 1995. He proved his worth in his only near-full season in 1997, when he stole 56 bases for Cincinnati.[2]

The man they called Neon Deion—for his embracing of the spotlight and unabashed confidence—was born on August 9, 1967, in Fort Myers, Florida. He was playing organized baseball and football by age eight. Sanders played cornerback and quarterback at North Fort Myers High School and was all-state in football, baseball, and basketball. He dropped the latter at Florida State, joining the Seminoles' track and field team instead.

Sanders helped the track team win a conference championship and specialized in stealing bases for the Florida State nine. But it was his football talent that inspired the most attention. He earned consensus All-American status, won the Jim Thorpe Award in 1988, recorded 14 career interceptions, and played a significant role in a Sugar Bowl victory in 1988. He led the nation in punt return average that year. It was no wonder that Florida State retired his jersey in 1995. It was also no wonder that he was selected fifth overall by the Falcons in the 1989 NFL draft.[3]

POINT TOTAL EXPLANATION

Achievements: 34/35

Though the claim that Sanders is the greatest cornerback ever is certainly a subjective one, it is widely accepted. He was a good baseball player, not a great one, but the mere fact that he sustained a viable major-league career while doubling as an All-Pro defensive back is incredible. He did not often lead the NFL in any category, but there are no statistics that accurately rank the stickiness of cornerbacks. And Sanders was at least the best in coverage from his generation.

Athleticism: 23/25

All that Sanders lacked was pure power—he slugged few home runs during an era of major-league baseball in which even weak hitters were regularly blasting them out of the park. But the rest? You name it—Sanders had it. He was blurry fast, and his quickness, balance, and agility as a cornerback and return man are legendary.

Athletic Requirements of the Sport and Position: 19/20

The durability required from Sanders to play two sports extensively for a decade results in nearly a perfect score in this category. Cornerback is among the most athletically challenging positions on the football field, while outfielders and base stealers such as Sanders need speed and quickness to succeed.

Clutch Factor/Mental and Emotional Toughness/ Intangibles: 15/15

Sanders performed his best with the most at stake. He intercepted five passes and recovered a fumble in his first ten NFL playoff games and batted .533 with five stolen bases in his only extensive postseason baseball series. His tremendous confidence, a necessary ingredient for any cornerback, translated into far more success than failure. Sanders's undying self-assurance resulted in his establishing himself as one of the greatest players in NFL history.[4]

Versatility: 5/5

Sanders was arguably the finest defensive back ever, a major-leaguer, and a college track standout. What else is there? If Sanders doesn't deserve every point available here, who does?

TOTAL POINTS: 96

7

LEBRON JAMES: THE CHOSEN ONE

Basketball

LeBron James. © Ken Blaze—*USA TODAY Sports*

To find fault with LeBron James on the basketball court is to nitpick. He struggles at times with his foul shots. It took him years to upgrade his outside jumper from acceptable to deadly. Aside from those details, he is a flawless player. Not only is James perhaps the most gifted player in NBA history, but his work ethic, unselfishness, motivation, and innate sense on the court can hardly be believed by his contemporaries.

Playing against James is akin to competing against Bobby Fischer, especially when passing the ball. He is one or two moves ahead of the game. He always knows where his teammates and the opposing players are going to be. And his passes are perfect.

Northeast Ohio knew about James by the eighth grade. Whispers about a kid born and raised in the inner city of Akron with otherworldly talents began to circulate around the area. Soon he was on the cover of *Sports Illustrated*, the most celebrated American high school athlete of all time. He had overcome the lack of an active father in his life to emerge as a dedicated, straight-and-narrow teen with the ability even as a junior in high school to compete at the highest level. That James was destined to be the number-one pick in the draft after his senior year when the NBA still allowed high school players to skip the college game completely was a foregone conclusion.

The struggling hometown Cleveland Cavaliers tanked the 2002–2003 season to maximize their opportunity to land James, and they indeed lucked into the top selection. Their choice of James was as surprising as the sun rising in the east. He almost immediately transformed the woebegone franchise into a playoff contender, eventually turning it into the best regular-season team in the NBA. His spellbinding performance in Game 5 of the 2007 Eastern Conference Finals in Detroit—in which he scored 28 of the last 29 Cleveland points to will the team to victory and set it up for its first NBA Finals berth—remains among the most legendary performances in basketball history.

But the Cavaliers could not supply James with enough surrounding talent to win a title. He burned his bridges in a highly publicized and regrettable event called "The Decision" on ESPN in 2010, where he announced he was joining fellow superstars Dwyane Wade and Chris Bosh in Miami. At the peak of his game, James won two NBA championships in four seasons with the Heat.

But his reputation had suffered. Though James tried to explain that he left home not just with the intention of snagging a title, but with the same mind-set as a college kid yearning to explore, he apologized for the way he left Cleveland and announced in 2014 that he was returning home to try to lead the Cavaliers to their first championship since they entered the league in 1970. James nearly did just that in his first season back, guiding the team into the NBA Finals against Golden State. Despite the loss of premier teammates Kyrie Irving and Kevin Love to injuries, James won two games in the series with virtually no help before succumbing to the superior foe. Many believed the fact that James did not win Finals Most Valuable Player honors was a travesty, but it mattered little to him. He stated categorically that he did not want it if his team did not win.

A return to health of Irving and Love allowed James to maximize his vast array of talents as the Cavaliers swept into the title round against Golden State again in 2016, then became the first team in league history to rebound from a 3–1 series deficit to capture the crown. Among the most memorable plays was a chase-down block of an Andre Iguodala layup with the taut and nerve-racking Game 7 tied and two minutes remaining. And

> ### They Said It
>
> *He's arguably the best athlete that any of us have ever seen in terms of size and speed and strength. I mean, he's a force.*—Golden State Warriors coach Steve Kerr
>
> *All your life you are told the things you cannot do. All your life they will say you're not good enough or strong enough or talented enough. They will say you're the wrong height or the wrong weight or the wrong type to play this or be this or achieve this. They will tell you no. A thousand times no. Until all the no's become meaningless. All your life they will tell you no. Quite firmly and very quickly. And you will tell them yes.*
> —LeBron James

when it was over—after James had this time won the MVP he had so richly deserved a year earlier—he dropped to his knees and sobbed with joy. He had achieved his goal of leading his hometown team to the title.

There would be much more to accomplish. James appeared on target to become the league's all-time leading scorer. He was rising toward the top in many career statistical categories. He yearned to win more championships. It seemed likely that he could achieve whatever he set his will and mind to.

POINT TOTAL EXPLANATION

Achievements: 34/35

The only lost point here is because, unlike Michael Jordan, James has lost more Finals than he has won. But the fact that he led his teams to seven consecutive title-round appearances since leaving for Miami—and eight overall—is remarkable and speaks to his overwhelming physical and emotional influence. He is among the league leaders in nearly every career statistical category.

Athleticism: 25/25

James is listed as 6-foot-8, 240 pounds, but some estimate another inch and 20 more pounds. His muscular physique simply overpowers hapless defenders near the basket, but what is most remarkable about him, given his size, is his quickness and mobility. James can outmaneuver opponents from the perimeter in drives to the hoop or on the block with quick-steps that lead to easy layups despite tight coverage. Though Jordan is considered by most to be the most athletic basketball superstar in history, his combination of strength and quickness certainly puts James in the conversation.

Athletic Requirements of the Sport and Position: 19/20

James likes to say he plays every position. That is not far from the truth. He has guarded smaller centers, performs brilliantly as a point guard, defends burly power forwards on post-ups, and is peerless among those in his generation as an off-guard or small forward. That James has excelled at every position on the court, both offensively and defensively, makes him the only basketball player on the list to earn a perfect score in this category.

Clutch Factor/Mental and Emotional Toughness/ Intangibles: 13/15

Those comparing the greatest players in NBA history will claim that this category marks the biggest difference between the wildly clutch Jordan and James, who has risen to the occasion with the big shot in pressure situations less frequently. He has also at times allowed his teams to sink into a morass. One must consider that James has built his game on a team-oriented mind-set that does not always result in individual success. Jordan, on the other hand, was an assassin in both mind and body with games on the line. That James led earlier Cavaliers teams with little other talent to greatness speaks volumes about his mental and emotional resolve. He's no Jordan as a clutch performer—but then, who is?

Versatility: 4/5

James was a sensational high school wide receiver and very likely could have excelled as a tight end in the NFL. His brilliance on the gridiron earned him first-team all-state honors at Akron St. Vincent-St. Mary and showed his diverse athletic ability. Add his versatility on the basketball court and the result here is a near-perfect score.

TOTAL POINTS: 95

JACKIE JOYNER-KERSEE: MAGNIFICENT HEPTATHLETE

Track and Field

Jackie Joyner-Kersee. © Darr Beiser—USA TODAY Sports

Jackie Joyner-Kersee required no other heptathlete to set records for her to break. She just kept breaking her own. It is no wonder she is considered by many the greatest female athlete in American history.

Joyner-Kersee was indeed in a league by herself in the seven-event test of endurance, versatility, and athleticism. She became the first woman to shatter the 7,000-point mark by scoring 7,148 at the 1986 Goodwill Games, but she was merely warming up. She destroyed that mark with 7,161 later that year in Houston, then again with 7,215 in the scorching heat of Indianapolis at the 1988 Olympic Trials, then yet again by securing Olympic gold months later with 7,291. That total remains unsurpassed at the greatest feat in heptathlon history.[1]

Born in East St. Louis, Missouri, during the Kennedy administration on March 3, 1962, she was named Jacqueline after the First Lady because her paternal grandmother believed she would then be destined for greatness. Her grandmother was indeed prophetic. Joyner-Kersee began training and competing in track and field at age ten, in an era in which women's sports received little attention. Though some perceived female athletes as unfeminine, she proclaimed her view of them as beautiful, elegant, and graceful.[2]

She won four consecutive junior pentathlon championships starting at age fourteen, but also excelled in high school at volleyball and led her basketball team to a state title. She landed a basketball scholarship at the University of California, Los Angeles (UCLA), then dropped that sport after emerging as one of the greatest college track and field standouts ever. Joyner-Kersee twice earned the Broderick Cup as the most outstanding track athlete in the country.[3]

Joyner-Kersee gained momentum in her career by earning the silver medal in the heptathlon at the 1984 Summer Games, then proceeded to win gold in both the long jump and heptathlon at the 1988 Olympics in Seoul, South Korea. Her dominance in the latter included first-place finishes in the 100-meter hurdles, 200 meters, long jump, and high jump as well as, astoundingly, a second in the shot put. She placed no worse than fifth in any event in one of the most dominant performances in Olympic history. She had peaked, but she remained strong enough to capture gold in the heptathlon at the 1992 Games in Barcelona.

Her greatness was evident not only in Olympic competition. Joyner-Kersee won four gold medals at the World Outdoor Championships and earned the national crown in long jump nine times and in heptathlon eight times. Most amazing is that her records have stood the test of time and the brilliance of other athletes. Her world record in the heptathlon and long jump remained standing for three decades, through 2017, while her

---

They Said It

Age is no barrier. It's a limitation you put on your mind.—Jackie Joyner-Kersee

This gifted athlete and this brilliant young coach have done the same thing the Cubists did in art. They've taken their set of abstractions run them through their own process, established a world record in the heptathlon and given us a new athletic form.—Former Olympic coach and Stanford University track and field director Brooks Johnson

American indoor marks in the long jump (7.13 meters), 50-meter hurdles (5.57), and 55-meter hurdles (7.37) have been current for at least twenty-two years.

While other Olympic gold medalists her age were simply enjoying their memories, Joyner-Kersee continued to thrive. She won the gold medal in the heptathlon at the 1998 Goodwill Games at the age of thirty-six, retired briefly, then returned to nearly earn a spot on the US Olympic team in 2000.[4]

POINT TOTAL EXPLANATION

Achievements: 34/35

Others have won more Olympic gold, but the feat of dominating the record books twenty to thirty years later in the mentally, emotionally, and physically demanding heptathlon cannot be diminished. That Joyner-Kersee also earned a spot on the top step of the victory stand in the long jump is incredible. She won medals in three Olympic games and participated in four (nearly five), a remarkable achievement for a track and field athlete. She deserves nearly all the points in this category.

Athleticism: 24/25

Joyner-Kersee's dominance in such wide-ranging and physically tough competitions proves her athleticism. Winning events such as the long jump, hurdles, sprints, and high jump against the best in the world is amazing enough, but placing second among her fellow heptathletes while displaying her strength in the shot put is even more remarkable. Joyner-Kersee proved her speed, quickness, agility, and power in the Olympics and beyond.

Athletic Requirements of the Sport: 19/20

Joyner-Kersee competed at the highest level for almost two decades in the seven-event heptathlon. Every one of the events is athletically demanding, though the lack of physical contact costs her one point. Throw in the athletic challenges of her significant hoops career, which included a short stint in the American Basketball League, and one cannot deny her almost all the points available here.

Clutch Factor/Mental and Emotional Toughness/ Intangibles: 14/15

Joyner-Kersee generally rose to the occasion with the eyes of the world upon her. She maximized her opportunities in the Olympics and in lesser competitions. That she won only one gold medal aside from the heptathlon cost her a perfect score.

Versatility: 4/5

Landing a basketball scholarship at UCLA before discovering she was better at track and field? Establishing world records in the heptathlon? It all speaks to her versatility.

TOTAL POINTS: 95

RAFER JOHNSON: RENAISSANCE MAN

Decathlon

The decathlon is not a battle for victories. It is a test of talents and wills. It is the pursuit of gold medals by attrition. The athlete who performs well in the most events generally finds himself on the top step of the platform. And at the Rome Olympics in 1960, that man was Rafer Johnson.

Johnson, who had earned a silver in the Melbourne Games four years earlier, finished among the top five in nine out of ten decathlon events in Italy. In a tremendous show of versatility, he won the shot put and placed second in the long jump; third in the 100 meters, 400 meters, high jump, pole vault, javelin, and discus; and fifth in the 110-meter high hurdles. So distance running wasn't his strong suit—he finished fifteenth in the 1500-meter run. But his overall performance established an Olympic record and topped the field, just ahead of Yang Chuan-kwang of China, who won five events and became a lifelong friend.[1]

The discrepancy in event victories proves the value of depth of talent. Johnson had followed a similar path to the silver medal in Melbourne, placing no worse than sixth in all but one event. It proved to be the only time he did not win a decathlon in which he participated. That he could win the long jump that year and the shot put in 1960 speaks volumes about his depth as an Olympic athlete. He might have won the individual long jump in 1956 had an injury not forced him to withdraw. But Johnson had already proven himself by the time he reached Australia, capturing the decathlon at the 1955 Pan American Games, where he set the first of three world records. He won the Amateur Athetic Union (AAU) decathlon in 1956, 1958, and 1960.[2]

Johnson had come a long way from an impoverished early childhood. He was born on August 18, 1935, in a tiny Texas town, where he lived in a shack with no indoor plumbing or electricity. Yearning to make a better life, in 1944 his father, Lewis Johnson, he moved the family out of the segregated state to Kingsburg, California, where they were the only black family in town. The elder Johnson had good intentions, but his alcoholism and the violence it inspired resulted in beatings for his son, who took blame even for incidents he did not cause so he could take thrashings for his brothers. He realized that he could endure pain, a trait that would serve him well in the ultimate physically strenuous Olympic event that is the decathlon.

The younger Johnson did not simply survive—he thrived. He was elected class present in both junior and senior high, a remarkable achievement given the racism of the times. He was greatly admired for his character and the traits that would carry him far beyond the athletic fields later in life. Further inspiration occurred at age sixteen, in 1952, when track coach Murl Dotson drove him to the hometown of hero Bob Mathias. Johnson had shown some promise in track and field, but it was this experience that convinced him that he could be a great decathlete. Mathias, after all, had always espoused the philosophy that kids should work to be the best they could be. This would become Johnson's life mantra; his 1999 autobiography was titled *The Best That I Can Be*.

Johnson used the inspiration to become an incredible athlete. He was offered a football scholarship to UCLA but declined it to focus on track and field. He played briefly for John Wooden and the Bruins basketball team and captained the school's track squad. He was also named student body president.[3]

Johnson did not fade into obscurity after retirement in 1960. He became an actor, sportscaster, and activist. It was Johnson who helped wrestle the gun away from Robert Kennedy's assassin, Sirhan Sirhan, on that fateful and tragic night in Los Angeles in 1968, and he was chosen to light the Olympic flame at the opening ceremonies of the 1984 Games in that city. He also aided in the creation of the California Special Olympics.

POINT TOTAL EXPLANATION

Achievements: 33/35

Johnson was not quite as dominant as other decathlon gold medalists and managed just a silver at Melbourne, but that falls into the category of nit-picking. The 1956 Games proved to be his lone decathlon defeat—and a minor one at that. That he also excelled in football and basketball must be credited here as well.

Athleticism: 24/25

Johnson's score here is a reflection more on his athletic depth than on his brilliance in any one area. He might not have boasted the talent to win gold in an individual event, but his all-around talent cannot be underrated. He boasted the speed, quickness, leg strength, and balance to either win or place among the top three in the sprints, jumps, and hurdles and possessed the sheer power to take first in the shot put. That is a rare feat.

Athletic Requirements of the Sport: 20/20

It's the decathlon. It's the Olympics, the most challenging of all international competitions. Twenty points here.

Clutch Factor/Mental and Emotional Toughness/ Intangibles: 14/15

Nobody who earns gold in the decathlon can be docked too many points in this category, and Johnson showed enough grit in 1956 to compete despite a knee injury that required having his knee drained, then he re-injured it during pole vault practice. He also tore a stomach muscle. That he won a silver medal—in the decathlon, no less—despite those issues proves his determination.

Versatility: 4/5

Johnson cannot be punished much here simply because he did not play another sport beyond high school. He was a good enough basketball player to dabble in that sport under John Wooden at UCLA, which had offered him a football scholarship. His versatility as a decathlon gold medalist speaks for itself.

TOTAL POINTS: 95

MUHAMMAD ALI: THE LOUISVILLE LIP

Boxing

Muhammad Ali. *Library of Congress*

The image of heavyweight boxers had been cemented in the minds of sports fans for generations before Muhammad Ali burst upon the scene in the 1960 Summer Olympics. They were slow-moving, hunched-over behemoths who battled face-to-face in the middle of the ring. They boasted the mobility of a statue. Then along came Ali, who tossed all the perceptions and stereotypes out the window.

Ali changed boxing. He changed America. But his impact on black self-image and the antiwar movement of the 1960s would never have materialized had he not taken the sport by storm and emerged as a heavyweight champion. His brashness, brazen disregard for the feelings of foes, and fascinating personality would have meant nothing had he been just another contender or even had he fit that pigeonholed image of a heavyweight. Ali was a revolutionary figure both inside and outside the ring. He did not merely fit the turbulent sixties; he helped create the unrest of the decade. But it was his talent that made it all possible.

It is no wonder that Kentucky city of Louisville, in which the man formerly known as Cassius Clay was born and raised, still embraces that connection. His career was launched there by unusual circumstance after his bike was stolen at age twelve. Clay angrily entered the Columbia Auditorium to find the thief and told a cop he was going to "whup" the perpetrator. The officer suggested to the 89-pounder that he should learn to box first. Clay did just that, and within weeks had won his first bout.[1]

Clay embraced the sport, setting himself apart from the competition with his bravado and work ethic. The result was six Kentucky Gold Gloves and two National Gold Gloves—and, eventually, a gold medal at the 1960 Rome Olympics.

Boxing fans will always revel in his talent and most shining moments, which included his unmerciful taunting and mocking of hapless opponents who vainly attempted to strike more than a glancing blow as he danced about the ring with grace never before witnessed in a heavyweight fighter. He bragged that he would "float like a butterfly and sting like a bee." It was indeed an apt metaphor for his style and success in the ring.

Clay was thrust into the spotlight in a seventh-round knockout of heavily favored Sonny Liston in 1964, before his religious conversion and name change. He continued to dominate. Ali won his first 29 fights before being stripped of his title and banned from the sport for his refusal to fight in Vietnam. Ali insisted he had no problem with the Vietcong, who, he stated in one of his most famous declarations, "never called me nigger."

Ali won his first two bouts upon his return. His most legendary battle— perhaps the most anticipated fight of all time—was his first defeat, which occurred on March 8, 1971, at New York's "Mecca of Boxing," Madison Square Garden, against archrival Joe Frazier. In what was promoted as the "Fight of the Century," Ali was sent to the canvas by a vicious Frazier left hook to the jaw in the fifteenth and final round, marking the first time he had been knocked off his feet in any fight.

Nine months after Ali wrested the heavyweight title away from Frazier in early 1974, he defeated upstart George Foreman in a battle in the African nation of Zaire that became known as "The Rumble in the Jungle." Ali's last memorable fight was a technical knockout of Frazier in temperatures that soared over 100 degrees, in what was later called the "Thrilla in Manila." Ali secured that victory when a dazed and exhausted Frazier couldn't answer the bell for the fifteenth round.

Ali ended his career with a record of 56–5, but it should be remembered that he lost three years of his prime to forced retirement and might conceivably have remained unbeaten had he been allowed to continue.[2]

> ### They Said It
>
> *Float like a butterfly, sting like a bee. His hands can't hit what his eyes can't see. Now you see me, now you don't. George thinks he will, but I know he won't.*—Muhammad Ali before his fight against George Foreman
>
> *He is America's Greatest Ego. He is also . . . the swiftest embodiment of human intelligence we have had yet, he is the very spirit of the twentieth century, he is the prince of mass man and the media.*—Writer Norman Mailer in a 1971 essay on Ali
>
> *If you even dream of beating me you'd better wake up and apologize.*—Muhammad Ali

POINT TOTAL EXPLANATION

Athletic achievements: 33/35

Ali lost just two bouts until age really began taking a toll, and he was defeated in three of his last four fights as he approached forty years old. His dominance of the heavyweight division from 1960 to 1967 was complete—he was never even sent to the canvas until the Frazier fight eleven years after he launched his professional career. The defeats of the late 1970s and early 1980s preclude Ali from earning all the points in this category, but he deserves all but two for his record of 29–0 with 22 knockouts or technical knockouts before he was stripped of his crown.[3]

Athleticism: 25/25

Heavyweight boxing has never experienced a more well-rounded athlete than Ali. His amazing mobility in the ring did not revolutionize the division, because it remains unmatched. His ability to dance around opponents, thereby avoiding solid strikes to the head, as well as his lethal jabs made him easily the most athletic heavyweight of all time. Ali used the entire ring to literally run circles around most overmatched foes.

Athletic Requirements of the Sport and Division: 18/20

Though Ali moved better in the ring than any other heavyweight champion in history, boxers in that division require less agility and mobility than those who fight in lighter weight classes. It has been said, however, that boxers are the greatest athletes in the world. There is certainly an argument to be made for that; they compete infrequently in comparison to basketball or hockey players, but the pounding they must endure certainly offsets that consideration.

Clutch Factor/Mental and Emotional Toughness/ Intangibles: 15/15

Ali did much to place the spotlight on himself. He thrived in the spotlight, invited the attention. But he also rose to the occasion despite the pressure of the most significant publicity ever given to a boxer, perhaps any athlete. He was both revered and reviled, but he lived up to the hype. Sure, he lost five fights, but he also lost his prime to suspension. One can never know if he would have beaten Frazier had he not been forced into retirement for three years. And one can never know if he would have ended his career undefeated.

Versatility: 3/5

Ali was considered the finest athlete of his high school class, but he was so dedicated to boxing and his championship aspirations that he never embraced other sports. Though capability of versatility should not equal achievement in a variety of athletic endeavors, it should also not prevent Ali from earning some points here.

TOTAL POINTS: 94

██

WILLIE MAYS: THE SAY HEY KID

Baseball

Willie Mays. *Photos used with permission of the National Baseball Hall of Fame Museum (Cooperstown, NY)*

The only image of Willie Mays that younger generations have had the privilege of seeing is that of "The Catch," so titled because it has been deemed the greatest grab in baseball history. Viewers have watched Mays many times sprint toward the center field fence at the Polo Grounds in the eighth inning of a tied Game 1 of the 1954 World Series to haul in a line drive 460 feet from home plate off the bat of Indians slugger Vic Wertz to save the New York Giants from defeat and catapult them into an unlikely sweep of their heavily favored foe.

It's a sensational play, but it seems a shame that those too young to have marveled at the greatness of Mays during his storied twenty-three-year career have only that aging film to catch a glimpse of his immense talent. Mays remains arguably the most complete player ever to lace up a pair of cleats. One needn't ask what Mays could do brilliantly on the diamond. The only question is what he could *not* do brilliantly—and the answer is "nothing."

Willie Howard Mays was born on May 6, 1931, in Westfield, Alabama. The stifling restrictions of the Jim Crow system did not prevent him from maximizing his athletic potential at an early age. He certainly had it in his blood—his mother had been a championship sprinter in high school and his father played semipro baseball.

In fact, Mays competed with his dad in the Birmingham Industrial League. He also starred for the football and basketball teams at Fairfield Industrial High School. But his talents on the diamond shone so brightly that he received an opportunity to play on weekends for the Negro League Birmingham Black Barons at age sixteen in 1947, the same year Jackie Robinson boldly integrated Major League Baseball.

The growing presence of black players at the highest level of the sport helped motivate the Giants to sign Mays to a contract in 1950 and place him in their minor-league system. He posted video game numbers with the Triple-A Minneapolis Millers the following year, batting a ridiculous .477 in thirty-five games despite segregated living conditions and derision from racist fans. The Giants wasted no time promoting Mays three weeks after his twentieth birthday. After a slow start, he hit safely in twenty-one of his next twenty-three games and maintained consistent production, earning National League Rookie of the Year honors.[1]

Military obligations interrupted his career until 1954, when he won his first of two Most Valuable Player awards. He finished among the top six in the MVP voting in twelve of the next thirteen years.[2]

POINT TOTAL EXPLANATION

Achievements: 34/35

Mays led the National League in home runs and stolen bases four times and slugging percentage five times from 1954 to 1965 and won the Gold Glove in center field every season from 1957 to 1968. He finished his career with 660 home runs—not bad considering he played in the most dominant pitching-rich era in baseball history. Mays was arguably the greatest all-around player to ever grace a diamond. He ranked first in the National League in WAR nine times and third in career home runs behind Hank Aaron and Babe Ruth before the steroid era skewed the totals. He was also among the greatest defensive center fielders ever. The only point deducted here was for his inability to lead the Giants to more than one World Series title. But one cannot greatly punish any player much for that because baseball is not an individual sport; Mays could not be

> ### They Said It
>
> *There's absolutely no comparison to me or anyone else to Willie Mays. Willie Mays, he's the greatest baseball player of all time.*—Former Mariners and Yankees superstar Alex Rodriguez
>
> *As much as I loved Jackie Robinson, Roy Campanella, Junior Gilliam, and Don Newcombe, I loved watching Willie Mays play more than all of them combined, even if he played for the "bad guys"!*—Comedian Cheech Marin

blamed for any shortcomings of his teammates, and he did help his teams win four pennants.[3]

Athleticism: 25/25

Mays excelled in every athletic endeavor he attempted. He boasted tremendous power in spite of his 170-pound frame, played a role in changing the dynamic of baseball with his tremendous speed and quickness in tracking down balls slugged to distant parts of the outfield, and owned one of the premier throwing arms in the sport. The definition of "five-tool player" in a baseball dictionary later featured a picture of Mays.

Athletic Requirements of the Sport and Position: 18/20

Baseball does not rank high in this category, but the need for speed and quickness in center field gives Mays a bit of an edge here, as do all the requirements of a power hitter and base stealer, both of which helped make Mays arguably the most athletic player in baseball history.

Clutch Factor/Mental and Emotional Toughness/ Intangibles: 13/15

Mays cannot be judged by his four hits in fourteen at-bats in his lone World Series appearance. He excelled in clutch situations throughout his career, which explains his exceptional runs batted in (RBI) totals. Big-league manager Gene Mauch once proclaimed Mays the best clutch hitter in history.[4]

Versatility: 4/5

Mays did not play football or basketball beyond high school, but he performed well in both sports at that level. He deserves some credit for that. After all, he began his baseball career right out of high school and landed in the big leagues soon thereafter.

TOTAL POINTS: 94

12

BABE RUTH:
THE SULTAN OF SWAT

Baseball

Babe Ruth. *Library of Congress*

Major League Baseball was not in its death throes in 1920, but its image had been severely weakened by a scandal in which players on the Chicago White Sox conspired to lose the 1919 World Series to the Cincinnati Reds. The sport needed a shot in the arm, and it came in the form of a stubby-legged superstar named George Herman Ruth.

Some credit the launching of the "lively ball era" for the explosion in home runs early in the Roaring Twenties, but a glance at the home runs leaders in 1919 and 1920 prove that Ruth deserved most of the credit. He shattered the all-time single-season mark with 29 in 1919, more than doubling the total of Gavvy Cravath, who managed the second-highest total with 12. Ruth then destroyed his own mark in 1920 with 54 home runs, almost tripling that of George Sisler, who hit 19.

Ruth indeed revolutionized the game. He led both leagues in home runs twelve times in fourteen years from 1918 to 1931. But those who think of Ruth as merely a slow, overweight basher of baseballs should think again. Ruth boasted enough speed to reach double figures in stolen bases five times, finish his career with 136 triples, and lead the league in runs scored eight times. He was also a pitcher with Hall of Fame credentials whose career on the mound was cut short after the Red Sox traded him to the Yankees, who yearned to keep him in the lineup every day.[1]

The man who would gain fame for slugging home runs and eating hot dogs was born on February 6, 1895, in Baltimore. His reputation as a cantankerous figure began as a child who often skipped school and caused trouble in the neighborhood. A desire to find a stricter environment for their son motivated his parents to dispatch him to St. Mary's Industrial School for Boys, which was run by Catholic monks. It was there that Ruth developed a passion for baseball. He toiled tirelessly on the diamond, refining his skills in all areas of the game.

Ruth became so adept that one of the monks invited Orioles owner Jack Dunn to watch him play in 1914. Dunn became so impressed after less than an hour of scouting the nineteen-year-old Ruth that he offered him a contract. Baltimore players who gained familiarity with Ruth called him "Jack's newest babe," thereby creating the most famous nickname in American sports. But Ruth was sold to the Boston Red Sox before he could make his major-league debut that same year.[2]

The rest is history. Ruth established himself as a pitching standout, forging a mark of 18–8 in 1915, winning 23 games and the American League earned run average (ERA) title the next season, and compiling a record of 78–40 over a four-year period. But his hitting—and particularly his penchant for power—became intriguing. He batted .300 for the first time in 1917 and that percentage never dipped lower until 1925. He led the league with 11 home runs for the Red Sox despite just 382 at-bats in 1918.

Ruth had become a star. And soon he was among the most famous people in America: a prodigious figure, prodigious eater, and prodigious slugger. His statistics are even more impressive in a modern light. Ruth owns the best career slugging percentage and on-base plus slugging (OPS) percentage in the history of Major League Baseball. So fearful were opposing pitchers of Ruth that he led the league in walks eleven times.[3]

Ruth finished his career with 714 home runs, a record that stood until Hank Aaron broke it in 1974. It was considered the most hallowed mark in sports. And though Ruth no longer owns it and he has not played a game for more than eighty years, he is still the most legendary player ever, arguably the most famous American athlete of all time.

They Said It

The harder you grip the bat, the more you can swing it through the ball, and the farther the ball will go. I swing big, with everything I've got. I hit big or I miss big. I like to live as big as I can.—Babe Ruth

No one hit home runs the way Babe did. They were something special. They were like homing pigeons. The ball would leave the bat, pause briefly, suddenly gain its bearing then take off for the stands.—Teammate and Hall of Fame pitcher Lefty Gomez

POINT TOTAL EXPLANATION

Achievements: 35/35

One can argue that Ruth does not deserve every point available in this category given that he played in an era in which black players were still banned from Major League Baseball. But each athlete is judged in the era in which he or she competed—and Ruth simply dominated his. The 1920s and 1930s were replete with sluggers, including Yankees teammate Lou Gehrig. Ruth not only overshadowed them all statistically, he played the biggest role in launching a Yankees dynasty that did not end until the mid-1960s.

Athleticism: 24/25

Ruth could do everything on a baseball field, though his overall talents waned as he got older and bigger. He was far more quick and agile in the outfield and on the bases than he has been credited for, and his power is legendary.

Athletic Requirements of the Sport and Position: 17/20

Baseball does not require the same level of athleticism as the other major American sports, but Ruth deserves credit for excelling both as a pitcher and everyday player. That he had the balance and precision necessary to thrive on the mound coupled with the speed, quickness, power, and hand-eye coordination necessary to become an all-around position player cannot be overlooked.

Clutch Factor/Mental and Emotional Toughness/ Intangibles: 15/15

The eyes of the sports world were always on Ruth and he most often came through, particularly in the World Series. He was deadlier at the plate with championships on the line than he was in the regular season. Ruth owned a .326 batting average with 15 home runs in just 129 at-bats in the World Series, and he allowed just 3 earned runs in 31 innings pitched for Boston in World Series competition. Whether he actually called his blast against the Cubs in 1932 has been debated ever since. But what cannot be debated is that Ruth never faded in the spotlight as a player, nor has he faded from it as an American legend.[4]

Versatility: 3/5

Ruth did not play other sports, but it should be noted that his upbringing was not conducive to such athletic versatility and that baseball was the only professional sport not in its infancy when Ruth was active. His talents as a pitcher and everyday player must be taken into consideration here.

TOTAL POINTS: 94

ASHTON EATON: WHEELS

Decathlon

Ashton Eaton. © John David Mercer–USA TODAY Sports

Ashton Eaton was called "Wheels" as a little kid running around the playground in his hometown of La Pine, Oregon. He was tagged with the complimentary nickname because of his speed, but it was not merely his speed that would gain him fame. It was his all-around brilliance as an athlete that earned Eaton Olympic gold in the decathlon in 2012 and 2016.[1]

It was, however, his speed and powerful legs that put him over the top in both London and Rio de Janeiro. In the former, he beat the competition in the 100 meters, long jump, and 400 meters, placing second in the 110-meter hurdles. In the latter, he again won the long jump and 100 meters while finishing second in the 400 meters and 110-meter hurdles. But his brilliance extended far beyond those events that tested his short-distance speed. Eaton finished among the top three in the high jump and pole vault and took fourth in Rio in the 1500 meters. He even placed first in his group in the shot put and discus.[2]

Eaton was born in the track-happy town of Portland, Oregon, on January 21, 1988, but his mother, Roslyn, moved the family to La Pine. The folks of the tiny, economically struggling logging town are virtually all white. Eaton's father, who left when he was two years old, was black, and he was raised by a white mother who instilled in him a sense of pride and motivation. She taught him humility and the importance of making commitments and sticking to them. Life was a series of crossroads, she explained, and it was up to her son to choose the right path.

Eaton gained inspiration at age eight from watching American gold-medal sprinter Michael Johnson in the 1996 Summer Games. It was then that he realized he too yearned to participate in the greatest international competition. He maximized his athletic skills by playing baseball, soccer, football, and basketball, and even earning a black belt in tae kwon do. That versatility would serve him well in the Olympics. He also gained a reputation as a supremely gracious sportsman, congratulating winners in the face of his own infrequent defeats.

His potential as a decathlete emerged when he won the high school state championship in both the long jump and 400 meters. He earned a scholarship to the University of Oregon, which boasts a hallowed legacy in track and field. Soon he was winning the US Olympic Trials, taking first place with a shockingly strong performance in the 1500 meters. Eaton had not only proven himself as an Olympic decathlete, but he had proved to himself that he could thrive in events outside the sprints. He had even placed a respectable fifth in the javelin.[3]

The rest is history. Eaton took his momentum and confidence and ran with them to London. He alone won three events among the thirty-one decathletes there. He outdistanced the silver medalist—American teammate Trey Hardee—by nearly 200 points. He then set an Olympic record in Rio, tallying 8,893 points to edge out Kevin Mayer of France.[4]

POINT TOTAL EXPLANATION

Achievements: 34/35

Only the lack of top-three finishes in the field and distance events prevents Eaton from earning a perfect score in this category, but that's nit-picking. Winning two Olympic decathlons speaks for itself: taking two gold medals in the most grueling competition against the best in the world is an incredible accomplishment.

Athleticism: 23/25

Eaton overcame a childhood in which he was exceedingly skinny to become a tremendously well-rounded athlete. His speed, quickness, and leg strength keyed his victories in the Olympic events that put him over the top. A bit more upper-body strength and power would have resulted in even greater dominance, but not everyone can be Jim Thorpe in comparison to the competition of the era. Nobody who wins two gold medals as an Olympic decathlete should be docked more than two points here. The categories of athletic achievements and athleticism go together when it comes to the decathlon; the former assumes the latter.

Athletic Requirements of the Sport: 20/20

The versatility of decathletes is a given, but far more is required of them to capture Olympic gold medals. One must boast speed, quickness, agility, lower- and upper-body strength, power, and endurance to reach a spot atop the podium while one's national anthem is playing.

Clutch Factor/Mental and Emotional Toughness/ Athleticism: 13/15

His dash to the finish line in the 1500 meters at the 2012 Olympic Trials is all one needs to know about the grit of Ashton Eaton. He has not always performed up to peak efficiency, but it can be argued that participating in ten events on that stage and coming out on top requires more mental and emotional toughness than any other athletic activity.

Versatility: 4/5

Eaton performed well enough on the gridiron to consider college football. He was also a black belt in tae kwon do and played a variety of sports. He would have earned five points here had he taken any other sport to a level beyond high school, but "versatility" and "decathlete" are practically synonymous.[5]

TOTAL POINTS: 94

BABE DIDRIKSON ZAHARIAS: THE MASTER OF ALL

Track and Field/Basketball/Golf

The question of what sports Babe Didrikson Zaharias excelled in is easy to answer: "Whatever she attempted." The list is long.

The most compelling and impressive feats in the career of the woman born Mildred Ella Didrikson were achieved at the 1932 Summer Olympics in Los Angeles. At the time, female athletes could enter only three events, but Didrikson certainly maximized her opportunity. She had called attention to herself at the 1931 Women's AAU track meet, during which she won eight events, and then again by dominating the same competition in 1932.

Her performances had track and field fans anticipating greatness at the Olympics—and she delivered. Didrikson broke four world records and showed remarkable versatility by winning the javelin throw with a heave of 143 feet, 4 inches, twice breaking the world record in a gold-medal effort in the 80-meter hurdles, and initially overtaking the world mark in the high jump. (Her leap was disallowed, and she was awarded the silver medal.)[1]

Her Olympic feats were stunning, even in the light of her previous athletic successes. Didrikson excelled in basketball at Beaumont Senior High School in Texas. She proved so talented that coach Melvin McCombs secured a job for her with an insurance company with the express purpose of placing her on its Golden Cyclones basketball team, which proceeded to win three consecutive national championships. Didrikson was twice named an All-American forward.

Following her Olympic accomplishments, she became a jack-of-all-trades. She formed the Babe Didrikson's All-Americans basketball team, on which she was the lone female, and played baseball for the House of

David. Her talents on the diamond became evident when she pitched an inning for the St. Louis Cardinals in an exhibition game. She was reputed to have thrown a baseball over 300 feet.

She also became a deadly golfer. Didrikson had taken up that sport around the same time she was training for the Olympics. She won the Texas State Women's Championship in April 1935 but did not embrace golf as a potential career until a decade later. She emerged as arguably the greatest female golfer of all time, as both an amateur and professional, winning the 1946 US Women's and 1947 British Ladies amateur events to become the first American to capture both. She was the leading money winner on the Ladies Professional Golf Association (LPGA) circuit during its first four years of existence, from 1948 to 1951. Included among her triumphs were the 1948, 1950, and 1954 US Open. She was also a four-time Western Open champion and three-time Titleholders winner.

Didrikson seemed destined to continue her dominance on the links. But colon cancer took her life at the tender age of forty-five, in September 1956. Her legacy includes six Female Athlete of the Year awards by the Associated Press; that organization voted her the Woman Athlete of the 20th Century in 1999.[2]

POINT TOTAL EXPLANATION

Achievements: 34/35

Had all her greatness been accomplished on the golf course, Didrikson would be far lower on this list. But her achievements in the Olympics and even basketball warrant a high ranking and all but one point available in this category. Didrikson not only captured three medals, including two gold, but her shattering of world records is most impressive. She is easily the premier two-sport female athlete in history.

Athleticism: 25/25

Didrikson showed her immense and diverse athletic skills by winning both the javelin and 80-meter hurdles at the 1932 Games. That display of both strength and speed, as well as the agility and quickness needed to excel on the basketball court and the hand-eye coordination necessary to become a golfing champion, all add up to a perfect score here.

They Said It

My main idea in any kind of competition always has been to go out there and cut loose with everything I've got. I've never been afraid to go up against anything. I've always had the confidence that I was capable of winning out.—Babe Didrikson Zaharias

She is beyond all belief until you see her perform. Then you finally understand that you are looking at the most flawless section of muscle harmony, of complete mental and physical coordination, the world of sport has ever seen.—Legendary sportswriter Grantland Rice

Athletic Requirements of the Sport: 15/20

This is a tough one in the case of Didrikson. Should she be judged mostly by one brilliant performance as a track and field athlete in the Olympics? Or should she be judged by her longer and more prominent career in golf, which ranks quite low in athletic requirements? Let's go with a combination of the two here.

Clutch Factor/Mental and Emotional Toughness/ Intangibles: 15/15

Golf indeed requires far less athleticism than other sports, but there is no less mental and emotional toughness needed to slam home those title-winning putts. Didrikson not only proved her mettle by winning medals in the Olympics, but she displayed it as well on the courses as perhaps the finest female golfer ever.

Versatility: 5/5

Didrikson excelled in two wildly varying Olympic sports, as well as basketball, golf, and even baseball. She was even a sewing champion in her day. If she doesn't deserve all five points here, nobody does.

TOTAL POINTS: 94

WILT CHAMBERLAIN: WILT THE STILT

Basketball

Wilt Chamberlain. *Library of Congress*

Few athletes in American history conjure up such strong and specific thoughts as Wilt Chamberlain. Four come to mind immediately:

- A 100-point performance against the New York Knicks in Hershey, Pennsylvania, in 1962
- His ridiculous average of 50.4 points per game that same year
- Epic NBA playoff battles and defeats against Bill Russell and the Boston Celtics
- Boasts about his prolific sexual activity

Thankfully ignoring the last one, Chamberlain's career always been defined by his grandiose achievements and showdowns with Russell. He was simply the most overwhelming offensive force in basketball history. His accomplishments have led to misconceptions, such as claims that Chamberlain camped in the lane and that the center position was weak in his days. Untrue on both counts—the league had instituted the three-second clock nearly a quarter century before Chamberlain arrived, and anyone who witnessed such talents as Walt Bellamy, Nate Thurmond, Wes Unseld, and Willis Reed (as well as Kareem Abdul-Jabbar, later) cannot doubt the level of competition.[1]

Chamberlain compiled statistics with the Philadelphia/San Francisco Warriors, Philadelphia 76ers, and Los Angeles Lakers that today boggle the mind. He played virtually every second of every game in his first twelve seasons, leading the league in minutes played in nine of those years. He paced the NBA in scoring in each of his first six seasons, averaging about 38 points a game during that stretch. Those who claim he was merely an offensive juggernaut should note that he led the league in rebounding in eleven of his sixteen years and finished his career with an absurd average of 22.9. Though he scored often on finger-rolls and dunks, Chamberlain was deadly on short jumpers. That he led the NBA nine times in field goal percentage is no small feat. He even dished out 7.8 assists per game in back-to-back years.[2]

His legacy, however, has been tarnished by his seemingly annual defeats to Boston. His teams managed one playoff victory over the Celtics, a 1967 triumph in the Eastern Conference Finals. History has turned many of those losses into personal failings against Russell. Ignored is that Chamberlain outscored and outrebounded Russell head-to-head in playoff matchups. That Russell was the superior defender is undeniable. But Chamberlain earned spots on two all-NBA defensive teams. It can be argued that the Celtics dominated Chamberlain's teams because they boasted better all-around talent.[3]

Chamberlain's talent was not pronounced in his early years—he scoffed at basketball as a game for sissies and leaned toward track and field. Born on August 21, 1936, into a family of nine children, he was a frail child who

They Said It

Everybody pulls for David, nobody roots for Goliath.—Wilt Chamberlain

One time, when I was with Boston and he was with the Lakers, Happy Hairston and I were about to get in a scrape. All of a sudden, I felt an enormous vise around me. I was 6–7, 235 pounds, and Wilt had picked me up and turned me around. He said, "We're not going to have that stuff." I said, "Yes, sir."—NBA power forward Paul Silas nearly died of pneumonia. He eventually embraced basketball—and that was bad news for Overlook High School's competition. The still-skinny Chamberlain had grown to 6-foot-10 and developed a penchant for scoring and blocking shots.

Chamberlain led his team to a 56–3 record over three years. He exploded for games of 90, 74, and 71 points during his prep career and averaged 44.5 per game. He once even tallied 60 points in one half.

He proved nearly as dominant at the University of Kansas. He scored 52 points in his debut for the Jayhawks and led his team into the NCAA Finals. They lost to North Carolina, but Chamberlain earned Most Outstanding Player honors for the tournament. Most impressive, however, was that as a junior, the same year he was named an All-American in basketball, he won the high jump at the Big Eight Track and Field Championships.

Chamberlain skipped his senior season to turn pro but lost that year due to an NBA rule that prohibited players from competing until their class graduated. Chamberlain joined the Harlem Globetrotters to stay in basketball shape before launching his career with the Warriors.[4]

POINT TOTAL EXPLANATION

Achievements: 34/35

That Chamberlain was the greatest offensive player in NBA history might be argued, though nobody else but Michael Jordan can be considered in the conversation. Nobody—even Jordan—was more statistically dominant. It can also be argued that until he joined Jerry West, Elgin Baylor, and the Lakers, he simply did not boast the surrounding talent to compete with Boston. That he annually led his team into the playoffs and won two titles was an achievement.

Athleticism: 25/25

Chamberlain boasted tremendous strength and durability—Celtics forward Tom Heinsohn marveled at the number of brutal fouls he endured. Few knew that he could bench press over 500 pounds. His power, agility, and leaping ability allowed him to get open, score, rebound, and block shots. His speed and leg strength were evident when he competed in the 440 meters, broad jump, and high jump in youth and college competitions.

Chamberlain has been called one of the greatest pure athletes in American sports history. He loses one point here only because he could never find the touch on his foul shots.[5]

Athletic Requirements of the Sport and Position: 18/20

Centers in the days of Chamberlain and Russell did not require tremendous mobility—they competed almost exclusively close to the basket. But agility and strength were certainly needed, and NBA players in general—especially Chamberlain—sat only briefly and often played entire games.

Clutch Factor/Mental and Emotional Toughness/ Intangibles: 13/15

Chamberlain sometimes did not perform as well with a playoff series on the line, resulting in a reputation as a poor clutch player, at least in comparison to his immense talent. But such assertions can be argued. His numbers matched up favorably in the postseason, and his rebounding was significantly better.

Versatility: 4/5

Chamberlain competed in the 440, shot put, broad jump, and high jump at the Big Eight Track and Field Championships, winning the latter. Given his height, weight, and overall basketball talents, his fine score in this category cannot be contended.

TOTAL POINTS: 94

JACKIE ROBINSON: THE BARRIER BREAKER

Baseball

Jackie Robinson. *Library of Congress*

Jackie Robinson would have made a significant impact on American sports even if he had proven to be a mediocre ballplayer lacking the temperament and courage to endure the torrent of abuse heaped upon him. But his brilliance at the plate and in the field and, more impressive, his ability to withstand the verbal and even physical torment make him one of the most admired and re-markable athletes ever. His imprint not only on the sport, but on society, is why Major League Baseball permanently retired his uniform number 42.

His imprint on the nation had to be quite powerful to prove itself stronger than his positive effect on the Brooklyn Dodgers from 1947 to 1956. Robinson changed the sport with his daring and speed, leading the National League in stolen bases twice in his first three seasons. He won the Rookie of the Year award in 1947 by batting .297 with 125 runs scored, the first of seven seasons in which he tallied at least 99. He was voted NL Most Valuable Player after moving to the cleanup spot in 1949, when he led the league with a .342 batting average, exceeded 200 hits, and drove in a career-high 124 runs.

Robinson proved tremendously consistent during his ten-year playing career. He hit between 31 and 38 doubles every season but one from

They Said It

A life is not important except in the impact it has on other lives.—Jackie Robinson

Thinking about the things that happened, I don't know any other ball player who could have done what he did. To be able to hit with everybody yelling at him. He had to block all that out, block out everything but this ball that is coming in at a hundred miles an hour. To do what he did has to be the most tremendous thing I've ever seen in sports.—Teammate and supporter Pee Wee Reese

The way I figured it, I was even with baseball and baseball with me. The game had done much for me, and I had done much for it.—Jackie Robinson

1947 to 1953 and slugged double-figures home runs every year but one. He owned a keen eye at the plate, averaging 87 walks and 34 strikeouts throughout his career. His on-base percentage of .409 included a league-best .440 mark in 1952.[1]

His credentials as a player warranted Hall of Fame consideration, though the shortness of his career might have kept him out if not for his greatness as a man. The journey of Jack Roosevelt Robinson began on January 31, 1919, in Cairo, Georgia. His family soon moved to California. Robinson did not need to grow up in the Jim Crow South to become familiar with racism and discrimination; the Robinsons were the only black family on the block in Pasadena, and they encountered plenty of it. But it served only to strengthen their bond and provide Jackie with the determination to succeed.

Robinson emerged as a brilliant and versatile athlete. He lettered in football, basketball, track, and baseball at Muir Tech. He even won the junior boys singles championship in the Pacific Coast Negro Tennis Tournament. He participated in the same four sports at Pasadena Junior College, breaking the school broad jump record set by his brother Mack, who went on to win a silver medal in the Olympics.

His amazing versatility continued at UCLA, where he became the first athlete to earn varsity letters in four sports—baseball, basketball, football, and track. He was named to the All-American football team before spending two years in the army. His military career ended when he was court-martialed for protesting racial discrimination.

Robinson then embarked on a baseball career. He played one season in the Negro Leagues with the Kansas City Monarchs. Soon Dodgers president Branch Rickey began searching for the ideal candidate to break the color barrier in Major League Baseball. He believed Robinson boasted the talent to thrive and temperament to handle the inevitable abuse. Rickey could not have selected a worthier athlete. Robinson dominated at Triple-A Montreal in 1946, batting .349, and arrived in the big leagues with great fanfare to start the 1947 season.

The journey was treacherous. Though some teammates and opponents accepted him, others (particularly from the South) proved unmerciful in their torment. Bench jockeys spewed forth racial epithets and pitchers sometime even threw at his head. Both he and Rickey understood that if he returned their verbal abuse, the integration of the sport, at least at that time, might fail. But Robinson handled it all with great aplomb. He answered with his play on the field.[2]

POINT TOTAL EXPLANATION

Achievements: 34/35

Robinson might have been only a borderline Hall of Fame candidate had he not courageously and with amazing composure broken the color barrier. But that is more a reflection on the comparatively short length of his major-league career. Modern statistical analysis proves his worth. He twice led the National League in WAR—three times among position players. And he was considered a fine defender at second base. He also deserves credit earning multiple letters at UCLA.[3]

Athleticism: 24/25

Robinson's speed, quickness, and agility were evident not only on the baseball diamond but also on the track, where it has been argued that he could have followed his brother on to the US Olympic team. Only a lack of power comparative to the major-league sluggers of his day prevents Robinson from earning all the points here.

Athletic Requirements of the Sport and Position: 7/20

Robinson gained fame as a baseball player. He played second base, which necessitates the quickness to track down grounders and popups as well as the agility to turn double plays. He also played first base, which requires far less athleticism. Again, however, one must consider his accomplishments in track, football, and basketball, all of which demand a higher level of athleticism than baseball.

Clutch Factor/Mental and Emotion Toughness/ Intangibles: 14/15

The mental and emotional toughness part? Robinson would get 100 out of 15 points if it was mathematically feasible. It's the clutch factor that costs him a point. He simply did not perform well in six World Series clashes against the archrival New York Yankees. His .234/.335/.343 slash line in the Fall Classic is one reason the Dodgers emerged with just one victory in those battles.[4]

Versatility: 5/5

Baseball? Football? Track? Basketball? Tennis? No discussion here. Robinson deserves a full load in this category.

TOTAL POINTS: 94

17

RICKEY HENDERSON: THE MAN OF STEAL

Baseball

Present any comparison that results in ranking players throughout baseball history and you have quite a conundrum—or least a heated debate. The greatest power hitter. The greatest pitcher. The greatest whatever. There is going to be wide disagreement.

There is one exception. Just declare that the greatest leadoff hitter of all time was Rickey Henderson. Crickets. Nobody will argue. His combination of speed and power from that spot certainly got starting pitchers nervous from their first windup. Walk him—and Henderson walked a lot—and it could be the equivalent of a triple. Throw him a strike anywhere in the zone and the pitcher risks straining his neck watching how far over the fence the ball traveled.

Henderson compiled outrageous numbers in an epic career—mostly with the Oakland Athletics and New York Yankees—that did not end until well past his forty-fourth birthday. Most impressive was his thievery—he set a record that might stand forever by stealing 130 bases in 1982, swiped 100 or more three times, led the league in that category seven years in a row and 12 times overall, and hung up his spikes with 1,406 steals. That is 468 more than anyone else. Absurd.

But his greatness extended far beyond those thefts. Henderson finished thirteen seasons with at least 100 runs scored and concluded his career atop the list in that critical statistic as well, with 2,295. His career .401 on-base percentage speaks of his batting eye and the dangers of pitching to him despite the threat of steals. His career batting average of .279 was weakened by a poor mark after the age of forty. His 1,406 total stolen bases ranks first in baseball history and 2,190 walks places him second. But most impressive, considering his 5-foot-10, 180-pound frame, was his power.

Henderson crouched low in stands, then uncoiled with tremendous bat speed, resulting in 297 career home runs.[1]

And to think he nearly pursued a football career. Born Rickey Nelson Henley in Chicago on December 25, 1958, he was abandoned by his father at age two. His mother, Bobbie, soon moved the family to her mother's farm in Pine Bluff, Arkansas. They lived there for a short time during the tail end of the Jim Crow era before Bobbie sought greater opportunities in Oakland, California.

It was there that Rickey blossomed athletically. He starred in baseball, basketball, and football at Oakland Technical High School. Football rival Ronnie Lott, who later starred with the San Francisco 49ers, recalled Henderson taking a sweep 80 yards against his team to the end zone. But Henderson's baseball coach had fonder memories of the young athlete working hard and remaining upbeat. Henderson could have accepted a football scholarship—he believed himself to be a potential All-American—but left the decision to his mother. She chose baseball. Opposing pitchers would have hated her for that had they known.

Henderson was chosen in the fourth round of the 1976 draft and excelled in the minors immediately. He batted .345 with 104 walks, 11 home runs, 120 runs scored, and 95 stolen bases at Class A Modesto in 1977. Within two years he was making a tremendous pest of himself in the major leagues.[2]

POINT TOTAL EXPLANATION

Achievements: 34/35

The only factor that prevents Henderson from nailing down a perfect score here is that he had occasional mediocre years in the 1990s and beyond. But he enjoyed mostly incredible seasons, and his career statistics as a combination base stealer, run scorer, and power hitter compare with those of nearly anyone in the history of the sport. He was even a strong left fielder who invariably got a good jump on the ball and used his speed to track down potential extra-base hits.

Athleticism: 25/25

Henderson earns every point here for not only his speed and power, but his acceleration and agility on the bases and in the field. He boasted tremendous upper- and lower-body strength and even a vertical leap that took home runs away from frustrated batters.

Athletic Requirements of the Sport and Position: 17/20

Left field is among the least athletically challenging positions on the field, and baseball is the least athletically challenging of the major American team sports. But Henderson cannot be punished severely in this category given that he utilized his athleticism, particularly as a base stealer, to go beyond what the sport requires to be successful.

Clutch Factor/Emotional and Mental Toughness/ Intangibles: 14/15

Henderson performed brilliantly with the most on the line, particularly in his prime. He smoked 14 hits in 34 at-bats in the 1989 and 1990 World Series combined with 6 stolen bases and 14 runs scored in just eight games. He struggled a bit in the postseason late in his career, which costs him a point. But though he was self-centered and brash, those who played with Henderson praised him as fine teammate.[3]

Versatility: 4/5

Henderson did not play another sport beyond high school, but he did also compete at that level in basketball and football and was talented enough in the latter to consider scholarships. And given his tremendous versatility on the diamond, his score in this category should is well deserved.

TOTAL POINTS: 94

BO JACKSON:
THE FREAKISH TALENT

Football, Baseball

Those unfamiliar with Bo Jackson might glance at his pro football statistics and shrug. The same reaction could follow upon examination of his baseball statistics. After all, his careers in both sports were comparatively short. But those numbers were impressive enough to place Jackson among the greatest American athletes of all time. And so is the old "eye test": one view of Jackson running through and around tacklers or bashing a baseball over a center-field wall is all anyone would need to confirm that status.

Jackson boasted a combination of speed and strength unseen in any sports figure of his generation, arguably unmatched among American athletes until LeBron James came along. Those traits were borne out in the numbers he combined in his (albeit short) professional career, which he launched with the Kansas City Royals as a classic slugger and speedster. Jackson averaged 27 home runs and 20 stolen bases in his four full seasons as a classic slugger with Kansas City. Most awe-inspiring was his 448-foot home run to dead center in the 1989 All-Star Game, but he displayed his speed as well with a stolen base and was voted the game's Most Valuable Player.

A few months later he was running wild for the NFL's Los Angeles Raiders. Jackson spent four years with that team, where he again showed off his athletic versatility. He averaged 5.4 yards per carry, a statistic buoyed by his penchant to use his power and speed to break off marathon runs. Jackson led the league in longest rush from scrimmage in three years with jaunts of 91, 92, and 88 yards. He ran for 77 yards on just six carries in his only playoff appearance.[1]

Jackson ended his football life after hip replacement surgery, but—remarkably—worked his way back to baseball, playing two years with the

Chicago White Sox. He finished his run in 1994 by achieving career highs in batting average (.279) and on-base percentage (.344).[2]

A tough upbringing without a father in the steel town of Bessemer, Alabama, could have ended in tragedy had Jackson not embraced sports. He sometimes beat up other kids and stole their lunch money to secure a bite to eat. His grades were poor, but not his performances on the gridiron, diamond, or track. Jackson won two high school decathlon championships, averaged nearly 11 yards per carry for the football team as a senior, and slammed 20 home runs in just twenty-five games for the baseball team to tie a national prep record.

Jackson turned down an offer from the Yankees to accept a scholarship to Auburn University, where he rushed for 4,303 yards and 43 touchdowns during regular-season competition. His 1,786-yard senior season landed Jackson the Heisman Trophy, but he also batted .401 with 17 home runs in forty-two games for the Tigers baseball team and rejected an offer by the Tampa Bay Buccaneers in order to play baseball, declaring that sport his first love. He joined the Royals after they selected him in the fourth round of the 1986 draft, then played a mere fifty-three games in the minor leagues before his promotion to the majors. Jackson thus launched an amazing two-sport career that ended with his retirement from baseball after the work stoppage that nearly ruined that sport in 1994 and early 1995.[3]

POINT TOTAL EXPLANATIONS

Achievements: 32/35

Jackson was certainly no Hall of Famer in either sport, though one can argue that he boasted the talent to be had injuries not taken a toll and had he concentrated on just one sport. But he deserves credit for accomplishing what he did at the highest levels of two sports, as well as against the best college athletes at Auburn, and for winning two decathlons in high school. Though this category is generally based on professional or Olympic achievements, Jackson deserves strong consideration here.

Athleticism: 25/25

You name it, Jackson had it: speed, quickness, power, agility, hand-eye coordination, arm strength, leg strength. His achievements in football and baseball were based on supreme athleticism. He is simply among the best pure athletes in American history.

> ### They Said It
>
> *When people tell me I could be the best athlete there is, I just let it go in one ear and out the other. There is always somebody out there who is better than you are.*—Bo Jackson
>
> *How can you turn down the NFL as the Heisman Trophy winner and go play for the Kansas City Royals? And on top of that, go play in [Double-A] Memphis?*—Royals superstar George Brett

Athletic Requirements of the Sport and Position: 18/20

Jackson spent more years in baseball than in any other sport, which costs him just a bit here. NFL running backs require supreme athleticism to excel, but Jackson played only four years in the league and was not a full-time starter. But he receives some consideration here for his achievements as a decathlete, which requires the wide-ranging athletic skills Jackson possessed.

Clutch Factor/Mental and Emotional Toughness/ Intangibles: 14/15

Jackson hit for a higher average with runners in scoring position, and particularly with two outs. He performed well in the only postseason football game in which he participated and against the premier competition in college, especially archrival Alabama in the Iron Bowl. Such efforts indicate an ability to rise to the occasion, and his physical style of running shows a high level of toughness.[4]

Versatility: 5/5

Jackson remains the only athlete to earn a spot in both the Pro Bowl and Major League Baseball's All-Star Game. He won two decathlons in high school. Enough said—he gets all the points here.

TOTAL POINTS: 94

19

JESSE OWENS: TO HELL WITH HITLER

Track and Field

Jesse Owens. *Library of Congress*

Never in Olympic history have gold medals been wrapped in heavier symbolism than the ones earned by Jesse Owens in 1936. Though he wore an American uniform, he didn't perform for a country that still treated his people as second-class citizens. Though he competed in Berlin in front of fans who appreciated his brilliance and roared their approval, he didn't perform for a Nazi regime that embraced a doctrine of racial inferiority. Rather, Owens represented himself and every black person in the world.

Owens gave African Americans in particular a sense of pride when he shattered not only Olympic records but also the racial myths perpetrated by German dictator Adolf Hitler and the trumpeters of his half-baked racial theories, which were also embraced by many in the United States. And he accomplished his feats not with braggadocio and vengeful rhetoric, but with grace and humility.

It all began in Jim Crow Alabama, where James Cleveland Owens was born the son of a sharecropper and the grandson of a slave on September 12, 1913. His family moved nine years later to Cleveland, Ohio, where he wasted little time establishing his athletic greatness. Owens set junior high

They Said It

The battles that count aren't the ones for gold medals. The struggles within yourself—the invisible, inevitable battles inside all of us—that's where it's at.—Jesse Owens

When he enters a room, he doesn't so much take it over as envelop it. —*Track and Field News* writer Jon Hendershott

When I came back, after all those stories about Hitler and his snub, I came back to my native country, and I couldn't ride in the front of the bus. I had to go to the back door. I couldn't live where I wanted. Now what's the difference?—Jesse Owens

school records in the high jump and long jump before dominating high school competition, including three consecutive years at the Ohio state championships. He blazed the track at 9.4 seconds in the 100-yard dash at the National Interscholastic event in Chicago during his senior year to tie a new high school world record, then set a new one in the 220 with a time of 20.7. He had already broken the prep mark in the long jump with a leap of 24 feet, 11.75 inches.

Despite an inability to offer track scholarships, Ohio State managed to win the recruiting war for Owens, who provided a preview of his Olympic heroism throughout the 1935 Western Conference Outdoor Track and Field Meet at the University of Michigan. A sore back threatened to undermine Owens's participation, so he urged coach Larry Snyder to allow him to run the 100-yard dash as a test. He tore up the track at 9.4, equaling a world record and embarking on the most dominant stretch in the history of college track and field. Ten minutes later, he leaped 26 feet, 8.25 inches to break the world long jump record. Nine minutes later, he slashed three-tenths of a second off the world mark in the 220-yard dash at 20.3, beating the second-place finisher by 15 yards. And twenty-six minutes later, he buried the competition in the 220 low hurdles with a world-record time of 22.6.[1]

Owens soon had a decision to make. Should he accept the invitation to Germany over the protests of those who believed it would serve to support the Nazi regime? Owens indeed decided to compete, and his performance made a far more poignant statement. He rose to the occasion under an international spotlight the pressure of representing the entire black race, as well as the United States. Owens competed in four events (three individual and the 400-meter relay) and captured gold in all of them. He won the 100 meters before setting a world record in the 200 and the Olympic mark in the long jump. His incredible performance and engaging personality motivated the throngs in Berlin to express their appreciation, much to the dismay of Hitler and other Nazi officials.[2]

From a purely physical standpoint, it was among the most amazing athletic feats ever. But that pales in comparison to its historical significance in what was arguably the most momentous event in the history of sports.

POINT TOTAL EXPLANATION

Achievements: 34/35

Though compared to other athletes in other sports Owens was a flash in the pan—his greatest achievements coming over a one-year period—what he accomplished during that time deserves great consideration here. Owens proved so dominant over the competition, setting world records along the way, that it makes perfect sense to dock him only one point in this category.

Athleticism: 23/25

Owens loses a bit here as strictly a sprinter and jumper. Granted, he was among the best who ever lived, but one cannot give him the same point totals as, for instance, gold-medal decathletes. His sheer speed, leg strength, and agility cannot be questioned, but other athletic traits went unproven. This is not his fault, but reality nevertheless.

Athletic Requirements of the Sport and Events: 18/20

There is no questioning the athletic difficulty of thriving as a sprinter, jumper, and hurdler. The quickness necessary to get an ideal jump off the blocks and the timing needed to make a perfect jump cannot be denied. And of course one must be blazing fast. Brute strength such as is required in the field events is all that is missing.

Clutch Factor/Mental and Emotional Toughness/ Intangibles: 15/15

One can only imagine the pressure on Owens from all sides when he lined up for his events at the 1936 Olympics. That he won the gold medal in all of them is a testament to his mental and emotional strength. His was among the most inspiring efforts in sports history.

Versatility: 3/5

Owens proved versatile within the track and field world. After all, there is a difference between hurdlers, sprinters, and long jumpers. He did not play other sports, but one wonders whether in a later era he might not have excelled, for instance, as a wide receiver or point guard.

TOTAL POINTS: 93

20

HENRY AARON: HAMMERIN' HANK

Baseball

Henry Aaron. *Photos used with permission of the National Baseball Hall of Fame Museum (Cooperstown, NY)*

Hank Aaron received many cards and letters before 1973 turned into 1974. They were not wishing him a merry Christmas. They were ugly. They were profane. They were hate letters. Some were even death threats. Why? Because Aaron was a black man on the precipice of breaking the most hallowed record in sports. And that record was held by a white man.

Aaron had slugged 713 home runs at that point, just one shy of the mark held by the legendary Babe Ruth. Aaron had kind of snuck up on immortality. Most believed for years that Mickey Mantle or Willie Mays was destined to challenge the home run record. But Aaron rolled merrily along, slamming at least 24 home runs every season from 1955 through 1973, peaking at 47 in 1971. By that time, as Mantle had retired and Mays had slowed down, all eyes had shifted to Aaron.

And the worst of America came crawling out of the gutter. They threatened to do Aaron harm if he continued his march toward the home run mark. One even warned that he would bring a gun to the ballpark and gun Aaron down on the field. Aaron was frightened and disgusted, but determined. He crashed number 714 in Cincinnati on Opening Day, then hit the record-breaker off Dodgers left-hander Al Downing on April 8 in Atlanta. The same fans who once would have refused Aaron restaurant service before the civil rights movement were not giving him a rousing ovation—but, thankfully, nobody had followed through with any of the threats against him.[1]

Aaron finished his career with 755 home runs, which is still considered by many the all-time mark given the assumption that Barry Bonds, who eventually passed him, used performance-enhancing drugs to get there. But Aaron was not merely a slugger. He was a complete ballplayer, even a three-time Gold Glove outfielder. He concluded his epic career with a .305 average and two batting titles. He exceeded 100 runs scored fifteen times, including every season from 1955 to 1967. He led the National League in total bases eight times and doubles and runs batted in four times. He owns the Major League Baseball career mark in RBI (2,297) and total bases (6,856).[2]

The racism Aaron faced in the early 1970s was not unfamiliar to him. He was born on February 5, 1934, in Mobile, Alabama, where the Ku Klux Klan and segregation reigned. His family moved to a home in rural Tomlinville that had no indoor plumbing, windows, or electricity. While Aaron earned money mowing lawns, picking potatoes, and delivering ice, his uncle Bubba taught him the finer points of baseball. Hank played the sport with neighborhood kids in an open field, but since baseballs were so expensive, he substituted golf balls covered with nylon panty hose.

Black schools in the Jim Crow South did not field baseball teams, so Aaron played organized fast-pitch softball. He did play for the high school football team and was named to the all-city squad. Fear of injury in foot-

They Said It

I'm hoping someday that some kid, black or white, will hit more home runs than myself. Whoever it is, I'd be pulling for him.—Henry Aaron

Trying to throw a fastball by Henry Aaron is like trying to sneak a sunrise past a rooster.—All-Star pitcher Curt Simmons

ball motivated him to quit that sport and concentrate on baseball. He was expelled during his junior year for skipping school to listen to Dodgers games on the radio and follow his hero Jackie Robinson. Aaron performed so well against older local players that he was noticed by the manager of the Mobile Black Bears, an all-black semipro team. Aaron played shortstop and showed so much potential that he earned a contract with the Negro League Indianapolis Clowns. Clowns owner Syd Pollock soon contacted the Boston Braves, who signed Aaron to a minor-league contract.

Aaron landed on the Eau Claire Bears in 1952. His first experience on an integrated team was enriching. He gained confidence and was named Northern League Rookie of the Year. He continued his ascent and eventually moved to the outfield. He was promoted to the Milwaukee Braves in 1954 and quickly emerged as one of the premier players in the sport.[3]

POINT TOTAL EXPLANATION

Achievements: 35/35

What can be added to establishing the all-time home run record? Aaron is among the most accomplished athletes of all time. He even managed double-figure stolen bases in nine consecutive seasons during the meat of his career. He was voted National League Most Valuable Player only once but finished among the top ten in the balloting thirteen times. He earned a spot on the NL All-Star team twenty-one straight years. He's ranked seventh in baseball history in WAR. Aaron knocks this category out of the park.[4]

Athleticism: 23/25

Aaron lacked elite speed, and his power was greatly the result of quick wrists that generated tremendous bat speed. But those who perceive Aaron as merely a slugger should understand that he was a fine athlete. He boasted the quickness and timing to steal bases and perform well in the outfield and owned a strong arm.

Athletic Requirements of the Sport and Position: 16/20

A corner outfielder such as Aaron does not require the speed and mobility needed from a center fielder, but outfielders have historically been counted upon to provide power. Baseball players simply do not deserve the point total here that football, basketball, and even tennis players earn. But the athletic requirements of outfielders place them atop the list of those who compete on the diamond.

Clutch Factor/Mental and Emotional Toughness/Intangibles: 15/15

The grit Aaron showed in overcoming a mentally and emotionally torturous run to the home run record alone should provide him with a full point total here. But the cherry on top was his performance in three postseason series. Aaron rose to the occasion in the 1957 and 1958 World Series and the 1969 National League Championship Series, batting .357 with 6 home runs in 69 at-bats.[5]

Versatility: 4/5

Aaron did not compete in other sports at any level beyond high school, but his achievements on the football field as an all-city selection deserve merit.

TOTAL POINTS: 93

21

TOM BRADY: TOM TERRIFIC

Football

It took Tom Brady seventeen years to build his case as the greatest quarterback in National Football League history. It took him only twenty-two minutes of game time to clinch it in the hearts and minds of millions.

That many minutes indeed ticked off the game clock in a 2017 Super Bowl that seemed destined to be a blowout. The Atlanta Falcons, whose defense had stymied and sacked Brady repeatedly, testing his resolve, had stretched their lead to 28–3 by late in the third quarter. The New England Patriots appeared doomed, but appearances can be deceiving when your quarterback is Tom Brady. He engineered a comeback for the ages, completing 25 of 32 passes for 288 yards and two touchdowns the rest of the way. Included was a heady performance in an overtime drive that gave him an NFL-record five Super Bowl triumphs.[1]

Tom Brady. © Mark J. Rebilas–USA TODAY Sports

Not that the entire football world was shocked. Followers and insiders alike had grown accustomed to Brady's heroics. He had long since separated himself from the likes of Peyton Manning and Drew Brees as the most accomplished quarterback of his generation. Not bad, considering he was perhaps the most legendary afterthought in the history of

> ### They Said It
>
> *He has a presence, almost regal-like. It's the same presence of a JFK, someone like that.*—Former Patriots teammate Christian Fauria
>
> *Who would you rather have running your two-minute drill? I'll take Tom Brady 10 out of 10 times.*—Notre Dame football coach Charlie Weis

American sports: Brady was selected by the Patriots in the sixth round of the 2000 draft.

Thomas Edward Patrick Brady Jr. began his life journey on August 3, 1977, in San Mateo, California. His football accomplishments were unpronounced at an early age—many believed his greater talents were displayed on the baseball diamond. He slammed two home runs in a high school playoff game and was even drafted by the Montreal Expos in 1995. He struggled to earn playing time on the football field, but his passion for the sport would not allow him to quit and he finally secured the starting job as a junior. He was not heavily recruited but did land a scholarship at the University of Michigan, where his achievements were overlooked by scouts who deemed him too slow to thrive in the NFL.

Scouts have never been more wrong. Passed up round after round before he was snagged by the Patriots, he started the third game of his second season when he took over for an injured Drew Bledsoe—who became the football equivalent of Yankees first baseman Wally Pipp, whose headache and resulting absence from the lineup allowed Lou Gehrig to begin his string of 2,130 consecutive starts. Brady never relinquished the job. Two years later he guided the Patriots to a Super Bowl victory over the Carolina Panthers by throwing for 354 yards and three touchdowns.[2]

The rest is history. Brady was still going strong at age thirty-nine, leading his team to another championship in 2016. From 2003 to that year, his Patriots compiled a ridiculous regular-season record of 176–48 and failed to win the division championship just once. His playoff mark heading into 2017 stood at 25–9. Those who contended that Brady was not the greatest quarterback in NFL history must concede that he was the most successful at maximizing both his own talents and that of his offense. Many marveled at his ability to transform moderately talented receivers into Pro Bowlers—after all, the only all-time great pass catcher who graced a New England roster during his time as the starting quarterback was Randy Moss.[3]

POINT TOTAL EXPLANATION

Achievements: 35/35

Brady ranked first in all-time playoff appearances (34), second in interception percentage (1.8), third in passer rating (97.2), and fourth in touchdown passes (456) and passing yards (61,582) through the 2016 season. With New England coach Bill Belichick predicting that his quarterback could play another four or five years, Brady seemed destined to shatter several records. His prolific passing helped transform the NFL into what was either praised or lamented as a track meet. Brady set a league mark by throwing for 50 touchdowns in 2007. He led the NFL in that category four times through 2016, and five times exceeded 100 in passing efficiency. But nothing defines the greatness of Tom Brady more than his five Super Bowl championships.[4]

Athleticism: 20/25

The scouts were right about Brady: he proved to be slow in escaping pressure in the pocket. But his nifty footwork allowed him to avoid sacks, and his strength prevented extensive injury. Most impressive was his powerful and deadly accurate arm, which zipped footballs past the flailing arms of defenders and into the hands of receivers well downfield. Brady indeed lacked speed and quickness, resulting in fewer points in this category. But that he overcame those shortcomings to emerge as arguably the finest quarterback in NFL history makes his story even more impressive.

Athletic Requirements of the Sport and Position: 18/20

Brady proved that quarterbacks need not boast the same level of athleticism as those who play more mobile positions on the field, particularly running backs, wide receivers, linebackers, and defensive backs. But one must still possess a strong arm and requisite mobility to maximize one's talent. Few wholly unathletic quarterbacks can excel in the NFL.

Clutch Factor/Mental and Emotional Toughness/ Intangibles: 15/15

Perhaps nobody gracing the pages of this book possessed a higher level of mental and emotional toughness than Brady. He even had to overcome the pressure of having to prove himself all over again following the Deflategate scandal, in which he was accused of deflating footballs for his own benefit and for which he received a four-game suspension. His response was to lead the Patriots to another Super Bowl victory. Brady must be considered the greatest clutch quarterback ever, given his penchant for winning championships. A keen intelligence that allowed him to read defenses as well as any quarterback set him apart. His concentration level, intensity, and mental toughness were challenged time and again. And Brady rose to the challenge on every occasion.

Versatility: 5/5

One wonders if Brady could have forged a career in Major League Baseball had he not sought to realize his dreams on the gridiron. It matters not—his talents in that sport provide all the points available in this category.

TOTAL POINTS: 93

22

LAWRENCE TAYLOR: L.T.

Football

Asked who was the most dominant defensive force in NFL history, football experts might supply myriad opinions, but one should not be surprised if Lawrence Taylor's name was uttered more than any other. Taylor not only wreaked havoc on opposing offenses, but he forever changed the job description of outside linebackers. Where once they read play calls and reacted to the movements of receivers, running backs, and quarterbacks, they became relentless attackers. They can thank Taylor for that.

Not that Taylor's pure numbers weren't among the best ever recorded, and his impact on his New York Giants wasn't as profound as any a defensive player has ever made in the NFL. Taylor averaged 13 sacks a year and was among the most feared tacklers in the sport. He covered the field with rare mobility for an outside linebacker of his era and performed with incredible intensity and speed to outmaneuver linemen and chase down the premier skill position players in the NFL.

Taylor was fast enough to blanket receivers and strong enough to battle offensive linemen. He terrorized quarterbacks, finishing his career with 142 sacks to rank among the all-time leaders. The top linebackers, legends such as Dick Butkus, had always roamed the middle in the B.T. (Before Taylor) era. The most disruptive in the modern era play on the outside—some are even moved from one end to the other or are moved occasionally to defensive end.

In the process, he played the most significant role in transforming the Giants defense into one of the greatest that ever graced a football field. The unit was among the worst in football before the All-American from the University of North Carolina was selected with the second pick in the 1981 draft and immediately jelled. Taylor amassed 133 tackles and nine sacks as a rookie as the Giants jumped from twenty-seventh to third in the NFL

They Said It

Lawrence Taylor, defensively, has had as big an impact as any player I've ever seen. He changed the way defense is played, the way pass-rushing is played, the way linebackers play and the way offenses block linebackers.
—NFL coach and analyst John Madden

All you can do is put your story out there enough times and hope that a couple will understand that no matter why type of athlete you are—there were no better than I was, there was no one who had more going for him than I did, there was no athlete stronger mentally than I was.—Lawrence Taylor

in points allowed that year. They remained among the best defensively throughout his career, peaking in 1986 and 1990, when they won Super Bowl championships. Taylor became the first defensive player since 1971 to win the NFL Most Valuable Player award in 1986, when he racked up a career-best 20.5 sacks and recorded 105 tackles.[1]

Not bad, considering Taylor didn't even begin playing football competitively until his junior year at Lafayette High School in Williamsburg, Virginia, where he was born on February 4, 1959. Taylor lived in a tiny four-room house and grew up in a tough neighborhood that was riddled with drugs and crime. The late bloomer in football did not attract much attention from the premier college programs, but did show enough talent to land a scholarship to North Carolina.

It was there he blossomed. Taylor earned the nickname "Godzilla" with the Tar Heels for his relentless pursuit of opposing quarterbacks. The result was that he was taken second overall in the NFL draft, the highest pick of any player in North Carolina history. His greatness as a pro resulted in ten Pro Bowl appearances as well as Associated Press Defensive Player of the Year awards in 1981, 1982, and 1986.[2]

POINT TOTAL EXPLANATION

Achievements: 34/35

Only a lack of accomplishment at any level in any other sport and the fact that he led the NFL in sacks only once cost Taylor a perfect score here.

One would be hard-pressed to select a handful of NFL defensive players throughout the history of the league who achieved more or raised the level of his unit higher. Taylor was a perennial Pro Bowler and a Hall of Famer. There is little more he could have accomplished.

Athleticism: 25/25

Taylor was able to revolutionize the outside linebacker position because of the depth of his athleticism. He used his speed and quickness to track down ball carriers and quarterbacks, backs emerging from the backfield, or receivers running routes. He utilized his agility and strength to take on offensive linemen in run defense and in pass rush.

Athletic Requirements of the Sport and Position: 19/20

It can be argued that the point total here is due to Taylor, who set a new standard for the level of athleticism needed for an outside linebacker to thrive. No position on the defense requires a higher amount or wider range of athleticism, especially from the 1980s and beyond, when running backs were increasingly being utilized as dump-off receivers, and outside linebackers became greatly responsible for covering them as well as tight ends.

Clutch Factor/Mental and Emotional Toughness/ Intangibles: 13/15

Taylor gained a well-deserved reputation for the intensity with which he played. That does not always translate into clutch performances or mental and emotional toughness, however. And though Taylor managed 8 sacks in fifteen postseason games, he had none in the 1986 and 1990 Super Bowls. He did make a key stop that prevented Denver Broncos quarterback John Elway from scoring in the former, but though he continued to play at his typical high level and his team won both games, Taylor was no more a standout performer than usual.[3]

Versatility: 2/5

Taylor played some baseball in his youth, but that hardly qualifies here. He receives some consideration for his versatility as an outside linebacker, but not for any talents off the gridiron.

TOTAL POINTS: 93

23

CARL LEWIS: KING CARL

Track and Field

Thirty-five-year-old Carl Lewis burst forward and within two seconds was running full speed, his powerful legs churning, his arms moving in perfect harmony. He leaped forward with every ounce of power he could muster and flew through the air before landing in the sand. The huge crowd awaited the verdict, but Lewis already knew. He had won yet another gold medal.

It was the 1996 Summer Games in Atlanta, just a relative stone's throw from Lewis's Birmingham, Alabama, birthplace. Lewis had just soared 27.89 feet to capture the Olympic long jump for the fourth time. Some had believed he was too old to take gold. He had proven them all wrong.[1]

Lewis had cemented his legacy. Nobody could deny he was the greatest long jumper of all time. In fact, some believe him to be the finest track and field athlete ever. The gold medals he earned over four Olympics speak for themselves. Lewis accepted second place just once in Olympic competition between 1984 and 1996: a silver in the 200 meters in 1988.

The rest of his events speak for his greatness. Lewis won gold in the long jump as well as the 100 and 200 meters in 1984, establishing a new Olympic mark in the latter, and helped the 400-meter relay team set a world record. He snagged gold in the 100 meters and long jump in 1988, then again won the long jump in 1992 while aiding in another world-record effort by the relay team.[2]

His dominance is a bit less surprising given the athleticism that ran in the family. Frederick Carlton Lewis was born on July 1, 1961, in the segregated South, but eventually moved to New Jersey. His mother was a hurdler on the 1951 Pan American team, while his father was a track coach and his sister Carol was an Olympic long jumper who earned bronze in the 1983 World Championships at the age of sixteen.

They Said It

My thoughts before a big race are usually pretty simple. I tell myself: Get out of the blocks, run your race, stay relaxed. If you run your race, you'll win. . . . [C]hannel your energy. Focus. —Carl Lewis

My goal is to be respected. I would like to become the type of person that Jesse Owens was, a person influential in track and field who is a role model. That means more to me than being a rich man. —Carl Lewis

Carl took the local track world by storm. The school record in the long jump when he arrived was 21 feet, 6 inches. He destroyed it after his freshman year and continued to break it. He leaped 25 feet as a sophomore and reached 26 feet, 8 inches and earned a bronze medal in both the Pan Am Games and Spartakiad before taking his talents to the University of Houston. He was ranked fifth in the world in the long jump by 1979.[3]

Lewis dominated with the Cougars. Four decades later, he still holds their records in the indoor and outdoor long jump as well as the indoor 55-meter dash. The six-time All-American won six national championships and nine individual conference crowns during just two seasons at Houston. He burst upon the national scene by qualifying for the 1980 Olympics in the long jump and 400-meter relay but was sidelined by the US boycott of the Moscow Games.[4]

He made up for it in 1984. And 1988. And 1992. And 1996. Those who believe Lewis is the greatest track-and-field athlete in history certainly have plenty of ammunition to back up their contention. His four gold medals in 1984 matched the record set by Jesse Owens in 1936, and he also equaled the mark of capturing the same event in four straight Olympic Games when he won the long jump in 1996.[5]

POINT TOTAL EXPLANATION

Achievements: 34/35

Perhaps a few individual world records would have warranted a perfect score here, but Lewis can't be penalized greatly. He won nearly every World Championship and Olympic competition in which he participated and established Olympic marks in the sprints. Snagging gold in four consecutive Games speaks not only of his accomplishments but also his longevity.

Athleticism: 24/25

Lewis displayed nearly every athletic attribute possible. He boasted the speed to win sprints and gather the necessary momentum in the long jump and the timing and agility required in the relays. He was also a more powerful runner than most; he used his muscular legs to create long strides as he raced down the track.

Athletic Requirements of the Sport and Events: 18/20

The athleticism required of a sprinter and leaper is undeniable. One must be quick to achieve the key component of bolting off the blocks and blazing fast to win. The timing and leg strength necessary to take off for a gold-medal leap in the long jump also cannot be questioned. But one cannot award points for the raw power required of decathletes and others who compete in field events such as the shot put and discus. Also missing here is the daily grind of physical competition, such as what basketball and hockey players experience.

Clutch Factor/Mental and Emotional Toughness/ Intangibles: 15/15

Carl Lewis came, and he conquered. He won nearly every event he entered, including in Olympic competition with the eyes of the world upon him. And he did it for well over a decade. Perfect score here.

Versatility: 2/5

Lewis certainly boasted the athleticism to thrive in other sports, but he concentrated on the sprints and long jump. Perhaps if he had competed in the hurdles he would deserve more points in this category, but there is not much versatility here.

TOTAL POINTS: 93

24

REGGIE WHITE: THE MINISTER OF DEFENSE

Football

If *only*. Those are the two words Reggie White must have thought to himself after he retired. If only he had not played two meaningless years in the ill-fated United States Football League (USFL). If White had spent those seasons in the NFL, he would be its all-time sack leader. His 198 career drops of quarterbacks rank him as second in league history, just two behind Bruce Smith. White retired on top of the list, but Smith eventually overtook him.

But it's no biggie in the grand scheme of things. White's legacy as one of the greatest players ever will last decades beyond his tragic and untimely passing in 2004 at age forty-three. His consistent production for the Philadelphia Eagles and Green Bay Packers at defensive end resulted in ten All-Pro honors and thirteen Pro Bowl appearances.

White was not only a danger to quarterbacks; he was also among the premier tackling defensive linemen ever. While 100-plus-tackle seasons are common among linebackers, such is not typical for defensive ends in 3–4 or 4–3 alignments. But White registered at least 100 tackles in four of his first seven seasons and averaged 97 tackles a year from 1985 to 1993.[1]

And to think he could have opted for a basketball career if he'd been so inclined. Born Reginald Howard White in Chattanooga, Tennessee, on December 19, 1961, White was raised with an emphasis on religion by his mother and grandmother. Young Reggie was inspired by the Baptist ministers at his church and continued to embrace their teachings; he too became an ordained minister, fulfilling a promise he had made to his mother at age twelve. His other promise was to become an NFL player.

Football gave him the confidence he badly needed after having been verbally bullied as a young child. Other kids called him "Bigfoot" or "Land of the Giant," then they would run away. The taunts hurt his

They Said It

People consider me a success because I'm a good football player and make lots of money. But if my heart's not right, if I'm not living a life pleasing to God, I'm a failure.—Reggie White

He was the greatest, he was the most talented person I ever played against in the league, and you know I'm putting some unbelievable players in that category.—Giants quarterback Phil Simms

self-image—and football restored it. White boasted plenty of size and strength, but he believed it to be all God given. He never lifted weights or embarked on ambitious conditioning programs.

White excelled in both basketball and football at Howard High School, earning all-state honors in the former and gaining All-American status in the latter. He never wavered in his commitment to the gridiron, nor in his passion for the Volunteer State, accepting a scholarship to the University of Tennessee despite offers from elsewhere. He spent Saturdays on the football field and Sundays listening to sermons throughout the state. He played just two years in college and was named Southeastern Conference Player of the Year in his second season. He was also a finalist for the Lombardi Award, which is presented to the premier defensive lineman in the country.[2]

A desire to help his family financially motivated White to sign a $4 million contract with the Memphis Showboats of the fledgling USFL upon his graduation from Tennessee. He starred there, but the desire to compete against the best finally won him over and he defected to Philadelphia in 1985 after starting that year with Memphis. That short span likely cost White longevity as the all-time NFL sack leader, but it can be argued that it takes nothing away from his legacy.[3]

POINT TOTAL EXPLANATION

Achievements: 34/35

White must be strongly credited for averaging nearly a sack a game for his career, including a remarkable 70 in fifty-seven games during his first four seasons. His tackle numbers dropped considerably after he left Philadelphia for Green Bay, but that falls under the category of nit-picking. White is considered by many the greatest sacker of quarterbacks to ever grace a gridiron.[4]

Athleticism: 23/25

This 300-pounder was more a power rusher than a speed rusher, but he was agile enough not to simply bull-rush offensive linemen. His specialty was taking his inside arm and knocking an opponent on his butt with it. That required quickness to get off the ball on the snap and acceleration to absorb the initial contact and maintain momentum toward the quarterback. White also displayed great mobility for a man his size in tracking down running backs while moving laterally.[5]

Athletic Requirements of the Sport and Position: 17/20

Defensive ends who act both as pass rushers and run stoppers deserve high point totals here. They need a variety of athletic attributes to succeed, including speed, quickness, agility, and both lower- and upper-body strength. The lone drawback is that they play only sixteen games a year, but the collisions with opposing players on every down result in the requirement of durability as well.

Clutch Factor/Mental and Emotional Toughness/ Intangibles: 15/15

White collected three sacks in the Packers' defeat of New England in Super Bowl XXXI. It was among the most epic defensive performances of all time. Though that was his only overwhelming playoff performance, the mental and emotional toughness needed to record that many sacks over a career cannot be underestimated. White played with an incredible motor. He never took a play off.[6]

Versatility: 4/5

An all-state basketball player and Hall of Fame football player who played the run nearly as well as he sacked quarterbacks? White deserves a near-perfect score in this category despite having played just one sport past the high school level.

TOTAL POINTS: 93

25

BRUCE JENNER: BRUISER

Decathlon

Caitlyn Jenner will forever be better known as a transgender icon than an athlete who conquered the decathlon. Courageous personal decision aside, Caitlyn's transformation turned attention away from an incredible world-record performance at the 1976 Summer Olympics in Montreal.

Jenner did not appear destined to grace the top step of the podium that year after placing tenth in the decathlon at the Munich Games four years earlier. But he had turned his attention to that grueling event merely a year before, after previously focusing on football. That he qualified for the 1972 Olympics at all was quite an accomplishment.

Still, his leapfrog from tenth to first raised many an eyebrow and motivated some to consider Jenner the greatest athlete of his day. The variety of events in which Jenner won or placed high in Montreal was indeed inspiring. He won the discus and finished second in the 1500 meters, pole vault, 110-meter hurdles, 400 meters, high jump, and shot put. His success in such a wide variety of events resulted in a world-record point total.

The level of his domination was shocking, but he had achieved enough leading into the event to make his victory far less surprising. He had won the AAU title in 1974 and the Pan American Games championship a year later. He then established a world record that he would break in Montreal in a triangular meet against the Soviet Union and Poland.[1]

Jenner had taken an interesting path throughout his life. Born on October 28, 1949, in Mt. Kisco, New York, he was raised in Tarrytown, the son of a tree surgeon who had been a fine sprinter in his army days and a stay-at-home mom. The child's energy motivated his dad to nickname him "Bruiser." The young Jenner showed athletic ability as well, but also a curiosity about his sexuality and a penchant for trying on his mother's clothes.

> ### *They Said It*
>
> *Success is not measured by heights attained but by obstacles overcome. We're going to pass through many obstacles in our lives: good days, bad days. But the successful person will overcome those obstacles and constantly move forward.*—Bruce Jenner
>
> *The decathlon was the perfect distraction. Sports. It's not real life. You go out there, you work hard, you train your ass off, win the Games. I'm very proud of that part of my life. And it's not like I just want to throw it out. It's part of who I am.*—Caitlyn Jenner, reflecting on the 1976 Olympics

A reading disability caused Jenner to fail second grade and caused him embarrassment, which he sought to overcome through sports. After the Jenner family moved to Newtown, Connecticut, he proved his brilliance as an all-around athlete, winning pole vault and high jump championships in high school and even earning three water skiing titles. He also competed on the football and basketball teams.

Jenner performed well enough on the gridiron to land a small scholarship to Graceland College in Iowa. He then turned misfortune into opportunity. Sidelined his freshman season with an injury, Jenner became bored and began to train for the decathlon. He showed immediate talent, winning his first event with a school-record point total. His football career was over. He focused his energies on making the Olympic team, which he did a year later. His performance in Munich proved merely a stepping-stone to stardom. Little could anyone have imagined that stardom would take quite a different form forty years later.[2]

POINT TOTAL EXPLANATION

Achievements: 32/35

Jenner would deserve closer to the maximum point total had he excelled beyond the 1976 Games. He also won just one event in two Olympic decathlons. But he deserved credit not only for setting a world record in the decathlon in Montreal but winning three water skiing championships and landing a football scholarship, no matter how minor. Such accomplishments extend beyond the "Versatility" section here.

Athleticism: 24/25

The variety of events in which Jenner placed first or second is downright amazing, proving his power (shot put, javelin), speed (110 and 400 meters), leg strength and balance (high jump, pole vault), and endurance (1500 meters).[3]

Athletic Requirements of the Sport: 20/20

Jenner excelled in the Olympic decathlon, an event that tests the all-around skills and talents of the best in the world. That it requires every athletic attribute to thrive is undeniable.

Clutch Factor/Mental and Emotional Toughness/ Intangibles: 12/15

The drive Jenner displayed to turn a football injury into qualifying for the 1972 Olympics after one just year of training must be rewarded in this category. That excuses his mediocre showing in Munich. But Jenner simply did not participate in enough sporting events at a high level of competition to earn a great score in this category.

Versatility: 4/5

Jenner deserves a perfect score here for excelling not only in the huge array of athletic challenges in the decathlon, but also for his talents as a youth in several sports. He was a championship water skier and performed well enough on the football field to earn a scholarship. He also played basketball in high school.

TOTAL POINTS: 93

RAY ROBINSON: SUGAR

Boxing

Sugar Ray Robinson held aloft by other boxers. *Library of Congress*

Those who claim that old-school athletes were tougher than the new breed might cite Sugar Ray Robinson as evidence in favor of their argument. Boxers in the modern era require months to prepare for fights. The welterweight and middleweight many claim to be the finest to ever lace up a pair of gloves boasted a record of 128–1–2 through the first eleven years of his career. And he often fought two weeks or even one week apart.

Robinson thrived during the heyday of the sport, when bouts were regularly listened to by millions on the radio and later witnessed by equal numbers on television and fought in sold-out arenas and even stadiums. The sport was second only to baseball in popularity among American fans. Robinson fought twenty bouts in 1941 alone. He won them all, remaining unbeaten until losing a unanimous decision to Jake LaMotta (whom he had beaten four months earlier) in February 1943.

Despite his incredible record, Robinson did not receive a crack at the welterweight title until he defeated Tommy Bell nearly four years later, almost eight years into his professional career. Robinson did not lose again until 1951, at the age of thirty. He continued to fight until he was forty-four. Five of his nineteen career defeats occurred during the last six months of his career, in 1965.[1]

The need for an African American athlete to continue earning money in an era of limited opportunities was certainly a motivating factor for

> ## They Said It
>
> *Rhythm is everything in boxing. Every move you make starts with your heart, and that's in rhythm or you're in trouble. Your rhythm should set the pace of the fight. If it does, then you penetrate your opponent's rhythm. You make him fight your fight, and that's what boxing is all about.*—Ray Robinson
>
> *You are the king, the master, my idol.*—Muhammad Ali, speaking to Ray Robinson

Robinson, who was born Walker Smith Jr. in Detroit on May 3, 1921, but grew up in Harlem. He borrowed a new name from a local boxer as a teenage amateur and began battering one foe after another.

Robinson was well established when he boxed in exhibition tours of military bases during World War II along with heavyweight champion Joe Louis, who had been a neighbor in Detroit and an inspiring force in his life. Robinson displayed pride in his heritage and a militancy that was ahead of his time. He refused on one occasion to appear until attendance was open to black soldiers, and he scuffled with an army policeman who threatened him with violence for using a whites-only phone booth.

He maintained a heavy fight schedule during the war. He averaged one fight every three to four weeks over the next seven years and did not lose again until 1951. His skills eventually waned, but he still managed to go unbeaten in ten consecutive fights at age forty-three. That longevity is a comparatively minor factor in the belief of many boxing experts that he was the greatest fighter of all time. Rather, it was the immense talent he showed during his prime that motivates such praise.[2]

POINT TOTAL EXPLANATION

Achievements: 34/35

Robinson held the world welterweight crown for five years after World War II and was middleweight champion for five different periods from 1951 to 1960. He only once suffered a technical knockout in his two hundred bouts despite fighting into his midforties. Though Rocky Marciano retired unbeaten, one can claim that Robinson was as accomplished a boxer that ever lived. After all, he fought nearly four times as often as Marciano.

Athleticism: 23/25

Robinson was known for his footwork and knockout power with either hand. His hand speed and leverage were strengths, and his quickness allowed him to avoid hard contact. He even became an inspiration for Muhammad Ali as he trained for his career-altering fight against Sonny Liston in 1964. Robinson did not fight like Rock 'Em Sock 'Em Robots—he moved about the ring and looked for an opening. He used his footwork to separate himself from opponents, then put them away with combinations.[3]

Athletic Requirements of the Sport and Division: 19/20

Robinson earns an extra point here for his brutal schedule, which sometimes included up to four fights in a month. Boxing is a brutal sport and anyone who can survive and thrive having fought two hundred bouts deserves a little more consideration in this category. It requires remarkable elusiveness and durability to make like the Energizer Bunny and keep going for a quarter century.

Clutch Factor/Mental and Emotional Toughness/ Intangibles: 14/15

Robinson generally rose to the occasion in the biggest bouts, especially in his prime. He beat LaMotta twice after his initial defeat and defeated the likes of Henry Armstrong, Rocky Graziano, and Gene Fullmer. His intelligence as a boxer has been overlooked due to his physical greatness. And though he lost several battles in his forties, that he remained active and won his share at that age only serves to strengthen his case here.[4]

Versatility: 2/5

Like many boxers from difficult circumstances, especially African Americans in a greatly segregated society with few opportunities, Robinson had tunnel vision. His athletic versatility in the ring earns him a couple points here despite his lack of participation in other sports.

TOTAL POINTS: 92

DON HUTSON: THE ALABAMA ANTELOPE

Football

Those familiar with statistics-based website Pro Football Reference know that numbers with which featured athletes led their leagues in various categories are shown in bold. A study of the Don Hutson page screams out his dominance as a wide receiver for the Packers in the 1930s and 1940s. Bolded numbers can be seen all over the place. Hutson played eleven years, giving him thirty-three total opportunities to pace the NFL in receptions, receiving yards, and touchdowns. On Football Reference, twenty-four of those numbers are bolded.

Hutson led the league eight times in receptions, seven times in receiving yards, and nine times in touchdowns. In an era during which the forward pass was still in its infancy and the ground game reigned supreme, Hutson averaged nearly 70 yards receiving per game, which in today's schedule translates into more than 1,000 yards a season. He is considered the inventor of pass patterns. Nobody of his era approached his level of production at that position. And his 1942 season was arguably the greatest ever for a wide receiver in relation to his era. Hutson caught 74 passes for 1,211 yards and 17 touchdowns in just eleven games that year.

And by the way—he also played defense (like most NFL players of that time) and served as the team's placekicker for most of his career. Hutson was both a defensive back and defensive end. He twice earned the Joe F. Carr Trophy as the outstanding player in the NFL and earned All-Pro status five times.[1]

Not bad for a guy better known for his collection of pet rattlesnakes as a teenager. Born January 31, 1913, in Pine Bluff, Arkansas, Hutson played only one year of high school football. He could thank prep teammate Bob Seawall for the opportunity to play at the University of Alabama; Seawall insisted that Hutson be included in the package if he was to play for the Crimson Tide. Ironically, Hutson stuck around longer than Seawall, who dropped out after two years. Hutson played opposite side of fellow wide receiver Bear Bryant, who became perhaps the greatest coaching legend in college football history at Alabama.

Hutson performed well enough there to earn All-American status in 1934. His talent piqued the interest of Packers coach Curly Lambeau, who climbed the wall during a secret Crimson Tide practice before the Rose Bowl that year and came away particularly impressed with Hutson's shiftiness, sure hands, and elusiveness. The brilliant wideout didn't disappoint Lambeau in the game either. He caught seven passes, including two for touchdowns, in an Alabama rout of Stanford. Soon he was earning $175 per game for the Packers, nearly twice the amount most NFL starters were paid. Hutson snagged an 83-yard touchdown pass against the Chicago Bears on the first play of his first game. He was already the greatest wide receiver in the NFL.[2]

POINT TOTAL EXPLANATION

Achievements: 34/35

Hutson was the Jim Brown of wide receivers until Jerry Rice came along. He thoroughly dominated the position in his era. The only slight drawback was his comparative lack of production in championship games aside from

They Said It

Don had the most fluid motion you had ever seen when he was running. It was like he was going just as fast as possible when all of a sudden he would put on an extra burst of speed and be gone.—Alabama teammate and future coach Bear Bryant

For every pass I caught in a game, I caught a thousand in practice.—Don Hutson

I just concede him two touchdowns a game, and I hope we can score more.—Legendary Chicago Bears coach George Halas

his fine performance in a victory over the Boston Redskins in 1936. One can only speculate whether conservative game plans or an inability to separate from defensive backs explains his struggles in his four title games to follow.[3]

Athleticism: 23/25

Hutson boasted enough speed and elusiveness to beat defenders, and his huge hands were soft and sure. His athleticism was wide ranging enough for him to run track for the Alabama team and earn a baseball scholarship as well. But it was not his athleticism that made him arguably the greatest wide receiver ever; rather, it was his innovative approach to the game.

Athletic Requirements of the Sport and Position: 17/20

Wide receivers require as high a level of athleticism as any position player in major American team sports. They must outrun and outleap defenders while trying to separate from them with their quickness and shiftiness. They need strong legs and tremendous balance and agility. The only points lost here are because they use those skills rather infrequently. Hutson played an average of fewer than eleven games per year in just eleven seasons. He loses a point for that in comparisons to the modern players.

Clutch Factor/Mental and Emotional Toughness/ Intangibles: 14/15

Though indeed his production slipped after 1936 in championship games, Hutson earns massive credit for revolutionizing the wide receiver position. Prior to his arrival, the NFL single-season record for receptions was 22. He broke that in his second season and more than doubled *that* total in 1942. Hutson created the art of route running. He designed the first buttonhook, hook-and-go, and Z outs. And it has been claimed that not one defensive back in his era could cover him.[4]

Versatility: 4/5

Hutson landed a partial baseball scholarship at Alabama as a center fielder after a standout high school career. He also ran track for the Crimson Tide. He certainly deserves a strong score here.[5]

TOTAL POINTS: 92

28

BOB HAYES: BULLET BOB

Track and Field, Football

Bob Hayes had already snagged the gold medal in the 100 meters at the 1964 Summer Olympics, tying the world record at 10.0. He had beaten the silver medalist by a ridiculous seven meters. But his task was not complete, and it was about to become far more daunting. He was ready to anchor the US 400-meter relay team. And it was running fifth when he received the baton.

Hayes took off and soon reached his typical blur-like speed. He bolted past one, then another, and when it was over he had turned a three-meter deficit into a two-meter triumph. His time was unofficially clocked at 8.6 seconds as the team established a new world record at 39.0.

"You haven't got anything except Hayes," said French anchor Jocelyn Delecour. "That's all we need," replied Hayes's teammate Paul Drayton.[1]

Drayton was not the only colleague to thank his lucky stars that Hayes was on his side. The athlete known as the World's Fastest Human proved it in the Olympics. But he continued to prove it as a wide receiver for the Dallas Cowboys. His blazing speed forever changed how defensive backs covered receivers. What was once solely a one-on-one task was transformed into the art of double-teaming and the need for safety help. Safeties who once focused on stopping the run were forced to prevent Hayes from blasting past cornerbacks for easy catches and scores. Zone defenses were popularized as well due to the talents of Hayes.[2]

Not that it helped all that much. In an era in which 1,000-yard receivers were rare, Hayes exceeded that total in his first two NFL seasons, leading the league in receiving touchdowns in both of those years. He averaged an absurd 26.1 yards per catch in 1970 and 24.0 the following season. He concluded his career as one of five receivers to average more than 20 yards per reception. He was also a feared kick returner.[3]

His athletic brilliance became apparent soon after he was born on December 20, 1942, in Jacksonville, Florida. He gained a reputation by beating the top sprinter on the high school track by five yards. Hayes quickly emerged as a track standout but was recruited by Florida A&M as a fullback. He ran track as well—did he ever. He managed a 9.1 in the 100-yard dash to establish a world record that stood for eleven years. He soon shattered the world indoor mark in the 60-yard dash at 6.0.[4]

Hayes then went on to Olympic and NFL glory. He earned All-Pro status four straight seasons and helped the Cowboys win the 1972 Super Bowl. It came as no surprise when he was elected into the Pro Football Hall of Fame.

POINT TOTAL EXPLANATION

Achievements: 33/35

Hayes participated in only two Olympic events and played only ten full seasons in the NFL. But combine the two, and consider his two gold medals and Hall of Fame credentials, and he simply cannot be penalized much here.

Athleticism: 24/25

Hayes was no diminutive speedster. He weighed in at 190 pounds and bolted by the competition on the cinders and the gridiron with a powerful

---

They Said It

After me, everybody started drafting speed. But they used to laugh at a lot of those guys because they couldn't catch. [Browns quarterback] Otto Graham once said that I had 9.1 speed and 12-flat hands, but I proved him wrong. I was the leader of the pack.—Bob Hayes

Fans used to boo me when he got behind me, but how can you cover him running backward when he's the fastest guy in the world.—NFL cornerback Dick Lynch

stride. He boasted a strong upper body and overcame skinny ankles and calves to support his weight. He lifted his knees high as he ran. He was not a strictly a blow-by, straight-ahead runner on the football field; he could cut inside or out while taking short passes a long way.

Athletic Requirements of the Sport and Position: 19/20

Hayes must once again be credited for being a two-sport athlete here. The combined athleticism required of Olympic sprinters and NFL wide receivers cannot be underestimated. There is not much sheer power needed in either endeavor, so Hayes does not receive all the points available. But he's as close as one can get.

Clutch Factor/Mental and Emotional Toughness/ Intangibles: 12/15

Winning two golds and saving the relay team from oblivion in the Olympics is no small feat. But Hayes didn't do much in the NFL playoffs, catching four passes in his last four postseason games and scoring just two touchdowns in thirty-one playoff appearances.

Versatility: 4/5

It is tempting to give Hayes five points here because of his Olympic and NFL feats. But he was basically an incredibly fast man who used that speed to excel in two sports. Five points are generally reserved for decathletes and more well-rounded standouts.

TOTAL POINTS: 92

29

BILL RUSSELL: MR. 11 RINGS

Basketball

Five players grace the basketball court at any one time. It's six in hockey, nine in baseball, and eleven in football. One can therefore argue that the most dominant defensive player in the NBA is the most dominant defensive player in major American sports. And that man is Bill Russell.

It is a shame that blocked shots were not counted by statisticians during the era in which Russell led his Boston Celtics on their annual runs to the championship. They called journeyman 1970s and 1980s center Marvin Webster "The Human Eraser," but that moniker rightly belonged to Russell, who was not only proficient at blocking shots but proved to be such a defensive force that opponents grew fearful of attacking the basket. He would quite commonly block five or more shots in a game, but it was his overall defensive brilliance that made the difference in his frequent battles against archrival Wilt Chamberlain in the Celtics' many title-round triumphs.

Russell was arguably also the finest rebounder in NBA history. He led the league five times in that category and averaged more than twenty per game in each of his first eleven seasons. Though offensive rebounds were also not charted during his career, which ran from 1956 to 1969, it has been estimated that he yanked down about seven a game, giving his team extra chances to score.

And though Russell was outscored by other centers of his era—such as Chamberlain, Willis Reed, and Walt Bellamy—he could not be ignored offensively. He averaged 15.1 points per game throughout his career and was a willing and proficient passer. His assist totals rose later in his career. His Celtics won eleven championships in his thirteen seasons, and he was named NBA Most Valuable Player five times.[1]

William Felton Russell was born in segregated Monroe, Louisiana, on February 12, 1934; his family later moved to the San Francisco Bay Area. Russell had yet to blossom on the basketball court in high school, but he showed enough promise to land a scholarship at the University of San Francisco. It was there that he emerged as a defensive force. At 6-foot-9 he was shorter than other centers of his era, but he still averaged 20.7 points and 20.3 rebounds per game in his three-year career with the Dons. His brilliance on the defensive end played the most critical role in his team's winning national championships in both 1955 and 1956. He was named Most Outstanding Player in the 1956 NCAA Tournament.

Celtics coach Red Auerbach was licking his chops. He yearned to land Russell but understood quite well that he would need to move up in the 1956 draft to snag him. Auerbach already boasted offensive firepower in Bob Cousy and Bill Sharman, and he believed a defensive stalwart such as Russell would transform the Celtics into NBA champions. So he sent all-star Ed Macauley and promising rookie Cliff Hagan to St. Louis for the rights to draft Russell.

The Celtics also landed K. C. Jones—Russell's college teammate—and Tom Heinsohn in that draft. It proved to be one of the greatest draft hauls ever and resulted in a dynasty that ranks only behind the New York Yankees of the 1940s through the early 1960s as the most dominant in American sports history. And though many of his teammates played

They Said It

The idea is not to block every shot. The idea is to make your opponent believe that you might block every shot.—Bill Russell

We were forced to play the Celtics 11 to 13 times during the regular season. And if you think that wasn't enough, then we have another seven games against them in the playoffs, if it went seven games. So I had a chance to see William Felton Russell much more than I wanted to.—Wilt Chamberlain

Success is the result of consistent practice of winning skills and actions. There is nothing miraculous about the process. There is no luck involved. —Bill Russell

significant roles in that success, Russell was the proverbial straw that stirred the drink. The first-ballot Hall of Famer whose name graces the NBA Finals MVP trophy even served as the team's player-coach for two championship seasons.[2]

POINT TOTAL EXPLANATION

Achievements: 34/35

Bill Russell was the most important player on a team that won NBA championships as a matter of course. His contributions to the Celtics dynasty cannot be understated. He is still considered the most dominant defensive player in history. Athough he was no weak link offensively and was a fine passer and offensive rebounder, his comparative lack of scoring costs him a point here.

Athleticism: 23/25

Russell used his quickness, agility, balance, and leaping ability to prove himself as one of the greatest shot blockers and rebounders in NBA history. His quickness allowed him to leave opposing centers and cover their teammates or swat away shots by opponents who dared to enter the lane. He didn't boast the same level of strength as other premier centers historically, but he changed forever how NBA teams evaluated and valued defense.

Athletic Requirements of the Sport and Position: 18/20

It can be contended that NBA players are required to be the best athletes in American sports. Those in Russell's era were in constant movement for well over forty minutes a game and eighty-two regular-season games a year (they get far more rest now). Though centers are not quite as active and mobile as point guards, for instance, they must use their strength and quickness to battle near the basket and challenge penetrators.

Clutch Factor/Mental and Emotional Toughness/ Intangibles: 15/15

Russell performed his best with championships on the line. His battles against Chamberlain were epic, but he consistently emerged as the winner.

His scoring, rebounding, and assist totals were all higher in the postseason despite the raised level of competition. He averaged at least 20 rebounds per postseason game every year. Russell was a winner. He deserves every point in this category.

Versatility: 2/5

Russell did not explore his athletic potential until high school, and when he did he concentrated strictly on basketball. He developed into a proficient golfer later in life, but that does not earn him much here.

TOTAL POINTS: 92

DEACON JONES:
THE SECRETARY OF DEFENSE

Football

It's too bad about NFL statistics. The league was late catching up; it treated defensive players with disdain in that era. It did not count sacks when Deacon Jones was terrorizing ball quarterbacks. If it had, perhaps Jones—and not Bruce Smith—would be recognized as the all-time leader in that department.

Heck, Jones was the one who coined the term "sack" to describe what he did so often. He was the premier player in the Fearsome Foursome of the Los Angeles Rams—which also included Merlin Olsen, Rosey Grier, and Lamar Lundy—and was cited by no less an authority than Dick Butkus as the most dominant defensive line in NFL history.[1]

And to think that Jones was nearly bypassed in the 1961 draft, perhaps destroying his opportunity to display his enormous talent. The credit goes to two Rams scouts watching film of a college opponent when they noticed a 6-foot-4, 272-pound tackle chasing down the running backs on whom they were focusing. The scouts recommended Jones as a sleeper pick, leading their team to pluck him in the fourteenth round.

Jones hadn't previously made a name for himself. He played the 1958 season with South Carolina State and didn't return to the game until hooking up with Mississippi Vocational in 1960. It was not exactly four standout years at Alabama with Bear Bryant—but then, he wasn't exactly recruiting African American players back then.[2]

The Rams switched Jones from tackle to end, a move that proved quite beneficial. He teamed with the fellow perennial All-Pro Olsen on the left side to give the Rams half of their Fearsome Foursome. Jones earned unanimous all-league recognition every year from 1965 to 1970 and played

They Said It

When I first came up, defensive linemen were dull as hell. Some were great performers, but nobody knew who they were. I set out to change that.—Deacon Jones

There has never been a better football player than Deacon Jones.—Merlin Olsen

I'm the best defensive end around. I'd hate to have to play against me! —Deacon Jones

He was fantastic coming off the ball. He had the greatest head slap anyone could have. Our right tackle Cas Banaszek had ice bags on his head after every game against the Rams. . . . Deacon hit him so hard.—49ers tight end Bob Windsor

in eight Pro Bowls. He was named the premier defensive player in the NFL in both 1967 and 1968. A blockbuster trade to San Diego in 1972 did not slow him down, despite his advancing age. He led his team in tackles and was again selected to the Pro Bowl. Upon retirement, he had missed just five games in his fourteen-year NFL career.

He had come a long way from Eatonville, Florida, where he was born David Jones on December 9, 1938, to parents who ran a barbecue stand. One of ten children, Jones played football, baseball, and basketball at Hungerford High School. One traumatic and profound experience in his life came at age fourteen, when he witnessed a carload of laughing white teenagers hit an elderly black woman with a watermelon. The woman later died, and police declined to investigate. Jones took out the anger he felt as a black youth on the football field. He found another outlet during his year at South Carolina State, when he became involved in lunch counter demonstrations to promote integration. His activities, which landed him in jail, played a role in his departure from that school. Few could have imagined then that Jones would eventually blossom into arguably the greatest defensive end of all time.[3]

POINT TOTAL EXPLANATION

Achievements: 33/35

Though it is impossible to pinpoint a deserving point total here statistically, what is certain is that the Rams went from woeful to wonderful defensively by the mid-1960s upon the blossoming of Jones and his fellow Fearsome Foursome mates. That Jones was a disruptive force and among the top sackers in NFL history cannot be disputed.

Athleticism: 24/25

Jones used speed, agility, and quickness over power in tracking down quarterbacks and ball carriers, but he could also overpower tackles on occasion. He was simply one of the most athletic defensive linemen ever.

Athletic Requirements of the Sport and Position: 18/20

The deep involvement in all run and pass plays requires defensive ends to boast tremendous durability and conditioning. They can't take plays off. They also need great balance, quickness, and upper- and lower-body strength. Football players in Jones's era faced just a fourteen-game schedule, which weakens the score a bit here. But the depth of the in-game athletic requirements of those at his position are undeniable.

Clutch Factor/Mental and Emotional Toughness/ Intangibles: 14/15

Jones was the fiercest of the Fearsome Foursome. His motor and relentlessness were legendary. He attacked on every play. His "head slap" technique against offensive linemen was deemed so dangerous that is was banned by the NFL in 2009. Jones embraced the violence of football.[4]

Versatility: 3/5

Jones did not focus solely on football. He also played basketball and baseball in high school. He deserves a few points here.

TOTAL POINTS: 92

31

SANDY KOUFAX: THE LEFT ARM OF GOD

Baseball

Something clicked for Sandy Koufax in 1961. That was the year he began finding his control. And that was the year National League hitters descended from hoping for a walk to hopelessness.

Koufax locked in. He already boasted the premier fastball in the sport and a fall-off-the-table curve. But his newfound ability to pinpoint his pitches resulted in arguably the most dominant stretch by a hurler in the history of the sport. That period started in earnest in 1962. The Dodgers left-hander led the NL in earned run average in each of the next five seasons, won at least twenty-five games three times, and compiled an absurd record of 111–34. His ERA during that period was 1.95. Not bad for a guy whose college scholarship was in basketball and who had considered a career in architecture.

There were times in the late 1950s and beyond that Koufax might have wished he had become an architect. His balance and release point often eluded him, resulting in wildness that prevented him from living up to his vast potential. His annual performances were steeped in mediocrity. Koufax managed a 36–40 record and 4-plus ERA from 1955—when he launched his career as a nineteen-year-old bonus baby—through 1960. He averaged five walks per nine innings.

That he began his major-league career so young allowed him to correct his flaws and remain viable. Koufax won eighteen games in limiting his walks in 1961, then spearheaded pennant drives in 1963, 1965, and 1966, after which he retired at age thirty to save his elbow from the painful traumatic arthritis that he feared would cause permanent disability. Koufax was done, but not before he won three Cy Young Awards and one

National League Most Valuable Player over a four-year span. After Koufax sizzled with a 25–5 record in 1963 and twice shut down the vaunted
Yankees in a World Series sweep, New York star Yogi Berra offered his
understanding that Koufax won twenty-five games. What he could not
fathom is that he lost five.[1]

The greatest southpaw ever was born Sanford Braun on December 30,
1935, in Brooklyn. He played stickball in the streets with his neighborhood
friends, but he pronounced an interest in architecture early in life and
began to embrace basketball after a move to Bensonhurst at age fourteen.
His jumping ability and proficiency as a rebounder later caught the attention of scouts. Koufax's pitching talents were noticed by sandlot baseball
manager Milton Laurie, who saw the boy in what was known as the Ice
Cream League. Laurie watched Koufax walk nine batters in two innings,
but was so impressed with his arm that he invited him to pitch for his team
in the Coney Island Sports League. Koufax would often strike out sixteen
to eighteen batters. His parents, who had previously expressed a belief
that spending on baseball was a waste of money and vowed that their son
would never pursue the sport professionally, were changing their tune. But

They Said It

*It's better to throw a theoretically poorer pitch whole-heartedly than to
throw the so-called right pitch with feeling of doubt—doubt that it's right
or doubt that you can make it behave well at that moment. You've got to
feel sure you're doing the right thing—sure that you want to throw the
pitch you're going to throw.*—Sandy Koufax

*It's a deception. I'm with the skeptics. Koufax's fastball did not go up. Of
course, he had such a good release, a smooth point of delivery, that pop of
the wrist at the end that projected the ball so strongly to home plate that
the ball never went down as most fastballs actually do. It lost no velocity
to gravity. That was different.*—Catcher Rick Dempsey on the legend of
Koufax's rising fastball

*I became a good pitcher when I stopped trying to make them miss the ball
and started trying to make them hit it.*—Sandy Koufax

it was in basketball that Koufax earned a scholarship from the University of Cincinnati, a feat that also excited his folks.[2]

Friends still believed his future was in baseball. They urged Koufax to go out for the high school team his senior year. He did indeed, playing first base. And when he performed well for the Bearcats as a freshman starting forward, an NBA career appeared possible.

But a twist of fate would alter the sports world. Cincinnati basketball coach Ed Jucker was also the baseball coach, and he needed pitchers. Koufax volunteered. Both his incredible velocity and erratic control were evident from the start. But he began to pique the interest of major-league teams, particularly the Giants, Dodgers, and Yankees, who were seeking Jewish players to attract the large numbers of Jewish fans in the Big Apple to the ballpark. The Dodgers signed him as a bonus baby in 1954. Koufax never spent a day in the minor leagues.[3]

POINT TOTAL EXPLANATION

Achievements: 31/35

If Koufax were judged here over his last four seasons, the temptation would have been great to give him 36 out of 35 possible points. He was simply the greatest lefty of all time and the most dominant pitcher in baseball history over that short stretch. But it was indeed a short stretch, which limits his point total in this category.

Athleticism: 23/25

Unlike many pitchers, Koufax was a well-rounded athlete. He was strong and quick enough to rebound and score inside with the big boys at just 6-foot-2 as a potential NBA player. He eventually found his balance and coordination on the mound as well.

Athletic Requirements of the Sport and Position: 20/25

This gets a bit tricky. It can be argued that pitchers can be the least athletic position players in major American sports. But Koufax *was* a fine athlete; he was simply not required to be one as a major-league pitcher. He does not lose as many points in this category as do other pitchers.

Clutch Factor/Mental and Emotional Toughness/ Intangibles: 14/15

Koufax performed brilliantly in the World Series. He won twice in the sweep of the Yankees in 1963 and finished his postseason career with a 4–3 record and 0.95 ERA. Both statistics speak volumes about the lack of hitting support he received with titles on the line. Koufax exhibited his best control in the World Series, walking just 11 and striking out 61 in 57 innings pitched.[4]

Versatility: 4/5

That Koufax was a key starter for a premier University of Cincinnati basketball team as a freshman is impressive. It indicates he could have emerged as an NBA standout. Little punishment here for not having played two professional sports. That he was capable of doing so provides a strong enough argument in favor of a near-perfect score.

TOTAL POINTS: 92

32

MICKEY MANTLE: THE MICK

Baseball

New York Yankee Mickey Mantle hitting home run in first inning of the Hall of Fame game August 9, 1954. *Photos used with permission of the National Baseball Hall of Fame Museum (Cooperstown, NY)*

Casey Stengel was sixty years old in the spring of 1951. He had played in the same era as Ty Cobb and Honus Wagner and managed the likes of Joe DiMaggio. He'd seen the greatest baseball players in the world come and go. But he had never laid eyes on a prospect such as Mickey Mantle.

The Yankees manager exclaimed wonderment and even confusion over the skill set of Mantle, who had yet to play in a major-league game. Stengel proved to be prophetic. Mantle boasted a combination of speed and power that eventually made him the first five-tool center fielder (with another one, Willie Mays, on the way).[1]

The nineteen-year-old Mantle wasted little time proving Stengel right as DiMaggio's replacement in center field. He lifted his average over .300 in mid-May and remained a Rookie of the Year contender until a slump in late June and early July prompted a demotion that devastated him. He returned to the Yankees in late August and hit well, then took off in 1952, batting .311, finishing third in the Most Valuable Player voting, and never again returning to the minors.

Mantle finished among the top five in MVP balloting eight times during his brilliant career, winning the award thrice, including back-to-back years in 1956 and 1957. He surpassed 100 runs scored every season from 1953 to 1961, leading the league in that category in five of those years. His

> ### *They Said It*
>
> *Sometimes I think if I had the same body and the same natural ability and someone else's brain, who knows how good a player I might have been.*—Mickey Mantle
>
> *Mickey Mantle is the strongest hitter in the game. He's the only one who hits the ball so hard, he knocks the spin off it. Catching a liner from him is like catching a knuckleball. It flutters all over.*—Journeyman center-fielder Jim Busby
>
> *Somebody once asked me if I ever went up to the plate trying to hit a home run. I said, "Sure, every time."*—Mickey Mantle

speed-power talents were evident not only visually but also through his statistics. He paced the American League in triples and stole 10 or more bases in six consecutive seasons. But he also exceeded 30 home runs nine times, leading the league four times and peaking at 54 in 1961 as he engaged in an epic battle for supremacy with teammate Roger Maris.

Modern statistics are also kind to Mantle and speak to his versatility. He led the AL in WAR six times and Offensive Wins Above Replacement every year from 1955 to 1962. Fearful pitchers and his patience and knowledge of the strike zone led to a tremendous .421 on-base percentage (OBP). Mantle earned an amazing .486 OBP in 1962, reaching base nearly half the time.[2]

Not bad for a guy whose family could barely afford baseball equipment during the Great Depression in the tiny town of Spavinaw, Oklahoma, where Mantle was born on October 20, 1931. It was before the advent of Little League baseball, so Mantle learned the game with friends on the sandlots, reluctantly becoming a switch-hitter at the urging of his father, who foresaw the possibility of his son finding a job as a platoon player. Little could he have imagined that Mickey, whom he named after premier major-league catcher Mickey Cochrane, would emerge as the greatest platoon player in history.

Mantle overcame osteomyelitis, a bone disease that nearly motivated doctors to amputate his leg. He was saved by the wonder drug penicillin, but the disease ended a promising football career and forced him to concentrate solely on baseball. He was playing shortstop for a semipro team with the colorful name the Baxter Springs Whiz Kids at age fifteen when he was discovered by Yankees scout Tom Greenwade, who had arrived to check out a teammate. Mantle picked the right time to slug two home runs, one from each side of the plate. Greenwade had to wait until Mantle graduated from high school to sign him, which he did the following spring. The rest is baseball history.

Though time has provided a perspective on Mickey Mantle, whose battle with alcoholism might have cut short his career and certainly cut short his life, he remains a legend and one of the most complete superstars ever to grace a diamond.[3]

POINT TOTAL EXPLANATION

Achievements: 33/35

Had Mantle maintained his brilliance beyond the age of thirty, he might have earned all the points available here. But injuries and the alcoholism that came to light after his career substantially weakened his statistics. He managed just one strong season after 1962 as his batting average and power numbers suffered. His downturn, which began in earnest in 1965, played a huge role in the collapse of the Yankee dynasty. History, however, cannot diminish the greatness of Mantle during his heyday. He was the most dominant player in the American League for more than a decade.

Athleticism: 25/25

Mantle could do it all. He was a five-tool player before the expression came into vogue. He boasted the power to blast home runs—his 565-foot shot in Washington against the Senators is still considered the longest ever hit. He was gifted with speed, a strong arm, tremendous hand-eye coordination, and the timing and quickness needed to steal bases.

Athletic Requirements of the Sport and Position: 17/20

The need for speed and quickness as a center fielder adds a point or two here, as does Mantle's penchant for power and stealing bases. His speed was required as a leadoff hitter (where he batted occasionally) and his power was greatly needed when he batted third or cleanup. Given that knowledge, one cannot punish Mantle too much for playing a sport that is not high on the required athleticism list.

Clutch Factor/Mental and Emotional Toughness/ Intangibles: 13/15

Mantle's efforts in the postseason spotlight were inconsistent. He was alternately productive and meager. He finished his career with a mediocre (for him) .257/.374/.535 slash line in World Series competition, but he also hit 18 home runs, slugging three each in 1956, 1960, and 1964. His abuse of alcohol costs him a bit here. Though alcoholism is a disease, his inability to conquer his issues when he understood the effect it had on himself and his team speaks of a lack of mental and emotional toughness.[4]

Versatility: 3/5

Mantle played football at a high level as a youth and must be credited for his tremendous versatility as a baseball player, but he cannot be awarded the same point total as those who played more than one sport competitively at the high school level or above.

TOTAL POINTS: 91

33

KAREEM ABDUL-JABBAR:
THE BIG "A"

Basketball

The National Collegiate Athletic Association did not name names when it banned dunking in 1967, but the motivation for the move was about as subtle as a Lew Alcindor dunk. It was because of the Lew Alcindor dunk.

Alcindor, who four years later would change his name to Kareem Abdul-Jabbar, had played one season at UCLA and proved to be such a dominant inside force that the NCAA took away one of his primary weapons. But the organization could not stop Alcindor for dropping in his deadly skyhook. Neither could anyone else.[1]

Abdul-Jabbar was the last NBA rookie to transform a loser into a championship contender practically by himself. The 7-foot-2 center was selected by the Milwaukee Bucks with the top pick in the 1969 draft. His team more than doubled its victory total from the previous year, and he finished second in the league in scoring, fifth in rebounding, and first among all centers in assists. His impact has proven greater than that of any rookie in league history.

And he was merely warming up. Abdul-Jabbar paced the NBA in scoring in each of the next two seasons, winning the Most Valuable Player award in both and guiding the Bucks to their first NBA championship in 1971. He earned four more MVPs before concluding his epic career. His yearning to play for the Lakers resulted in a trade to that team before the 1975–1976 season. The arrival of Magic Johnson helped Abdul-Jabbar secure five more crowns from 1980 to 1988.

His productivity, consistency, and longevity were stunning. Not only did Abdul-Jabbar average at least 21.5 points in his first seventeen seasons and 12.8 rebounds in his first ten years in the league, but he finished his career with a .559 shooting percentage, led the league in blocked shots four times, and earned a spot as the center on its All-Defensive team five times. Most impressive is that he is the all-time leading scorer in NBA history, with 38,387 points.[2]

But Abdul-Jabbar is far more than a basketball legend. His childhood experiences, thoughtfulness, reflectiveness, and intelligence, combined with the era in which he lived, all resulted in a social and political consciousness far exceeding that of most athletes. He was raised during the civil rights era but came of age during the black power movement. Even during his dominant years on the court at UCLA, he joined much older and more accomplished black athletes such as Jim Brown, Muhammad Ali, and Bill Russell to discuss black empowerment.

Ferdinand Lewis Alcindor Jr. was born in April 16, 1947, in New York City. The only child of an overprotective mother and a strict father was freakishly tall at an early age, but he put his height to good use at Power Memorial High School, which dominated area basketball. The young man who would become Kareem Abdul-Jabbar yearned to maximize his basketball talent and future, so he bolted across the country to play for coach John Wooden and his UCLA Bruins. His arrival marked the beginning of the greatest dynasty in the history of college basketball.

It also marked the beginning of his social and political activity. Though many decried the NCAA's ban on dunking as a shackle specifically on Alcindor, he claimed it targeted black athletes in general, many of whom used the dunk as a physical form of expression in the playgrounds of the inner city.

They Said It

I didn't really seek attention. I just wanted to play the game well and go home.—Kareem Abdul-Jabbar

Why judge anymore? When a man has broken records, won championships, endured tremendous criticism and responsibility, why judge? Let's toast him as the greatest player ever.—Former Lakers coach Pat Riley

I tell kids to pursue their basketball dreams, but I tell them not to let that be their only dream.—Kareem Abdul-Jabbar

Alcindor was arguably the most dominant college player ever, despite the disallowing of dunks. He was voted Player of the Year in both 1967 and 1969 by *Sporting News* and the most outstanding player in the NCAA Tournament in all three of his seasons, each of which concluded with a championship.[3]

By the time Abdul-Jabbar hung up his sneakers, no NBA player had scored more points, blocked more shots, captured more MVP awards, played in more All-Star games, or played more seasons. Despite the brilliance of Jordan and James, the defensive dominance of Russell, and the offensive supremacy of Chamberlain, an argument can be made that Kareem Abdul-Jabbar is the greatest player who ever lived.[4]

POINT TOTAL EXPLANATION

Achievements: 35/35

This stat-stuffing superstar was more than just a point scorer, rebounder, and shot blocker. He was a winner. His teams won six NBA championships and competed in eight Finals. Abdul-Jabbar did it all on the court. The records he set and the titles for which he was greatly responsible result in a perfect score here.

Athleticism: 23/25

Before his arrival, the general and accurate perception of NBA centers was that they were plodding behemoths with little mobility, though stars such as Bill Russell certainly did not fit that mold. Abdul-Jabbar used his long strides to get downcourt quickly when so motivated and position himself offensively to utilize his skyhook or get close enough to the basket to dunk or defensively to block shots. He was far from burly, but his arm length and strength prevented him from getting pushed around.

Athletic Requirements of the Sport and Position: 18/20

Nobody who plays in the NBA will receive fewer points. The constant action requires tremendous endurance, though the center position necessitates a bit less mobility, especially in the era in which Abdul-Jabbar played. Before the advent of the 3-point shot and 6-foot-9 centers who could shoot from beyond 15 feet (such as Boston's Dave Cowens), centers stayed close to the hoop.

Clutch Factor/Mental and Emotional Toughness/ Intangibles: 13/15

As noted in an odd and funny scene in the movie *Airplane*, Abdul-Jabbar did not always sprint downcourt on defense. Finding that motivation for at least forty minutes a night, three or four nights a week, and about one hundred games a year for an NBA finalist is not always easy. But Abdul-Jabbar was indeed at his best in the playoffs. He averaged about 30 points and 17 rebounds per game in his first seven postseasons and significantly raised his blocked shot totals. His teams won six of eight NBA Finals.[5]

Versatility: 2/5

The guy was 6-foot-8 in eighth grade. Did you expect him to concentrate on any other sports? Still, his focus strictly on basketball costs him here. He did boast some versatility on the court, so it's not a total washout.

TOTAL POINTS: 91

34

LOU GEHRIG: THE IRON HORSE

Baseball

Lou Gehrig was certainly displaying his courage and selflessness when, despite the knowledge of his impending death, he famously stated that he was the luckiest man alive. But his claim did not speak the whole truth. It was the New York Yankees that were lucky to have benefited from his greatness for seventeen years, and it was the baseball fans of America who were lucky to have witnessed that brilliance.

No hitter in history brought greater lineup protection to a superstar—in this case, Babe Ruth—than Gehrig. He exceeded 100 RBI in thirteen consecutive seasons, including an AL-record 185 in 1931. And it was Gehrig—not Ruth—who won Most Valuable Player in 1927, when the Yankees produced the greatest offensive machine in baseball history. Gehrig compiled a ridiculous stat line that year of .373/47/173 with a league-high 52 doubles.

And that is just scratching the surface when analyzing the greatness of a man whose 2,130-game playing streak was believed to be unbreakable until Cal Ripken Jr. finally seemed destined to shatter it. Gehrig reached triple figures in runs and RBI every year from 1926 to 1938 and likely would have continued to do so had he not fallen victim to the disease that bears his name. He was so feared by pitchers that he was walked more than 100 times in eleven seasons and led the league in on-base percentage five times, including four in a row late in his career. And he averaged 38 doubles and 12 triples per season.

Gehrig ranks among the best of all time in a slew of career statistics, both traditional and modern, including WAR, OBP, slugging percentage, total bases, and RBI. That at least a few productive years likely awaited him had illness not struck makes such achievements even more remarkable.[1]

They Said It

The ballplayer who loses his head, who can't keep his cool, is worse than no ballplayer at all.—Lou Gehrig

His greatest record doesn't show in the book. It was the absolute reliability of Henry Louis Gehrig. He could be counted upon. He was there every day at the ballpark bending his back and ready to break his neck to win for his side. He was there day after day and year after year. He never sulked or whined or went into a pot or a huff. He was the answer to a manager's dream.—New York Times *sportswriter John Kieran*

Fans, for the past two weeks you have been reading about a bad break I got. Yet today, I consider myself the luckiest man on the face of the earth.—Lou Gehrig

The character of Henry Louis Gehrig, who was born on June 19, 1903, in the Yorkville section of Manhattan, can be credited in part to his German immigrant parents. Lou was the only one of their four children to reach the age of three—though, of course, his life too would be cut short. Though his father struggled with a drinking problem and was often unemployed from his job as a sheet-metal worker, forcing his mother to serve as the breadwinner, he was protective of his son. His mother was more the disciplinarian.

The young Gehrig drew his first inspiration from baseball when the family moved to an apartment in Washington Heights that was a stone's throw from Hilltop Park, home of the American League New York Highlanders, and close to the legendary Polo Grounds, where the National League New York Giants played. He began to enjoy pickup games with neighborhood kids and soon established his superiority in talent. His parents were not turning cartwheels over his passion for baseball, however—they preferred that he set his sights on a business career and advised strongly that he concentrate on his school work. Gehrig did just that, but he still found time to play baseball in the summer and on weekends.

The result was a brilliant career at Commerce High School, where he also starred in football. He displayed his greatness on the diamond in a game in Chicago that pitted the champions of that city against his championship team. Gehrig iced the victory with a grand slam in the ninth inning. The New York media began comparing Gehrig to Ruth. But he did not let it go to his head. He continued to help his struggling family financially by washing dishes and holding down part-time jobs at butcher shops and grocery stores.

Gehrig soon landed a football scholarship at Columbia University, but baseball scouts still buzzed around him after his performance in the Windy City. Among then was Arthur Irwin, who worked for the Giants and asked Gehrig if he would like to play for his favorite team. Gehrig landed a tryout and hit six home runs in batting practice, but a fielding error caused Giants manager John McGraw to send him packing. McGraw's temper and impatience cost him one of the greatest players in baseball history.

That McGraw had erred became evident when Gehrig began destroying college pitching, batting .444 as a sophomore and slugging majestic home runs while doubling as Columbia's best pitcher. Soon a Yankees scout came calling. He watched Gehrig slug two home runs against Rutgers, then called Yankees general manager Ed Barrow and claimed he had discovered another Ruth. It turned out he was pretty much right.[2]

POINT TOTAL EXPLANATION

Achievements: 34/35

Gehrig remains among the most accomplished baseball players ever. His fielding at first base was merely adequate—he committed double-figure errors in eight seasons. But his hitting more than made up for it. Though Gehrig benefited from a tremendous lineup that precluded pitchers from pitching around him, his achievements at the plate rank among the best ever.

Athleticism: 23/25

Gehrig boasted such prolific power that his speed, which resulted in so many doubles and triples, as well as three double-figure stolen base seasons, is historically underappreciated. That Gehrig boasted the durability to play in 2,130 consecutive games is certainly worth something here as well.

Athletic Requirements of the Sport and Position: 15/20

Baseball is not the most athletically challenging of sports, and first base is perhaps the least athletically challenging position on the field. But batting takes tremendous hand-eye coordination and balance, while hitting for power takes, well, power.

Clutch Factor/Mental and Emotional Toughness/ Intangibles: 15/15

Gehrig deserves all the points in this category for his tremendous postseason production, the legendary toughness he displayed as the Iron Horse, and the courage he showed in battling his deadly illness.

Versatility: 4/5

Gehrig might have played in the NFL if his career had taken a different turn. That he was scouted as a pitcher for Columbia and proved versatile as a hitter and baserunner also earn him points here.

TOTAL POINTS: 91

35

EMLEN TUNNELL: OFFENSE ON DEFENSE

Football

Emlen Tunnell broke his neck playing football at the University of Toledo. Thereafter he became a pain in the neck to opposing offenses.

Tunnell is considered by many to be the greatest safety in football history. He thrived in the legendary "umbrella defense" utilized by the New York Giants in the late 1940s and 1950s. The 4–1–6 alignment in passing situations placed Tunnell in the back and allowed him to roam free. The result was 74 interceptions with the Giants (he picked up 5 more with Green Bay) in establishing a league record.[1]

And Tunnell boasted the elusiveness and strength to maximize his thefts. He scored three touchdowns off interceptions in his first two seasons. He peaked in 1949 with 10 interceptions for 251 yards and two scores. He recorded at least 6 interceptions in each of his first ten years. His 79 career picks remained an NFL record until broken nearly two decades later by Paul Krause. Tunnell is still second all-time in that department.

The nine-time Pro Bowler and four-time All-Pro was the first African American player in Giants history and the first voted into the Pro Football Hall of Fame. He performed admirably not only as a safety but also on special teams, leading the league in punt return yardage in 1951 and 1952. In the second of those seasons, he gained more yards on punt, kickoff, and interception returns than the NFL rushing leader.[2]

Tunnell was indeed a pioneer, but he did not embrace the distinction. His color-blind mind-set was forged growing up in an integrated neighborhood in Bryn Mawr, Pennsylvania. Better yet for his future relationships with people of all walks of life, he was a pleasant kid. His good nature helped make him one of the most beloved players to ever don a Giants uniform.

They Said It

I can make tackles until I'm 50. Your body may go, but your heart doesn't.—Emlen Tunnell

Quarterbacks at the time talked about Tunnell as one of the best at faking his intentions, disguising his intentions. A quarterback would wait all day, see that Tunnell didn't seem to be spending much time over in a certain area of the field and throw there and get burned for it.—Football historian Michael MacCambridge

Born on March 29, 1924, and abandoned by his father early in life, young Emlen was raised by his mother, who cleaned houses to make ends meet. She rejected the notion of putting her kids to work to supplement the family income, believing that they should be outside playing. Emlen did just that, honing his talents in baseball, softball, basketball, and football at nearby Villanova University and in what is now Emlen Tunnell Park. Sports simply came easily to him. He once claimed that he competed against college kids at age eight.

Tunnell landed on the varsity football team at Radnor High School as a freshman. He performed well enough there to convince University of Toledo officials to lure him to their school with a new suit, which his mother could not afford and was a prerequisite for college students at the time. He broke his neck as a freshman, yet played for the basketball team four months later. Rejected by the army and navy during World War II, he joined the US Coast Guard and beat out the flames engulfing a shipmate during a Japanese torpedo attack.

He finished his college career as a halfback at the University of Iowa before Giants owner Tim Mara, a man Tunnell greatly appreciated, decided he would be the player to integrate the team. It certainly worked out well for both sides.[3]

POINT TOTAL EXPLANATION

Achievements: 33/35

That Tunnell could set an NFL record for interceptions that lasted more than a decade during an era dominated by the ground game speaks volumes about his impact. His special-teams contributions cannot be overlooked either. The Giants finished among the top five in the NFL in points allowed every season but one from 1950 to 1958. Tunnell played a significant role in that accomplishment.

Athleticism: 24/25

Tunnell was a large safety, particularly in his era, at 6-foot-1, 200 pounds, but possessed great speed to complement his physical play and fierce tackling. He also boasted sure hands as an interceptor and kick returner, as well as elusiveness once he secured the ball in both pursuits. Athletically, Tunnell was close to complete.

Athletic Requirements of the Sport and Position: 17/20

Safeties such as Tunnell are the center fielders of the secondary. They require tremendous mobility, range, and quickness. They are involved not only in short and long passes but run plays as well. It's tough to give football players of that era more points than this because they played only twelve games a year.

Clutch Factor/Mental and Emotional Toughness/ Intangibles: 14/15

Tunnell was a great student of the game. Perhaps his finest attribute was an ability to read quarterbacks and receivers to place himself in the ideal position to make a tackle interception. He was noted for his preparation, spending an inordinate amount of time studying film to best understand what he could expect the following Sunday. He did not record a playoff interception in six games and he did fumble twice, which costs him a point here, but nobody has questioned his toughness.[4]

Versatility: 4/5

Tunnell thrived in a variety of sports in his youth and played basketball well enough to earn a spot on his college team. His excellence as both a safety and kick returner warrant a near-perfect score in this category.

TOTAL POINTS: 91

JERRY WEST: ZEKE FROM CABIN CREEK

Basketball

Jerry West was not literally from Cabin Creek—the West Virginia outpost was merely where his family picked up their mail. But this son of a coal miner did emerge from the backwoods to personify the ultimate rags-to-riches story, somehow grooming his talents to blossom into one of the greatest players in NBA history.[1]

Also known as "The Logo" because his image was adopted by the league as its symbol, West overcame the supposed limitations of his lithe, 6-foot-2, 170-pound frame to consistently attack the big boys under the basket to score and rebound. His consistency from season to season earned him twelve first-team All-NBA selections and fourteen All-Star Game appearances. In 1969 West became the last player to capture the NBA Finals Most Valuable Player award as a player on the losing team.

West led the league in scoring just once, averaging 31.2 points per game in the 1969–1970 season, but he scored at least 25.8 points a game every year from 1961 to 1972. He also shot .474 from the field throughout his career, no mean feat for a smallish guard who did most of his damage inside against the Bill Russells, Nate Thurmonds, and Kareem Abdul-Jabbars of the NBA world. West even averaged at least 7 rebounds per game in his first three seasons. His deft passing resulted in a career average of 6.7 assists per game despite spending much of his playing time as a shooting guard. His assist totals rose dramatically late in his career.[2]

That brilliance was the result of tireless work and motivation as a youth and beyond. Born on May 28, 1938, in Chelyan, West Virginia, he overcame poverty and tragedy to gain fame and fortune. The son of a coal mine electrician who returned home every day so exhausted that he rarely played with his kids, young Jerry was also forced at age twelve to

They Said It

Jerry, I love you.—Celtics star John Havlicek after his team beat West and the Lakers in the 1969 NBA Finals

When time is running out and the score is close, most players are thinking, "I don't want to be the one to lose the game," but I'm thinking, "What do I have to do to win?"—Jerry West

He took a loss harder than any player I've ever known. He would sit by himself and stare into space. A loss just ripped his guts out.—Lakers broadcaster Chick Hearn

deal with the death of his closest brother, David, who was killed in the Korean War.

Jerry used sports to channel his emotions in a positive direction. He practiced basketball on a hoop nailed to a storage shed outside a neighbor's house. It became his sanctuary. He dribbled and shot in the rain or snow, in the heat of summer and cold of winter. He played until his fingers bled. He taught himself the quick release that became legendary. And when he finally returned home, often hours after dinner, he would switch on the radio and listen to University of West Virginia basketball games. He ate so little that he lost enough weight to require vitamin injections.

His diligence paid off—and so did a six-inch growth spurt between his junior and senior years at East Bank High School, where West became the first prep player in West Virginia history to score 900 points in one season. He averaged 32.2 points per game in leading his team to the 1956 state championship.

That he would take his momentum and run with it to play for his beloved Mountaineers was a foregone conclusion. He scored 24.8 points per game there and twice earned All-America honors. West even helped his team reach the 1959 NCAA championship, averaging 32 points in five games during that tournament. (No surprise, given his later playoff heroics as an NBA player.) West and Oscar Robertson were soon leading the US Olympic team to a gold medal in the 1960 Games. Ironically, that same teammate was the only player selected before him in the 1960 draft. Who got the best of that deal can be debated forever.[3]

POINT TOTAL EXPLANATION

Achievements: 33/35

It's tough to deny West anything, but others had a bit more longevity, won more championships, and compiled slightly better statistics. West's accomplishments center on his all-around production; greatness as a scorer, passer, and leader; and brilliance in the playoffs.

Athleticism: 23/25

West boasted the balance and timing to release a picture-perfect jump shot and the lateral quickness, agility, and surprising strength to defend as a four-time All-NBA Defensive Team player and to attack the basket and score or get fouled. He averaged nearly 10 free throws a game throughout his career. He was also well conditioned, giving him stamina and durability.[4]

Athletic Requirements of the Sport and Position: 19/20

West played both guard spots in what is the most athletically challenging American team sport due to its potentially 100-game schedule and consistent action. One must realize that NBA players of his era usually played at least forty minutes per game, most of which required constant movement both vertically and laterally. This is especially true of point guards and shooting guards because they control the ball so much.

Clutch Factor/Mental and Emotional Toughness/ Intangibles: 14/15

West only once helped the Lakers to the top in nine NBA finals, but the finger of blame should not be pointed at him. He not only won the Finals MVP in 1969, but he led the NBA in playoff scoring four times, including in 1965, when he scored an incredible 40.6 points per game. West had steely resolve and was a fiery competitor in the regular season and beyond, and his leadership was unquestioned.[5]

Versatility: 2/5

West became so focused on basketball at such an early age that he did not turn any attention to other athletic activities. But his statistics as an NBA player scream out versatility, so he does deserve a couple points here.

TOTAL POINTS: 91

ANTHONY MUNOZ: THE GREAT PROTECTOR

Football

No position in major American sports is less tied to statistical analysis than offensive lineman. Even offensive team success or failure cannot be linked accurately to one guard, tackle, or center. After all, there are four other linemen and six skill position players on the field who one might argue play more significant roles.

What experts have left is a few numbers and the "eye test." How often does a lineman yield a sack? How well otherwise does he protect his quarterback? Does he consistently hold his ground or even push back defensive linemen? Does he open holes? Is he strong enough to get to the second level? Is he mobile enough to pull? Ask any of these questions with regard to Anthony Munoz and the answer is yes.

Munoz was the finest tackle in the game during his thirteen seasons with the Cincinnati Bengals. He is considered by many to be the greatest offensive lineman in NFL history. He ranks number one among all offensive linemen who have played the game in approximate value. Munoz placed first in that category among all NFL players in 1985, an incredible feat for an offensive lineman. He earned All-Pro status nine times and played in eleven Pro Bowls. He was also voted the top NFL tackle of the 1980s.[1]

Not bad for a Hispanic pitcher from Southern California. Michael Anthony Munoz was born on August 19, 1958, near Los Angeles. He was deemed too big to play Pop Warner football in his youth, so he focused on baseball. He eventually hurled for the University of Southern California national championship team in 1978, but it had become evident by that time that football provided his greatest athletic potential.

Munoz was raised with four siblings in a poor family by his mother after his father left during Anthony's early childhood. His mom toiled packing eggs at a local farm, where Anthony sometimes worked on weekends. She encouraged her son to pursue his sports dreams during his free time. He especially cultivated his talents in baseball and football.

So dominant was Munoz as a lineman in high school that he landed a scholarship to USC, but he stipulated before he accepted that he must be allowed to play for the Trojan baseball team as well.[2] Knee injuries suffered on the gridiron prevented him from playing baseball aside from his sophomore year. A severe knee injury that required reconstructive surgery all but destroyed his senior football season, but NFL talent evaluators who watched him after he returned for the Rose Bowl understood his potential. The Cincinnati Bengals selected him third overall in the 1980 draft.[3]

POINT TOTAL EXPLANATION

Achievements: 34/35

Munoz is widely regarded the most dominant offensive lineman ever. He earned All-Pro and Pro Bowl honors nearly every year. It is no coincidence that a Cincinnati team steeped in offensive mediocrity before his arrival ranked among the top seven in the NFL in points and yards gained nearly every year he played. He even scored four touchdowns on tackle-eligible plays. Munoz was a first-ballot Hall of Famer.

Athleticism: 23/25

Munoz boasted the power and leverage of a premier straight-on blocker and proved agile and mobile enough to handle more elusive defensive ends from his left tackle spot. Munoz is among the most athletic tackles in NFL history. It was this athleticism that made him great.[4]

They Said It

Why would an offensive lineman get all this attention? I don't know why, but I'm fortunate. I use it as a motivator.—Anthony Munoz

There is the drive to be great, and then there is a desire like Anthony's to be superlative. You won't know if you can get there, but you want to see how close you can come.—Bengals coach Sam Wyche

Athletic Requirements of the Sport: 17/20

The left tackle is more responsible than anyone on the field to protect the quarterback, who can be blindsided without effective blocking. They require the upper- and lower-body strength to fend off bull-rushing ends and the quickness and footwork needed to keep up with their pass-rushing moves. Not much speed required here—some linemen are a bit out of shape—but anyone who believes offensive linemen are not superior athletes should watch film of Munoz.

Clutch Factor/Mental and Emotional Toughness/ Intangibles: 14/15

Munoz established a demanding workout regimen when he installed a weight room in his home. He ran several miles daily and held himself to high standards. The toughness necessary to battle opposing linemen play after play as an undersized tackle (Munoz played at 278 pounds) cannot be questioned.[5]

Versatility: 3/5

Munoz was a two-sport star in high school. He didn't get much of a chance to show off his baseball talents at USC, but the fact that he played both sports at that level is worthy of a strong score here.

TOTAL POINTS: 91

38

OSCAR CHARLESTON: THE BLACK TY COBB

Baseball

It was the year 2000. A play focusing on the life of Ty Cobb—the belligerent baseball superstar of a bygone era—had opened in the Big Apple, and in the production, Cobb was compared to an under-the-radar Negro League player as a way to place their lives and opportunities in context. That player was Oscar Charleston.

An actor playing Charleston appeared on stage at various stages. He complained that nobody knew who he was, but everyone was aware of Cobb. He taunted his far more famous peer by informing the audience that he, not Cobb, had had the chance to compete against immortals such as Josh Gibson and Satchel Paige. *How could Cobb call himself the best without having played against the best?* he asked.[1]

The actor who played Charleston had researched the role. He told a newspaper reporter about his discovery that Charleston was equally as antagonistic and driven as Cobb. And a writer later offered that Charleston was not the black Ty Cobb, but rather Cobb was the white Oscar Charleston. After all, though Negro League statistics are sketchy, Charleston owned a career average of .339, including marks of .451 in 1925, .444 in 1921, and .395 in 1922. The jackrabbit stole 20 bases a year from 1921 to 1926 despite averaging about 250 at-bats.

Many of his single-season statistics were ridiculous. He drove in 94 runs in 308 at-bats with 26 stolen bases and 48 walks for Indianapolis in 1923. He slugged 20 home runs in 235 at-bats, registered a .552 on-base percentage, and scored 95 runs for Harrisburg in 1925. He boasted a combination of power and speed few players in the history of baseball could match.[2]

Oscar McKinley Charleston played several of his best seasons in his hometown of Indianapolis, where he was born on October 14, 1896. The

> ## They Said It
>
> *Oscar Charleston was Willie Mays before there was a Willie Mays, except that he was a better base runner, a better center fielder and a better hitter.*—Negro League player Ted Radcliffe
>
> *If Oscar Charleston isn't the greatest baseball player in the world, then I'm no judge of baseball talent.*—Giants manager John McGraw

headstrong fifteen-year-old ran away from home in 1912 to join the US Army and play baseball with the Negro 24th Infantry in the Philippines. He returned home three years later to sign with the Indianapolis ABCs. His combative nature soon emerged, such as when he punched an umpire and was charged with assault. Or when, according to Negro League legend James "Cool Papa" Bell, he yanked the hood of a Klansman and dared him to respond. Or when he duked it out with Cuban army members who arrived to stop a brawl; according to fellow ballplayer Ted Page, Charleston knocked out about a dozen of them.

Mostly, however, he knocked out pitchers. The left-handed Charleston was also a deft center fielder with tremendous range and tracking who played so shallow that opponents complained he was a fifth infielder. He was once clocked at 23 seconds in the 220-yard dash. His sister recalled during the Hall of Fame ceremony honoring Charleston that one game had to be halted so he could pick up the money thrown at him by appreciative fans after a particularly spectacular play.

Charleston, of course, never received an opportunity to play in the major leagues. But he did compete against big-leaguers in barnstorming exhibitions in the United States and Latin America, during which he batted .318 with 11 home runs in fifty-three games, and he batted .458 with 5 home runs in five games in a 1921 series against the St. Louis Cardinals.[3]

POINT TOTAL EXPLANATION

Achievements: 33/35

Though it's difficult to place Charleston's career into context statistically—there are no numbers associated with a few of his seasons—the longevity of his career and the accomplishments that have been recorded warrant a wonderful score here. That no less an authority than legendary John Mc-Graw cited Charleston the best player in the world speaks volumes about his talent.[4]

Athleticism: 25/25

All accounts indicate that Charleston was without weakness. He hit for power, ran like the wind, boasted the quickness to track down balls in the outfield and secure a great break in stealing bases, and had the durability to play into his midforties. What else is there?

Athletic Requirements of the Sport and Position: 16/20

Center field is a demanding spot that requires quickness, balance, agility, and speed. The comparative inactivity of baseball players, however, who mostly sit or stand around during games, precludes a great score.

Clutch Factor/Mental and Emotional Toughness/ Intangibles: 14/15

It is impossible to judge how Charleston's combative nature affected his game and relationships on the field, but what is known is that he rose to the occasion when needed the most. He boasted a reputation for hitting in clutch. The passion, intensity, and drive with which he played the game cannot be diminished.

Versatility: 2/5

Like many in his era, especially those from poor backgrounds, Charleston picked a sport and ran with it. He was tremendously versatile on the diamond, however, so he can't be judged too harshly in this category. And perhaps he should be counted as a boxer after knocking out a dozen Cuban soldiers![5]

TOTAL POINTS: 90

(39)

EARVIN JOHNSON: MAGIC

Basketball

The date was May 16, 1980. The city was Philadelphia. The venue was the Spectrum. The event was Game 6 of the NBA Finals. The Lakers were on the verge of winning their second championship, but they had a 7-foot-2 problem: future Hall of Famer Kareem Abdul-Jabbar, who had returned to Los Angeles nursing a sprained ankle. Who, wondered coach Pat Riley, would play center? To many, his answer seemed absurd. It would be rookie point guard Magic Johnson.

Johnson was a point guard in the body of a power forward who could play center. He could play all positions, which is what he did on that fateful night. He embarked on perhaps the most incredible performance in NBA playoff history, leading both teams with 42 points and 15 rebounds. The cherry on top was 7 assists in a 123–107 victory. Johnson hit 14 of 23 shots in the clincher and made all 14 of his foul shots.[1]

Even in the context of history, long after Johnson hung up his sneakers, the effort seems phenomenal. But Johnson was phenomenal, perhaps the greatest playmaker ever. He put the show in the Showtime Lakers with behind-the-back and no-look passes. He was the engine, the catalyst of a team that won five titles in ten years and reached the Finals eight times during that stretch.

Johnson left the game at age thirty-one after announcing to a stunned nation he had contracted HIV. But he had already compiled numbers that made Hall of Fame induction a lock. He led the league in assists four times and finished with the fifth-highest career total in NBA history despite his early retirement. He averaged nearly 20 points a game and shot a fine 52 percent from the field. Most importantly, he was a winner who played with joyous abandon every minute on the court.[2]

They Said It

Magic is who I am on the basketball court. Earvin is who I am.—Earvin Johnson

I don't think there will ever be another 6–9 point guard who smiles while he humiliates you.—Lakers teammate James Worthy

His story began on August 14, 1959, in Lansing, Michigan. Engrossed in basketball as a youth, Johnson practiced dribbling all day, then slept with his basketball. He earned the nickname "Magic" at the tender age of fifteen by a sportswriter who had watched him total 36 points, 16 rebounds, and 16 assists in one game. Johnson led Everett High School to a 27–1 record and the state title as a senior, averaging 26.8 points and 16.8 rebounds.

He next conquered the college game at Michigan State, where he established a career-long rivalry with budding Indiana State superstar Larry Bird. Johnson wasted no time displaying his talent and versatility, averaging 17 points, 7.9 rebounds, and 7.4 assists as a freshman in leading the Spartans to the Big 10 championship. He then guided his team to the national crown as an All-American sophomore, beating Bird's Sycamores in the most hyped and anticipated NCAA title game ever. Johnson had achieved all he could as an amateur. He was selected first overall in the 1979 draft by Los Angeles.[3]

The Lakers never regretted it. Johnson finished his career with three NBA Most Valuable Player awards and twelve All-Star Game appearances. Most important, however, was that the team would not have captured all those crowns without him.[4]

POINT TOTAL EXPLANATION

Achievements: 32/35

Johnson had an amazing career, but it was cut short, which precludes his reaching his full potential here. He was also a terrible long-distance shooter. Johnson was a good scorer but cannot be placed in the same ballpark with LeBron James, who could tally 30 points at will while also racking up huge assist totals.

Athleticism: 23/25

Johnson was a fine athlete, but his success was based equally on his cerebral approach to the point guard position. He was quick and shifty but did not boast the power of James. His incredible ball-handling and passing required tremendous agility and hand-eye coordination.

Athletic Requirements of the Sport and Position: 19/20

Thriving at point guard in the NBA requires tremendous endurance and all the qualities possessed by Johnson, such as shiftiness, quickness, elusiveness, and hand-eye coordination.

Clutch Factor: Mental and Emotional Toughness/ Intangibles: 14/15

His performance in Game 6 of the 1980 Finals was merely the first of many examples of Johnson's rising to the occasion. Johnson increased his assist and rebound averages in the postseason and decreased his turnovers against superior competition. He won Finals MVP awards in 1980, 1982, and 1987.[5]

Versatility: 2/5

Johnson was so engrossed in basketball that he never explored his talents in other sports at a high level. He receives points here because of his ability to excel in various position on the basketball court.

TOTAL POINTS: 90

JOE LOUIS: THE BROWN BOMBER

Boxing

Joe Louis. *Library of Congress*

Joe Louis will never be remembered most for his left hook or right jab. His name is not a hallowed one in sports specifically for his immense talents as a boxer. Rather, he is beloved for striking a blow against cockeyed Nazi racial philosophy and bringing pride to Americans during the Great Depression, especially the black population, who embraced him as a hero.

Louis will be forever linked with German heavyweight Max Schmeling, an unwitting and unwilling ambassador of the Aryan superiority theory espoused by the leaders of his country in the 1930s. The pair squared off in two bouts that remain legendary, not for the action in the ring, but for the social and political impact they had on their two nations.

The first was held at Yankee Stadium on June 19, 1936, after Louis had established himself as an undefeated contender and seemingly invincible. Schmeling stunned the world by winning the contest with a 12th-round technical knockout (TKO). The second took place in the same venue two years later with the heavyweight championship on the line, a year to the day after Louis had captured the crown with a knockout of Jim Braddock. Louis sent Schmeling reeling from the start with two left hooks, then put him away just two minutes into the fight. His victory set off celebrations in black communities around the country and struck a blow against Nazism.[1]

His success was a tribute to not only talent but also perseverance. Louis was born on May 13, 1914, in Jim Crow Alabama, where the fate awaiting many young black men was a life of picking cotton, which is what his father did for a living. The family moved to Detroit in 1924, and that is where Louis began to display his talents. He won the Golden Gloves as a light heavyweight in 1934, turned professional, and quickly ascended the ranks. He owned a 21–0 record with 18 knockouts or TKOs heading into a bout at Yankee Stadium against former heavyweight champion Max Baer, who had just lost the title to Braddock. Louis pummeled Baer so completely that rising journalist Ernest Hemingway claimed the fight to be "the most disgusting public spectacle outside of a public hanging."

Louis followed his famous knockout of Schmeling with a decade of dominance the sport has rarely experienced. He maintained his crown for the next twelve years, battering such notables as Tony Galento, Buddy Baer, and Billy Conn. Louis lost nearly three years to World War II as he toiled as a physical education teacher in the army. But he showed upon his return that he had not lost much, beating Conn again and twice defeating Jersey Joe Wolcott before announcing his retirement.

Idle for two years, Louis soon succumbed to the financial problems that beset most African Americans fighting a losing battle against racism and discrimination. He needed the money, so he agreed to a heavyweight title bout against Ezzard Charles. The result was a unanimous decision and

They Said It

I just give lip service to being the greatest. He was the greatest.—Muhammad Ali

Every time I hear the name Joe Louis, my nose starts to bleed.—Louis opponent Tommy Farr

He hit me 18 times while I was in the act of falling.—Louis victim Max Baer

second defeat. He won his next eight fights before ending his career with a loss to Rocky Marciano at Madison Square Garden.

Louis was done. He died in 1981, but he lives on in the hearts and minds of Americans who appreciate the impact he made on their country.[2]

POINT TOTAL EXPLANATION

Achievements: 35/35

Louis was not the most athletic heavyweight of all time—that distinction belongs to Ali—but he was arguably the most accomplished. That 52 of Louis's 66 victories were knockouts proves his greatness, as does the fact that he maintained his heavyweight crown for more than a decade following his pounding of Schmeling and after losing three years to the war.[3]

Athleticism: 19/25

Louis was not quick of foot and was not considered a premier defensive fighter, but his hands were quick, and both his left jab and hook packed a wallop. He was more a cerebral boxer than a physical or particularly athletic one. And though it has been claimed he had a glass jaw, he boasted the physical toughness to take a blow and remain standing and strong.

Athletic Requirements of the Sport and Division: 19/20

It has been claimed that boxers are the best athletes of all. One can argue the point, but the battering a boxer must endure, especially when a heavyweight lands solid blows, requires strength of body and character. Louis was a bit of an anomaly in that he thrived despite a lack of athleticism because his strengths as a knockout puncher were so overwhelming. But most heavyweights cannot survive without some level of agility and quickness.

Clutch Factor/Mentor and Emotional Toughness/ Intangibles: 15/15

No boxer deserves a full point total here more than Louis. The pressure on him to win, especially from the African American community and particularly in his second match against Schmeling, was enormous. Louis must also be credited for being a student of the sport, weighing the strengths and weaknesses of his opponents to become arguably the greatest heavy-weight champion ever.

Versatility: 2/5

Louis was so dedicated to his craft that he never dabbled in other sports. But it must be kept in mind that neither football nor basketball had hit yet its stride as a popular sport in the 1930s and that for a poor black man in a racist society, activities such as golf and tennis were out of the question.

TOTAL POINTS: 90

41

KOBE BRYANT:
THE BLACK MAMBA

Basketball

Kobe Bryant remains an enigmatic and polarizing figure. His place among the greatest NBA players of all time has been questioned. His critics cite personal drawbacks as well as statistics and other on-court issues.

They say he was not a great teammate. They point to his mediocre field goal percentage, particularly from three-point range. They claim he was a bit selfish. They stress his eventually unworkable relationship with Hall of Fame center Shaquille O'Neal and contend it is undeniable that the Lakers would have won more championships had Bryant not driven him away. They point to average assist and rebound totals. They mention as proof that their opinions are correct that Bryant only won one Most Valuable Player award in twenty seasons.

Such assertions are not without merit. But there is one thing that his critics never deny, and that is that Bryant was both immensely talented and an assassin with games on the line. They do not argue that he was among the greatest athletes ever to grace an NBA court. He was also a lockdown defender who was voted onto twelve All-Defensive teams.

Bryant was a prolific scorer. He twice led the league in scoring and finished his career averaging 25 points per game. But his most impressive feat was starring on five NBA championship teams. His overall play keyed all those title runs, with and without O'Neal. His supreme confidence drove him to take charge when playoff games and titles hung in the balance.[1]

The son of high-jumping NBA forward Joe "Jellybean" Bryant and named after a Japanese steak, Kobe was born on August 23, 1978, in Philadelphia. He spent six years of his childhood in Italy as his dad finished his basketball career. There, father and son played basketball together, and Kobe also learned the finer points of soccer.

They Said It

Losing is losing, there aren't different degrees of losing. You either win a championship or you're [crap]. It's very black & white to me.—Kobe Bryant

Kobe is one of those guys that every coach in the world says, "That would have been great to have an opportunity to coach that guy." That's the best thing I can say about him. It says everything. He's one of the greatest players of all time. It's not just his talent or his physical skills. His mind was on par with Michael [Jordan] and Larry [Bird] and Magic [Johnson], guys like that. They thought the game. They knew what was going on. And then on top of that, he had a really phenomenal competitiveness.—Spurs coach Gregg Popovich

Friends can come and go, but banners hang forever.—Kobe Bryant

The family returned to Philadelphia in 1991. They lived in the posh Main Line neighborhood, distant from African American friends who had embraced the new hip-hop culture with which the young Bryant was unfamiliar. The kids did not know what to make of the boy who spoke fluent Italian and lived in a comfortable home in a wealthy suburb.

Basketball helped close the gap at Lower Merion High School. Bryant's brilliance on the court had become pronounced and coach Gregg Downer encouraged him to follow in his father's footsteps by joining the professional ranks. Bryant concluded his high school career as the leading scorer in southeast Pennsylvania history with 2,883 points, easily surpassing the record set by the legendary Wilt Chamberlain. Bryant earned Pennsylvania Player of the Year honors as a junior and led his team to a 31–3 record and state championship a year later, averaging 30.8 points, 12 rebounds, 6.5 assists, 4 steals, and 3.8 blocked shots per game. It came as little surprise when he was named the winner of various national Player of the Year awards.

Locals yearned for Bryant to continue his career at a Philadelphia university such as La Salle, where his father served as an assistant coach. They were highly critical when he announced his attention to turn pro. Bryant had already proven himself worthy athletically, and his fine academic performance showed little necessity for a college education given his readiness to compete in the NBA. He was selected thirteenth overall by the Charlotte Hornets in the 1996 draft, then traded—much to that team's eventual chagrin—to the Lakers for center Vlade Divac.[2]

POINT TOTAL EXPLANATION

Achievements: 33/35

Bryant played twenty years in the NBA, winning five championships and averaging 25 points per game. He loses a couple points here to his average shooting numbers, especially from beyond the arc, but one cannot punish Bryant too extensively here. He finished his career as the third-leading scorer in league history despite tremendous defensive attention, especially following the departure of O'Neal.

Athleticism: 22/25

Bryant's greatness was not fully tied to his athleticism. He was more a fundamental player. He boasted tremendous footwork and an explosive first step to the basket, allowing him to post up against taller opponents and rise for dunks, but he managed to remain a prolific scorer as age crept up on him because he knew how to play the game. Bryant was incredible at contorting his body to avoid defenders. He was not as fast, quick, or strong as others, but his body control was legendary.[3]

Athletic Requirements of the Sport and Position: 19/20

No sport tests professional athletes more than pro basketball. Playing about 100 regular-season and playoff games every year is a greater physical challenge greater than that experienced by players in football or baseball. And those who handle the ball and drive to the basket as frequently as Bryant are challenged to an even greater extent. They must have great strength, quickness, agility, and endurance to thrive.

Clutch Factor/Mental and Emotional Toughness/ Intangibles: 14/15

Bryant was criticized for what many perceived as a "me-first" selfishness on the court and in the locker room. But others claimed his attitude was based on his teammates' dependence on him to lead them to victory. That is what made Bryant an enigma and a polarizing player. That he tried to put his team on his back is admirable. That he often succeeded—given the Lakers' five championships—is undeniable. Bryant was a fiery competitor. And he was a brilliant student of the game.

Versatility: 2/5

Bryant dabbled a bit in soccer and karate as a kid, but that doesn't qualify here. His versatility on the court earns him a couple points.

TOTAL POINTS: 90

42

SERENA WILLIAMS: MOMMA SMASH

Tennis

Serena Williams. © Robert Deutsch–USA TODAY Sports

Historically, individual dominance in tennis has often had the life span of the average housefly. Even the all-time greats—Jimmy Connors, John McEnroe, Björn Borg, and Ivan Lendl among the men in the 1970s and 1980s and Margaret Court, Chris Evert, and Billie Jean King on the women's side in the 1970s—remained on top only periodically as they jostled with others for supremacy.

There have been exceptions, players so dominant that they spent years at number one with only brief periods out of the top spot. The only American-born woman who fits that description is Serena Williams, who was threatening by 2017 to surpass Steffi Graf and Martina Navratilova as the longest-tenured top-ranked player ever. Williams had by that time 319 weeks atop the Women's Tennis Association (WTA) rankings, including a record-tying 186-week stretch from 2013 to 2015. She pulled within one Grand Slam championship of Graf for the career lead when she won her twenty-third at the 2017 Australian Open.[1]

Williams was born on September 26, 1981, in Saginaw, Michigan. She and sister Venus took an unusual path to greatness as they were home-schooled by their father, Richard, who mentored them in the sport. They moved to Florida at age nine so they could play year-round at a tennis academy. But they eschewed the junior circuit after Richard heard derogatory racist remarks hurled at them during tournaments. He also yearned for them to concentrate on their schoolwork.[2]

The lack of competition at an early age did not slow Serena. She emerged as a force on the court, winning her first Grand Slam before her eighteenth birthday. Williams has been called the "Tennis Playing Truck." Her powerful serve and ground strokes overwhelm most opponents. Her forehand is among the deadliest shots in the history of the sport. Her ability to blast through her forehand results in placement close to the baseline with tremendous pace, resulting in winners, unforced errors from opponents, and short points, allowing her to remain fresh. Her strong backhand is a product of a short, compact stroke and great extension.

Unlike superstars of the past, such as Evert, she often finishes off points and foes by attacking the net. Her hard ground strokes and deep approach shots prevent opponents from hitting accurate passes or lobs. She sometimes attacks off her serve, which features a smooth motion, tremendous racket acceleration, and placement depth.[3]

In other words, her style accentuates athleticism. But that does not always translate to success. It appeared when Serena and Venus exploded onto the scene, around the new millennium, that the latter would prove more dominant. But Serena soon separated herself from Venus and the rest of the tour competition. Though others—such as Justine Henin and Maria Sharapova—challenged her supremacy at times, Williams racked up Grand Slam titles at a furious pace after snagging the US Open in 1999. She won at least two each year in 2002, 2003, 2009, 2010, 2012, 2013,

They Said It

I am lucky that whatever fear I have inside me, my desire to win is always stronger.—Serena Williams

I've always looked forward to playing against her, because that's when you truly test yourself or your level. It's always exciting to me. In my mind, she's the greatest player ever, regardless of the record.—Tennis rival Victoria Azarenka

It's me, and I love me. I learned to love me. I've been like this my whole life, and I embrace me. I love how I look. I love that I'm a full woman and I'm strong and I'm powerful and I'm beautiful at the same time. There's nothing wrong with that.—Serena Williams

2014, and 2013, and she came within one crown of the coveted Grand Slam in 2002 and 2015. That gap alone explains much about her legacy and brilliance.[4]

Many believe Williams is the greatest female tennis player ever. Some even consider her the most dominant female athlete of all time. That debate will rage forever. But that she is the best tennis player of her generation is undeniable.

POINT TOTAL EXPLANATION

Achievements: 34/35

The sheer number of championships won by Williams (she was still active in 2017) earns her nearly every available point here. She even won four Olympic gold medals, including three in doubles partnered with Venus. She thrived on every surface, even the slow clay, which is not conducive to her power game. She is 13–3 in clay court finals, including four French Open titles. The ability to win whenever, wherever gives Williams an almost perfect score here.[5]

Athleticism: 23/25

Williams can play a bit heavy at times, not because she is lacking athletic potential but because she is not always in premier condition. That is somewhat understandable given her nearly twenty years on the tour. But she is sometimes unable to track down balls she is capable of reaching. Still, she boasts power on her serve and forehand that arguably exceeds all before her and enough quickness to cover the court and attack the net.

Athletic Requirements of the Sport: 18/20

If one does not maintain constant movement at the highest levels of tennis, one does not win. The sport requires tremendous hand-eye coordination and quickness, and some power. Even a high vertical leap can prove helpful on overheads, particularly in a lob-heavy women's game. There are no overweight tennis players. Williams is not always in peak condition, but there is a difference between getting a little winded and being out of shape.

Clutch Factor/Mental and Emotional Toughness/ Intangibles: 13/15

This is a tough one. Nobody who wins Grand Slam final after Grand Slam final should be punished here. Williams is gritty and determined. Her desire to win goes unquestioned. But she does allow herself to stray from the conditioning habits that could maximize her potential. It's not much—just enough to cost her at times.

Versatility: 2/5

The heavy concentration on tennis throughout her youth precluded Williams from developing other sports talents. And though she has admitted she's an awful basketball player, her athleticism indicates she could thrive in other endeavors if so motivated. She therefore gets a couple points here.

TOTAL POINTS: 90

43

HONUS WAGNER: THE FLYING DUTCHMAN

Baseball

Karl Kissner of Defiance, Ohio, was exploring his grandfather's attic one summer day in 2012 when he uncovered some old baseball cards. He knew which one was the gem. It was the Honus Wagner card, which has been valued at more than $2 million.

Granted, the card was old. But there are no mad scrambles for cards of ordinary ballplayers. It takes an exceptional talent for an artifact to be so highly sought after, and Honus Wagner was one hell of a talent.[1]

Wagner was among baseball's first superstars and is generally regarded as the greatest shortstop of all time, though he played multiple positions. He dominated the dead-ball era with his bat and legs. He was among the greatest doubles and triples hitters ever, slugged more home runs than most in his time, and was the most dangerous base stealer of the early twentieth century.[2]

Every year was another chance to dominate for Wagner, and he took advantage of it. He began his career with the Louisville Colonels in 1897 and quickly displayed his potential, driving in 219 runs in his second and third seasons combined. But a blockbuster trade involving pitching standout Jack Chesbro sent Wagner to Pittsburgh, where he became a legend. He led the National League in doubles in seven of the next ten years and batting average in eight of the next twelve. He also paced the Senior Circuit in stolen bases five times and in triples and home runs three times each. Modern analytics also smile upon his legacy Wagner ranks tenth all-time in WAR—seventh among position players.[3]

And to think his brother Albert was first considered the finest athlete in the family. Johannes Peter Wagner was born in the western Pennsylvania coal country village of Chartiers on February 24, 1874, less than nine years

They Said It

I don't make speeches. I just let my bat speak for me in the summertime.
—Honus Wagner

He was a gentle, kind man, a storyteller, supportive of rookies, patient with the fans, cheerful in hard times, careful of the example he set for youth, a hard worker, a man who had no enemies and who never forgot his friends. He was the most beloved man in baseball before Ruth.—
Baseball historian and author Bill James

after the Civil War guns fell silent. When Albert launched his career with Steubenville of the Inter-State League in 1895, he suggested to the powers that be that his little brother could help the team. Honus played with five teams in his first season of professional baseball, batting between .365 and .386 for all of them.

Early baseball scout Edward Barrow knew a good thing when he saw one. He signed Wagner to his Atlantic League team in Paterson, New Jersey. The twenty-two-year-old rewarded that faith by batting .313 and showing incredible defensive versatility as well as power and speed, and followed up by hitting .375 in 1897. Barrow soon contacted the woeful Colonels, who had finished the 1896 season with a 38–93 record. He fetched their manager and president to watch Wagner in person, but the two were not impressed, greatly because of his odd build, which featured a barrel chest, huge shoulders, muscular arms, gigantic hands, and bowed legs that made him quite ungraceful, as well as an odd split-handed grip on the bat. The Colonels took a chance anyway. They were rewarded when Wagner hit .335 in 62 games as a rookie. Little did the Colonels know when they made the mistake of trading him that such an average would be considered a slump season for the future Hall of Famer.[4]

POINT TOTAL EXPLANATION

Achievements: 34/35

Only two comparatively unproductive World Series performances prevent Wagner from nailing a perfect score in this category. His accomplishments in the regular season at the plate, in the field, and on the base paths were complete. One can argue that Wagner is the greatest player in National League history.

Athleticism: 24/25

The proof is in the pudding for Wagner. His speed and quickness are evident in one of the highest stolen base totals ever. His range was proven by his abilities in his positive defensive contributions in the outfield and at shortstop. And his balance and hand-eye coordination are a given considering his tremendous production at the plate.

Athletic Requirements of the Sport and Position: 16/20

The relative inactivity of baseball players when their team is at-bat (they are mostly sitting on the bench) and in the field (they are mostly just standing around) precludes a great score here. But Wagner was as active as they come, legging out doubles and triples, going from first to third, and stealing bases. He deserves some credit for that.

Clutch Factor/Mental and Emotional Toughness/ Intangibles: 14/15

Wagner gained a reputation as a great teammate who treated the young and experienced with kindness and understanding. He played aggressively from first pitch to last. He loses a point only for his comparatively mediocre performances at the plate in the two World Series in which he participated and for having won just one championship in twenty-one years.[5]

Versatility: 2/5

Wagner played in an era in which there were few options besides baseball—neither basketball nor football had come close to hitting their strides in the American consciousness, and the modern Olympics were launched the year before he played his first major-league game. His versatility as a hitter, base stealer, defender around the infield, and outfielder earns him a couple points here.

TOTAL POINTS: 90

44

JULIUS ERVING: DR. J
Basketball

One might be surprised to learn that what is generally accepted as the greatest basket ever scored by Julius Erving was not a dunk. After all, Dr. J helped turn the slam into an art form. He played above the rim with a style all his own, helping change the NBA forever.

The date was May 11, 1980. The venue was the Spectrum in Philadelphia. The stakes were high—it was the fourth quarter of Game 4 of the NBA Finals between the 76ers and Lakers. Erving drove toward the baseline past overmatched and undersized center Mark Landsberger. Kareem Abdul-Jabbar waited ominously on the other side of the basket. Erving swooped toward him from behind the hoop. Cradling the ball in his right hand, he leaped forward, extended his arm, evaded both defenders, released in a sweeping motion with his back turned to the target, kissed the ball gently off the backboard, and dropped it through the net.[1]

Incredible—but not shocking. The basketball world had learned never to be surprised by his brilliance. Before Erving wowed NBA fans, he had emerged as the biggest star in an American Basketball Association that had spotlighted so many stars until four of its teams—including Erving's New York Nets—were incorporated into the more established league in a merger his greatness helped force. Erving led the ABA in scoring in three of five seasons, peaking at 31.9 points per game in 1973. He also yanked down double figures in rebounds in all five years in which he played in the upstart league.

Erving proved tremendously productive and steady in eleven seasons with the Sixers. He scored at least 20 points per game in the first nine, played team-oriented basketball, and turned the ball over infrequently given the amount of time he handled it. He took smart shots, which resulted in a fine .506 career shooting percentage for a 6-foot-7 small forward. Also impressive considering his size was his career average of 8.5 rebounds per game. He exceeded 30,000 career points, which ranks him eighth all-time.[2]

Erving, however, will forever be best known for his high-flying dunks. He certainly had plenty of practice perfecting them as a youth. Born on February 22, 1950, in East Meadow, New York, he was refining his dunks on an eight-foot basket in sixth grade and was soon thereafter able to palm the ball. He worked tirelessly on his jump shot as well, practicing mostly by himself.

Though Erving was the best player on his Roosevelt High School team by his junior season, he came off the bench that year without complaint when his coached decided to start five seniors. He starred as a senior, earning spots on all-county and all–Long Island teams, as well as a scholarship to the University of Massachusetts. It was there that he blossomed into a star, compiling 51 double-doubles in just 52 games. He averaged 26.33 points and 20.2 rebounds a game at that level, becoming only one of five college players to reach the 20-20 mark for a career.

They Said It

There have been some better people off the court—like a few mothers and the Pope. But there was only one Dr. J, the player.—NBA coach Pat Riley

When I get a chance to power jump off both legs, I can lean, twist, change directions and decide whether to dunk the ball or pass it to an open man. In other words, I may be committed to the air, but I still have some control over it.—Julius Erving

No one has ever controlled and conquered the air above pro basketball like Julius Erving, the incomparable Dr. J. The Doctor not only leaps and stays aloft longer than most players dream possible, but he uses his air time to transform his sport into graceful ballet, breath-taking drama or science-fiction fantasy depending upon his mood of the moment and the needs of his team.—Newsweek writer Pete Axthelm

Erving joined the Virginia Squires as an undrafted free agent after leaving Massachusetts early. His immediate and profound impact helped that league establish its legitimacy in competing against the NBA. But Erving would have plenty of time to give NBA fans more than just a taste of his incredible talent.[3]

POINT TOTAL EXPLANATION

Achievements: 32/35

Erving did not lead the NBA in any statistical categories in any year during his eleven seasons with the 76ers. That costs him a bit here, but he still earns a fine score based on his consistent production in all areas of the game. He scored, rebounded, assisted, stole the ball, and even blocked shots. He struggled to shoot from downtown, but so did most players of his era, and that he shot 50 percent from the field for his career was a worthy accomplishment.

Athleticism: 24/25

The vertical leap that translated into memorable slam-dunks was only one athletic attribute owned by Erving. He boasted tremendous dexterity on the court and had enough quickness and strength to outmaneuver and outbattle taller and more powerful players for rebounds. Erving used his smarts to maximize his talent, but it was his athleticism that made him a legend.

Athletic Requirements of the Sport and Position: 18/20

Playing the small forward role in the NBA—one that particularly necessitates a high percentage of the ball possessions, passes, shots, and drives to the basket—requires a wide range of athletic skills and talents. Durability is a must for any NBA player in what can be a hundred-game schedule, but primary ball handlers such as Erving need a quick first step, the ability to maintain balance and control after contact, and great agility.

Clutch Factor/Mental and Emotional Toughness/ Intangibles: 14/15

Erving competed in four ABA and NBA Finals and performed admirably. He was especially dominant in the last ABA games ever played—the 1976 championship round against the Denver Nuggets. Erving hit an amazing 76 of 127 (60 percent) from the field in that victorious six-game series with an average of 14.2 rebounds per game. He also played brilliantly with little help from fellow superstar George McGinnis in the 1977 NBA Finals defeat to Portland.

Versatility: 2/5

Erving played only hoops at a high level, but his amazing versatility as a basketball player precludes him from earning a lower score here.

TOTAL POINTS: 90

45

GALE SAYERS:
THE KANSAS COMET

Football

He was a blip on the radar screen. He arrived, he conquered, he departed. Injuries sadly ended the career of Gale Sayers quite prematurely. But during that flash of time in the long history of professional football, his brilliance shone so brightly that he is still considered among the most talented players to ever wear a pair of shoulder pads.

Others have mimicked his running style, but none aside from perhaps Barry Sanders (who too often lost yardage) achieved his level of greatness with it. Sayers boasted the quickness and particularly the elusiveness that no running back has ever matched. He was a marvel in the open field, with an ability to shift horizontally while running practically full tilt. Nobody made more defenders miss.

The bottom-line numbers do not scream out, largely because he played just four full seasons in the NFL. Sayers twice led the league in rushing yards, peaking at 1,231 in 1966, his second year with the Chicago Bears. He paced the NFL three times in rushing yards per game and averaged a remarkable 6.2 yards per carry in 1968, a season that was cut short due to a knee injury. He bounced back the following year to lead the NFL in rushing again.

Sayers was also among the most feared returners of his generation. He returned eight kicks for touchdowns in his first three seasons, all of which he led the league in all-purpose yards. He even totaled 954 receiving yards in his first two years in an era in which running backs simply did not catch many passes.[1]

Gale Eugene Sayers was born on May 30, 1943, in Wichita, Kansas. His ancestors were among the first western settlers, and his great-uncle was

> ### They Said It
>
> *I had a style all my own. The way I ran, lurchy, herky-jerky, I kept people off-guard so if I didn't have that much power when I hit a man, hell, he was off-balance, and I could knock him down.*—Gale Sayers
>
> *His days at the top of his game were numbered, but there was a magic about him that still sets him apart from the other great running backs in pro football. He wasn't a bruiser like Jimmy Brown, but he could slice through the middle like a warm knife through butter, and when he took a pitchout and peeled around the corner, he was the most exciting thing in pro football.*—Legendary sportswriter Red Smith

the first black lawyer in the state. Sayers moved with his family to a farm in Speed, Kansas, at age seven. They then moved to Omaha, Nebraska. His poor father instilled in him a work ethic that remained with him for a lifetime.

Sayers embraced myriad sports in his youth. He participated in track, baseball, basketball, and football in Omaha city leagues, but he was most fond of football. His talent grew and his character strengthened through rough neighborhood competition, leading to success at the high school level. Sayers set the city scoring record and was voted onto the All-America team. He also won three gold medals at the state track meet and established a new state broad jump record.

The Gale Sayers Sweepstakes began. He received tremendous attention from college football programs, signing letters of intent to seventeen different schools. He chose Kansas. Sayers was disinterested in academics until he married his high school sweetheart and began to take college more seriously. Another issue was his weight. He weighed just 170 pounds when he began playing his sophomore season. He gained 15 pounds to add power to his speed and elusiveness. He led the Big Eight in rushing that year and finished third in the nation with 1,125 yards.

Sayers faded statistically his junior and senior years, but scouts were comparing him to the legendary Red Grange as the draft approached. The hometown Kansas City Chiefs of the American Football League offered him more money, but Sayers chose to play for the Bears, who selected him fourth overall.[2]

The rest is history. Sayers proved far deadlier to opposing defenses in the NFL than he did at the college level. Remarkably, he landed a spot in the Pro Football Hall of Fame despite having played less than four full seasons. At age thirty-four, he was the youngest inductee ever. That is a testament to his greatness.

POINT TOTAL EXPLANATION

Achievements: 29/35

The football world was left wondering what Sayers could have accomplished had he stayed healthy. What he accomplished in four seasons as a running back, pass catcher, and both punt and kickoff returner—especially considering he never played long enough to ever reach his prime—is incredible. The shortness of his career disallows a high point total here, but his achievements in track at the high school level are certainly worth consideration.

Athleticism: 24/25

Sayers was more about speed and quickness than power, which prevents him from earning all the points available here. But his elusiveness and acceleration were unsurpassed among NFL running backs, even to this day. He darted through the smallest of holes and wreaked havoc in the open field. Nobody could stop on a dime and shift like Sayers. And nobody could frustrate tacklers like him.

Athletic Requirements of Sport and Position: 19/20

Running backs—especially scatbacks such as Sayers—are the best of NFL athletes. They must be tough to endure hard tackles from hard-charging linebackers and safeties or linemen that weigh a hundred pounds more than them. Running backs of that era often handled the ball thirty times a game and took a pounding, though Sayers's ability to make tacklers miss allowed him to stay fresh.

Clutch Factor/Mental and Emotional Toughness/ Intangibles: 14/15

Sayers never played in a postseason game, so there is little to go on here. But his perseverance in returning from what could have been a career-ending knee injury in 1968 must be considered in this category. That he was able to return the next year and exceed 1,000 yards rushing to lead the league earned him the George S. Halas Courage Award as the most courageous player in pro football.[3]

Versatility: 4/5

Sayers did not participate in any sport but football beyond high school, so he cannot maximize his point total here. But his accomplishments as a prep track star leave little doubt about his athletic versatility.

POINT TOTAL: 90

46

MARY WAMBACH: ABBY

Soccer

Abby Wambach. © Bill Streicher–*USA TODAY Sports*

It was June 20, 2013. American striker Abby Wambach scored her second goal of the match against South Korea at Red Bull Arena in Harrison, New Jersey. The tally had little impact on the battle itself—just part of a blowout in an inconsequential friendly. But it had major implications on the history of soccer. It placed Wambach ahead of Mia Hamm in career goals scored among all female players ever.

Hamm had been the darling of women's soccer for years. She was the most significant athlete in popularizing the sport in the United States. But Wambach had emerged as a more explosive player. Her four first-half goals in the easy triumph over South Korea gave her 160, the most of any male or female player in international soccer. Hamm had retired with 158. Most impressive is that Wambach shattered the mark in 207 matches, while it took Hamm 275 to reach her final destination. Wambach finished her career with 184 goals in 252 matches.[1]

Not that Wambach was comfortable with the comparisons. She expressed thanks to Hamm for giving her something to shoot for—literally. Her feats stood on their own merits. She scored an incredible 23 goals in thirty-five Olympic and World Cup matches combined. Her total would have been higher had she not missed the 2008 Games with a broken leg. Her header goal in the 122nd minute of the 2011 World Cup quarterfinal against Brazil tied the match and allowed her team to win and advance to the finals. Wambach also earned FIFA World Player of the Year in 2012, following Hamm as the only other American to earn the award.[2]

It seemed Wambach was destined for such honors. Born Mary Abigail Wambach on June 2, 1980, in Rochester, New York, the youngest of seven children was raised in a sports-minded family. Her soccer talent emerged quickly—she scored 27 goals in three games against other girls, motivating the powers that be to transfer her to a boys' league. Her competitive drive was honed on the soccer field and in playing in a wide variety of other sports, including the popular street hockey, where she played goalie. She joked that her mother sent her kids out to play and would not let them return for any reason—they were forced to pee in the bushes. Her older brothers and sisters never let her win. Abby was victorious only when victory was earned. Eldest sister Beth, who played basketball and studied medicine at Harvard, held Abby to the highest athletic and academic standards.

The youngest Wambach maintained her wide-ranging athletic interests. She played basketball as well as soccer in high school. But it was her talents in the latter that were most pronounced. She later led the University of Florida to the NCAA championship in 1988 and four consecutive Southeastern Conference crowns. She remains the leading career scorer at that school with 96 goals. But it was her production in international competition that would make her arguably the greatest male or female American soccer player ever.[3]

They Said It

I don't care who scores the goals, I'm going to leave my humanbeingness on the field!—Abby Wambach

So proud of you, my friend. You are a warrior and true champion. Enjoy this.—Mia Hamm to Wambach after the latter broke her scoring record

No one individual is better than the team. I've scored no goals just on my own. Every goal I've scored has been because of someone else on my team, their excellence, their bravery. And I'm kind of the end product of a collection of a really good vibe, and feeling, and creativity on the field.—Abby Wambach

POINT TOTAL EXPLANATION

Achievements: 34/35

Though Wambach gained fame almost entirely as a point scorer—she had 75 assists as well—her tremendous ability to put the ball in the net is worthy of great consideration in this category. She helped the United States become the most dominant team in the world, a distinction that could not be claimed about its male counterpart. The competition level was not as strong internationally as what the men face, but she is the leading scorer in women's soccer history. Enough said.

Athleticism: 23/25

Wambach possessed the ability to outjump defenders and slam headers past goalkeepers with uncanny accuracy. All four of her goals in the 2011 World Cup came off headers. Her speed and footwork on the offensive end were among the best of her generation.[4]

Athletic Requirements of the Sport and Position: 17/20

The constant movement required of soccer players alone warrants significant consideration here. Footwork, quickness, speed, agility, leaping ability, durability, and endurance all come into play for strikers such as Wambach.

Clutch Factor/Mental and Emotional Toughness/ Intangibles: 13/15

Wambach gained her toughness competing against her siblings and others in her neighborhood. That toughness translated into a hard-nosed approach to soccer. She often sacrificed her body to score, leaping up on headers and throwing herself on the ground to boot the ball into the net. Wambach was also considered a vocal leader, but her talent spoke louder.[5]

Versatility: 3/5

The athletic endeavors of her youth, including high school basketball, provide a few points here. Wambach concentrated solely on soccer beyond her prep days, but her athletic versatility previous to that deserves recognition.

TOTAL POINTS: 90

47

JERRY RICE: FLASH 80

Football

Jerry Rice. © RVR Photos–*USA TODAY Sports*

One can argue that Jerry Rice was the greatest football player of all time. Not the finest athlete. Not the fastest. Not the quickest. Not the strongest. But possibly the best—only Don Hutson is in the same conversation. No skill position player proved more statistically dominant than Rice. And no wide receiver played a bigger role in his team's maintaining a Super Bowl dynasty.

The numbers are staggering. That Rice owns the NFL career record in receiving yards with 22,895 is impressive. That he bests second-place Terrell Owens by nearly 7,000 yards is amazing. But that is simply one example of his complete dominance. Rice sits atop the career receiving touchdown list with 197. Randy Moss is next, with a comparatively tiny 156. Rice ranks number one in career receptions with 1,549; next comes tight end Tony Gonzalez with 1,325.

Rice compiled records that might never be broken, even in the era that he helped launch a prolific aerial game. One glance at his annual production provides an explanation. He exceeded 1,000 yards receiving fourteen times, including eleven straight from 1986 to 1996. He racked up double-digit touchdowns nine times and led the NFL six times in one eight-year period. He managed at least 100 catches four times. Not bad considering Rice clocked in at a rather slow 4.71 in the 40-yard dash—and considering he did not take up the sport until his sophomore year in high school.[1]

Rice was born on October 13, 1962, in the small town of Starkville, Mississippi, and was raised in the much smaller town of Crawford. His unexpected football career began when the high school principal sidled up behind Rice when the student was playing hooky. Rice ran so fast that the principal informed the football coach, who convinced him to try out. The inhibited and shy Rice gained a sense of pride in his abilities on the gridiron and came out of his shell.[2]

With so little experience in football, he did not perform well enough to attract much attention, but he did land a shot with Division I-AA Mississippi Valley State. He blossomed as a sophomore in a high-powered passing attack, with 66 catches for 1,134 yards and seven touchdowns. He was establishing new I-AA records by the middle of his junior year, motivating *Sports Illustrated* to declare him the "Catch of the Year." He ended that season with 102 receptions for 1,450 yards. Rice snagged an absurd 24 for 279 yards in one game against Southern. He then shattered NCAA marks for receptions, yards, and touchdowns as a senior. So prolific were Rice and quarterback Willie Totten that Mississippi Valley State would later rename its home Rice-Totten Stadium. It is no surprise that Rice has since been named to the College Football Hall of Fame.[3]

They Said It

The enemy of the best is the good. If you're always settling with what's good, you'll never be the best.—Jerry Rice

Jerry Rice doesn't rank in the all-time greats. He is the greatest receiver and maybe the greatest football player of all time.—Pro Bowl safety Darren Sharper

I was always willing to work; I was not the fastest or biggest player, but I was determined to be the best football player I could be on the football field and I think I was able to accomplish that with hard work.—Jerry Rice

Many other honors had previously rolled in. Rice earned a spot in thirteen Pro Bowls and ten first-team All-Pro squads, was twice named NFL Offensive Player of the Year (an award most often reserved for quarterbacks), and was inducted into the Pro Football Hall of Fame in 2010.[4]

POINT TOTAL EXPLANATION

Achievements: 35/35

If Rice did not earn all the points here, nobody should. That he achieved more than any other player at his position is a given. One can even argue that he was the most dominant player at his position than any other athlete in a major American sport.

Athleticism: 20/25

Strangely, one of the "attributes" that made Rice so incredible was his *lack* of athleticism. He was slow of foot compared to most receivers. He was neither particularly strong nor particularly quick nor particularly elusive. But he ran impeccable pass patterns, knew how to get open, and found seams in the zone separate enough to add yards to the end of the catch. He knew how to use his body to ward off defenders and snag the ball when well covered. And, most incredibly, Rice was often double-teamed. Granted, playing catch with the likes of Joe Montana and Steve Young played a huge role in his success, but one should not minimize his contributions to one of the most prolific passing offenses ever assembled.[5]

Athletic Requirements of the Sport and Position: 18/20

Rice is admittedly an anomaly. Wide receivers are generally required to possess excellent speed and quickness to separate from secondary personnel. They must also boast a high level of endurance as they complete patterns or block on every play.

Clutch Factor/Mental and Emotional Toughness/Intangibles: 15/15

A career replete with explosive playoff and Super Bowl performances helps give Rice a perfect score here. He caught 11 passes for 215 yards and one of his six postseason touchdowns that year in the 1989 Super Bowl triumph over Cincinnati. He snagged three touchdowns in a Super Bowl rout of Denver the following season. He managed 10 receptions for 149 yards and three scores in a Super Bowl defeat of San Diego in 1995. That Rice produced such lofty numbers without the level of athleticism boasted by most of his contemporaries is remarkable and places a spotlight on his mental and emotional toughness.[6]

Versatility: 2/5

Rice did not play other sports at a high level. But his wide-ranging abilities on the football field allowed him to thrive despite a lack of athleticism and indicate some level of versatility.

TOTAL POINTS: 90

48

PETE SAMPRAS: PISTOL PETE

Tennis

One could hardly have imagined during the heyday of American men's tennis in the 1970s and 1980s, with Jimmy Connors and John McEnroe dominating the sport along with other stalwarts such as Björn Borg and Ivan Lendl, that another US player would soon emerge as the best of that country to ever grace a court. That player was Pete Sampras.

Connors won more matches, greatly due to his longevity. Sampras ranks third all-time with 14 Grand Slam titles—boasting an incredible record of 14–4 in Grand Slam finals—to just 8 for Connors. And though one can claim his level of competition was weaker than that of Connors, beating the likes of Andre Agassi and Boris Becker in those matches cannot be dismissed as a simple chore.

Sampras earned the top ranking in men's tennis every year from 1993 to 1998. His overall career match winning percentage of 84.23 tops all Americans. And only Rafael Nadal achieved at least one Grand Slam championship in more consecutive years than Sampras, who accomplished that from 1993 to 2000.[1]

He and Agassi engaged in a legendary rivalry. They represented the dying gasp of American men's tennis, at least for two decades. No US player who has competed since—not even Andy Roddick—could be considered among the world's elite during the fifteen years after Sampras defeated Agassi in the 2002 US Open championship for his last Grand Slam crown.

Sampras overpowered opponents with his serve and forehand, which was so deadly that he often moved around his backhand if given the time. He attacked the net and put away points with powerful and accurate volleys. He was a no-touch player and avoided long baseline rallies, but his shot accuracy made up for any deficiencies.[2]

The right-hander was born on August 1, 1971, in Washington, DC, but was raised in Southern California. His older sister Stella also played professionally, but it was Pete who developed into a champion. One critical turning point in his career proved to be his switch from a two-handed to a one-handed backhand, courtesy of a pediatrician who also served as his coach. Dr. Pete Fisher also convinced his protégé to play a more aggressive style by attacking the net rather than slugging back and forth from the baseline. Sampras developed a vicious serve, bringing it all together. He also embraced the legacies of yesteryear greats such as Rod Laver and Ken Rosewall.[3]

Sampras arrived on the professional scene during the waning years of those who had been dominating tennis since the 1970s. He helped hasten their departures, starting with the US Open in 1989 after falling in the first round of that event the year before. Sampras disposed of Mats Wilander in the fourth round of that event. Then, in 1990, he beat Lendl in the quarterfinals and McEnroe in the semis before destroying Agassi in straight sets for the championship. He had become the youngest US Open men's champion of all time. His defeat of Lendl was particularly impressive as he served 26 aces and held on after losing the third and fourth sets. He showed the grit that would become a trademark throughout his incredible career.[4]

They Said It

I never wanted to be the great guy or the colorful guy or the interesting guy. I wanted to be the guy who won titles.—Pete Sampras

He was always the argument you couldn't win. Tennis purists loved his skill, naturally, and they will unhesitatingly declare Sampras' second serve, his running forehand and his leaping overhead as treasures that belong under a museum glass. But for a public that didn't grow up playing, tennis becomes charismatic only when rackets are flying or fists are pumping or new ground in fashion is being broken.—Sports Illustrated *writer S. L. Price*

I made it look so easy on court all those years. No one realized how hard I had to work. No one realized how much I had to put into it. They underestimated my intensity.—Pete Sampras

POINT TOTAL EXPLANATION

Achievements: 33/35

Sampras is simply one of the most accomplished tennis players of all time. He burned out a bit sooner than some, which costs him a couple points here, but his record in Grand Slam finals speaks more about his greatness than any other statistic.

Athleticism: 24/25

Sampras was a complete player. He boasted tremendous strength that allowed him to hit extremely hard from the baseline and the net. He reached balls others could not with his speed and quickness. He used his strong legs to cover the court as well as anyone in his era. And his leaping ability resulted in overhead winners.

Athletic Requirements of the Sport: 17/20

The quickness, power, endurance, and hand-eye coordination necessary to compete at the top level in professional men's tennis result in plenty of points in this category. The only physical obstacle that tennis players are not required to overcome is body contact. It can be a grueling, tiring sport, especially when played outdoors in the summer months.

Clutch Factor/Mental and Emotional Toughness/ Intangibles: 14/15

Sampras has been disparaged by some for a perceived lack of toughness at the end of his career, but, if true, that can be excused a bit. Tennis players are notorious for eventually experiencing burnout—it happens to most everyone. His stoicism was mistaken for boredom, but that criticism had never been leveled at Borg. The fact that Sampras won 14 of 18 Grand Slam finals speaks for itself. His mental strength on critical points helped make him a champion, though his blistering serves certainly played a more significant role.

Versatility: 2/5

Sampras dropped out of high school to concentrate on tennis, but his versatility on the court as a strong baseline and net player with speed and power earns him two points in this category.

TOTAL POINTS: 90

49

ERIC HEIDEN:
THE RECORD BREAKER

Speed Skating

Runners and speed skaters generally specialize in short, intermediate, or long distances—think Wilma Rudolph and Bonnie Blair. They train for bursts of speed, endurance, or somewhere in between. Their concentration on a specialty allows them to maximize their potential for medals in national and international competitions.

Then there was Eric Heiden, who threw caution to the wind at the 1980 Winter Olympics in Lake Placid. Heiden skated the 500 meters. And the 1000 meters. And the 1500 meters. And the 5000 meters. And the 10000 meters. He probably would have skated the 100000 meters if there were such a thing. And he won them all. Not only did he stand on the top step of the podium after each event, but he set Olympic records in every one of them. Included was a world-record time of 14:28.13 in the longest and most grueling of the five. He had become the first athlete to win five individual gold medals in a single Olympics, Summer or Winter.

Not bad considering Heiden competed in only the 1500 and 5000 four years earlier at Innsbruck, placing seventh and nineteenth, respectively. But then, he was just seventeen years old at the time. In between the two Olympiads, he honed his craft, dominated the competition, and emerged as the clear favorite in 1980. He placed first in the 500 meters at the world championships following the 1976 Games and won the World Junior All-round, World Junior Sprints, and World Senior All-round in both 1977 and 1978. He captured the Sprints and Senior All-round in 1979, then became the first man since 1912 to win all four speed skating titles at the World Championships in 1979.

Heiden was the top-ranked speed skater in the world for nearly five years. He became the first ever to win the Oscar Mathisen Award—an

honor presented annually to the speed skater that provides the finest individual performance—four times. During his peak years, Heiden set eight
world records between the 1000- and 10000-meter distances.

Never one to shy away from a challenge, Heiden retired from speed
skating following his triumphs in Lake Placid and took up competitive cycling. He nearly landed a spot on the US Olympic team in that sport and
performed professionally for a brief time. He won the national professional
cycling crown in 1985 and even competed in the Tour de France (though
he failed to complete the race).[1]

A humble nature and a healthy set of priorities in life prevented Heiden
from allowing his success to massage his ego. Born on June 14, 1958, in
Madison, Wisconsin, he was raised to eschew fame and fortune for the
self-satisfaction that comes with dedication and accomplishment. Heiden
admitted that he embraced speed skating over hockey, at which he was
quite talented, so he could toil in relative anonymity. His Olympic success
spoiled that plan and made him feel a bit uncomfortable.

Heiden, who gained his perspective in life from his parents, began training in earnest at age fourteen. He worked five hours a day on his speed
skating, both on the ice and dry land. Among his exercises was simulating
skating in his socks on a six-foot-wide plastic sheet in his basement. Soon
he was doing the real thing at Innsbruck. Nobody—even Heiden himself—could have imagined that he would blossom into arguably the greatest speed skater in history.[2]

POINT TOTAL EXPLANATION

Achievements: 32/35

Heiden basically won every speed skating event in which he participated
following the 1976 Winter Games, including five at Lake Placid in Olympic-
or world-record time. The comparative shortness of his career precludes
him from matching the point total of athletes with greater longevity—that
is often the fate of Olympians—but he still gets a pretty healthy haul.

Athleticism: 22/25

Heiden was a muscular skater who used a wide array of athletic attributes
to thrive in both sprints and marathons. His rhythm, balance, and endurance all entered into his success in 1980 and beyond.

They Said It

Heck, gold medals, what can you do with them? I'd rather get a nice warmup suit. That's something I can use. Gold medals just sit there. When I get old, maybe I could sell them if I need the money.—Eric Heiden

What he did in 1980 was one of a kind, and we will probably never see it again.—Sportscaster Keith Jackson

Athletic Requirements of the Sport and Events: 18/20

Speed skaters who compete in both the short and long events deserve at least one more point here. They must boast a wider range of athletic talents, including speed, agility, lower-body strength, and stamina. Heiden simply had more of those traits than anyone else—perhaps in the history of the sport.

Clutch Factor/Mental and Emotional Toughness/ Intangibles: 15/15

Heiden won five gold medals in five events under the strongest spotlight in international sports. He set Olympic or world records in all of them. Such achievements are impossible without a high level of concentration and toughness. Perhaps what lessened the pressure was his attitude, a drive that was not centered on gaining fame and fortune based on self-importance. Whatever it was, he deserves all the points in this category.

Versatility: 3/5

His foray into and success in professional cycling after retiring from speed skating must be credited here. So should his versatility as a championship skater.

TOTAL POINTS: 90

SHAUN WHITE:
THE FLYING TOMATO

Snowboarding, Skateboarding

Shaun White. © Jerry Lai–*USA TODAY Sports*

Call them action sports or extreme sports—Shaun White played the most significant role in giving them legitimacy. His brilliance and the recognition of the athleticism required to perform well as a skateboarder and snowboarder helped motivate the sports' inclusion in the Summer and Winter Olympics, respectively. (Skateboarding was adopted for the Tokyo Games in 2020.)

White is considered the finest athlete to stand atop a board. So seamlessly has he transitioned back and forth that White, who at one time was better known for his skateboarding, emerged as the premier snowboarder in the world, earning Olympic gold medals in the half-pipe in both 2006 and 2010 and placing fourth in 2014.

His talent helped popularize the X Games and Winter X Games, both of which he dominated from the start of the millennium. He placed first in slopestyle at the winter event every year from 2003 to 2006 and again in 2009. He captured gold in the SuperPipe in 2003, 2006, and 2008 through 2013. He also topped the field at the X Games in 2007 and 2011.[1]

White did not emerge as the most recognizable skateboarder and snowboarder in the world based solely on his accomplishments. His long red hair earned him the nickname "Flying Tomato" and his engaging personality made him a media darling. In the process, he blazed new trails in both sports. He became the first snowboarder to nail successive double corks and the only skater to land the frontside heel-flip body varial, otherwise known as the Armadillo. The maneuver required White to flip his board while doing a backflip, catch it, and place it under himself. White also completed a McTwist, spinning around one-and-a-half times while doing a front flip. His Frontside 1080 required three 360-degree spins, while his Backside 900 landed him after two-and-a-half clockwise spins. Nobody could do what Shaun White could do at his peak.[2]

White had been training for such moments since he transitioned from skiing to snowboarding at age six. Born September 3, 1986, in San Diego, he suffered from a congenital disorder that lessened the supply of oxygen to his heart. He underwent two surgeries to correct the problem, motivating his parents to become far more protective. They did, however, encourage an active lifestyle. Young Shaun embraced surfing, soccer, trampolining, and skiing. His mother, who was concerned with his safety on the slopes, pushed him to eschew the latter for snowboarding, which she deemed less potentially dangerous. But her son had already established a love for speed and a bit of a reckless nature. The switch to snowboarding proved fateful.

He was a natural. White entered his first snowboarding competition at age seven—and won. The stunning victory earned him a spot in the United States Amateur Snowboarding Association National Championships, where

They Said It

What does it mean to be a snowboarder? It's about having fun with your friends or by yourself. It's about pushing yourself to try new things and do the unexpected. Finally, and most importantly, it's about being creative.—Shaun White

No one's done it. It's bad enough that Shaun White destroys everyone whenever he enters a snow contest, but now he's a pro vert skater and living out every rider's dream. How sick is that?—Transworld Snowboarding *editor Cody Dresser*

You know the best thing about competition? There's this whole strategy game, and when it all works out it's like solving this hard math equation. You finally get the answer and you're so happy.—Shaun White

he placed eleventh against far older competition. His battles against those sometimes more than twice his age raised his talent level and quickened his ascent through the snowboarding ranks. His fierce competitiveness became evident as the trophies piled up. His legend grew to the point that it reached skateboarding legend Tony Hawk, whose praise for White included the nickname "Future Boy." White had reached the point at which he could perform tricks five feet higher than everyone else.

The journey was far from easy. Along the way, he broke his hand and foot and fractured his skull. But he still won five national twelve-and-under championships in the mid- to late 1990s before turning professional at age thirteen. His dominance waned competing against older and more experienced snowboarders, including some of the best in the world, but soon he was beating them too. He placed second in the 2002 Winter X Games in both the slopestyle and SuperPipe. White was on his way to stardom.[3]

POINT TOTAL EXPLANATION

Achievements: 32/35

Shaun White holds the record for sixteen medals at the Winter X Games. That is a tremendous accomplishment, but it can be argued that it does not carry the weight of his two Olympic gold medals. Add his skateboarding achievements to the mix and White deserves a hefty total here.

Athleticism: 23/25

A higher level of athleticism than the competition proved most impactful in his dominance. White is not a powerful athlete, but he could jump higher with greater body control, reflexes, balance, and timing than his competition. Those traits allowed him to create greater speed on the boards, resulting in tricks that others simply could not achieve.[4]

Athletic Requirements of the Sport and Events: 18/20

That White participated in both snowboarding and skateboarding at the highest of levels helps his score here. Both require tremendous coordination and agility. Though upper-body power does not really enter into the equation, leg strength does, and so does every athletic quality required of gymnasts, who are some of the finest athletes in the world.

Clutch Factor/Mental and Emotional Toughness/ Intangibles: 14/15

White displayed the confidence to compete against those far older—and the concentration to beat them—in his midteens. He also proved his mettle by winning gold in his first Olympic event, then doing it again. The focus necessary to win championships in snowboarding and skateboarding, knowing that one fall can result in elimination, is intense. White earns a great score in this category.

Versatility: 3/5

White did not thrive in traditional sports but deserves a few points here for excelling in two (albeit similar) sports.

TOTAL POINTS: 90

51

SIMONE BILES: SIMONEY

Gymnastics

Simone Biles. © Robert Deutsch–USA TODAY Sports

The Olympics were not even a dream for Simone Biles. That she could compete on the biggest international stage as a gymnast never even entered her mind—at least not until 2012. That is when she took a break from her training at the Gymnastix Centre in Houston to watch the US team compete in the 2012 London Games.

Biles saw the American quintet of Gabby Douglas, McKayla Maroney, Aly Raisman, Kyla Ross, and Jordyn Wieber in action. She was impressed that they earned the all-around gold medal, but she realized that she had trained with Ross and Wieber. And she knew then that if they could compete and win at the Olympics, so could she.[1]

That confidence translated into dedication, which revealed her immense talent. Biles began making noise at the junior level. She embraced the floor exercises, balance beam, and vault, but also excelled in the individual all-around. She made her mark nationally before competing in her first World Championships in Antwerp, Belgium, in 2013. She called attention to herself with a brilliant performance and won four medals, including gold in the floor and individual all-around. She finished no lower than fourth in any event.

They Said It

My first Olympics and I've walked away with five medals: That's not disappointing at all. It shows dreams can come true. I'm not the next Usain Bolt or Michael Phelps: I'm the first Simone Biles.—Simone Biles

You feel the routine with her. You feel the moment before she mounts the balance beam or the uneven bars and you breathe with them because you anticipate everything they're doing and because your eye is used to seeing every angle, the momentum, enough spring going into a move. You are living it with them. You feel it with them.—Olympic gymnast Cathy Rigby

Biles continued to dominate both national and international competitions despite a shoulder injury that hindered her early in 2014. She rebounded to earn an incredible four golds, including three individuals, that year at the World Championships in Nanking, China. Biles topped the field in the individual all-around, floor, and balance beam (on which she had won only a bronze the year before), snagging a silver in the vault.

She then vaulted—pun intended—herself among the elite of all time at the 2015 World Championships in Glasgow, Scotland. Her third straight individual all-around crown in three years surpassed the feat of Russian legend Svetlana Korkhina, who needed five years to accomplish the feat. Biles also earned gold in the floor and balance beam. With fourteen medals, she had become the most decorated American female gymnast in the World Championships and was the first to win ten golds.[2]

The pressure to win in that annual event paled in comparison to the nerve-racking nature of Olympic competition. But her brilliance in the floor allowed her to open with arguably her best and most comfortable event. She blew away the field with a samba-inspired routine that captured the imagination of the crowd in Rio de Janeiro, helping the Americans take gold in the team competition. She won the individual all-around two days later, but she was merely warming up. Biles snagged her third gold with a score of 15.966 in the vault, then later matched that score in the individual floor routine to earn another. She had become only the fifth female gymnast—and the first American—to win four Olympic gold medals.[3]

Not bad considering her unstable beginnings. Biles was born on March 14, 1997, in Columbus, Ohio. Substance abuse prevented her biological mother from assuming parental responsibilities, so her maternal grandfather and his second wife summoned her to their home in the Houston suburb of Spring, where she taught herself to do backflips off the mailbox. A field trip at age six to the gym, where she watched older girls perform gymnastics routines, caught her attention. Soon after she began training, she caught the attention of gymnastics instructor Aimee Boorman.

It was a match made in gymnastics heaven. The two became inseparable, and Biles embraced Boorman like a second mom. She continued to train and improve until that fateful night in 2012 when she realized that she too could become an Olympian.[4]

POINT TOTAL EXPLANATION

Achievements: 31/35

Biles simply hasn't competed at a high level long enough to earn more points here, though she has been close to perfect so far. She has dominated every national and international competition in which she has participated, including the 2016 Summer Olympics. She has proven herself a gold medal winner or contender in every gymnastics event.

Athleticism: 24/25

For a diminutive 4-foot-9, 105-pounder, Biles boasts plenty of strength to go along with the agility, quickness, and balance needed to thrive in such events as the floor exercises, balance beam, and vault.

Athletic Requirements of the Sport: 18/20

Gymnasts are arguably the most underrated and least appreciated athletes in the world. They require wide-ranging athletic skills, including tremendous balance, quickness, agility, arm and length strength, and to some extent speed in the floor exercises. The timing necessary to complete perfect landings off the twists and turns in the air cannot be underestimated. The points deducted here are for a lack of physical contact and extensive daily competition throughout the year.

Clutch Factor/Mental and Emotional Toughness/ Intangibles: 14/15

Biles took it to another level in the Olympic spotlight, elevating her point total in this category in the process. The level of concentration needed in gymnastics, where one tiny slip can destroy all medal hopes, is astronomical. Biles has rarely faltered, indicating a mental and emotional strength that all gymnasts wish they possessed. She simply hasn't done it long enough to warrant a perfect score.

Versatility 3/5

Biles has not proven herself in any other sports—she hasn't even had the time. But gymnastics is all about versatility and she has excelled in all events. She deserves credit for that.

TOTAL POINTS: 90

52

STAN MUSIAL: STAN THE MAN

Baseball

To Stan Musial, hitting was like eating potato chips: Why stop at one when you can have two? Or three? Or four? Bases, that is. The Cardinals slugger ranks third in baseball history in extra-base hits. The only two ahead of him are the all-time leading home run hitters (one questionable, the other earned): Barry Bonds and Hank Aaron. Musial finished his career about 300 home runs behind them but was a doubles and triples machine.

Musial simply did it all. He ranks in the top ten all-time in hits (3,630), offensive WAR (124.7), runs scored (1,949), total bases (6,134), doubles (725), RBI (1,951), and a partridge in a pear tree. He led the National League in runs, hits, doubles, triples, batting average, on-base percentage, and slugging percentage at least five times each. And though he never led the National League in home runs, he slugged 475 for his career. It's no wonder he was a three-time Most Valuable Player and first-ballot Hall of Famer. And, by the way, he averaged about 30 strikeouts a season and led the Cardinals to four pennants and three World Series championships.[1]

That Musial forged an athletic career would not have surprised anyone who knew him growing up. Stashu Musial was born to Polish and Czech immigrants on November 21, 1920, in the western Pennsylvania town of Donora, twenty-five miles south and a bit east of Pittsburgh. Young Stan showed far less interest in his schoolwork than he did in sports. He honed his skills in baseball and basketball in high school and in local clubs. Stories abound about his father's reaction when the University of Pittsburgh offered a basketball scholarship. One claims that he tried to force Stan to accept, but the latter yearned to pursue a baseball career; another offers that his dad, like many immigrant parents of that time, greatly preferred that his son graduate and then take a "real" job in a steel mill.

In either case, Stan was the only one of the six Musial kids to complete his high school education. Legend has it that he had by then already signed a professional contract, having linked with Class D Monessen in the Cardinals organization in September 1937, which precluded him from playing college basketball. What is certain is that Musial hooked up with Williamson (West Virginia) of the Class D Mountain State League in 1938 and gave little indication on the mound or at the plate of his eventual greatness: the seventeen-year-old walked 80 batters in 110 innings and batted just .258.

But Musial's drive would not allow him to wallow in mediocrity. He toiled tirelessly on his batting stroke. He also worked on other sports while still at Donora High School, including basketball and even table tennis. His diligence paid off upon his return to Williamson, which had since joined the St. Louis organization. Musial still struggled to throw strikes as a pitcher, but he batted .352. Then everything came together the following year after graduation allowed him to play minor-league ball full-time. The southpaw showed potential as a pitcher, sporting an 18–5 record despite another bout with wildness, while batting .311 and establishing himself as a wonderful gap hitter. The power would come later. A shoulder injury late that season, however, ended his pitching career.

It was a blessing in disguise. Musial could now concentrate on his hitting and outfield play. He destroyed pitching at Class C Springfield the following

---

They Said It

I've had pretty good success with Stan by throwing him my best pitch and backing up third.—Dodgers pitcher Carl Erskine

I never realized that batting a little ball around could cause so much commotion. I now know how [Charles] Lindbergh must have felt when he returned from St. Louis.—Stan Musial

How good was Stan Musial? He was good enough to take your breath away.—Legendary baseball announcer Vin Scully

year, batting .379 and finally finding his power with a league-best 26 home runs. He batted .326 after a promotion to Double-A Rochester, then finished his meteoric rise by batting .412 in his first twelve games with the Cardinals while striking out just once in 47 at-bats. The twenty-year-old with the unorthodox crouch at the plate had completed one of the fastest single-season ascensions in baseball history. The best was yet to come.[2]

POINT TOTAL EXPLANATION

Achievements: 34/35

Only weak World Series performances prevent Musial from nailing a perfect score in this category. He is arguably the greatest hitter in National League history, one who consistently led the league in myriad offensive categories and played reliably both in the outfield and at first base. It can be argued that Musial owned the premier extra-base stroke ever.

Athleticism: 22/25

Musial did not boast the power of a Mantle or speed of a Mays, but his timing, balance, and hand-eye coordination at the plate were second to none and he could not be considered lacking in any one athletic attribute. He certainly proved himself to be fast enough to leg out triples, though the larger ballparks of his day provided gaps that aided in that pursuit. The shoulder injury he sustained in the minors resulted in a rather weak outfield arm, but he made up for it with strong fundamentals and a quick release.

Athletic Requirements of the Sport and Position: 16/20

Musial played every outfield position, which is a plus here, and first base, which is a minus. But that he did so for twenty-three seasons and played in virtually every game from 1941 to 1946 proves his durability and must be credited here.[3]

Clutch Factor/Mental and Emotional Toughness/Intangibles: 13/15

Musial was a tremendous teammate. He was not flashy like other stars of his and other eras, but his dependability stood out. He maintained an ideal disposition in a sport that can lead to frustration. He never even got ejected from a game. It should also be pointed out that Jackie Robinson cited Musial as one player who encouraged him during his breakthrough season of 1947. The lone drawback is that Musial batted just .256 with one home run in 99 World Series plate appearances.

Versatility: 4/5

Musial was a talented enough basketball player to be offered a major college scholarship. He also played all over the baseball field and boasted some promise as a pitcher in the minor leagues. He deserves a strong score here.

TOTAL POINTS: 89

53

WILLIE PEP: WILL-O'-THE-WISP

Boxing

Though the story remains more legend than fact, it was said that Willie Pep once bet Minnesota sportswriter Don Riley that he could win a round against Jackie Graves without throwing a punch. Riley informed the public after the bout that Pep won the round and the bet with a display of defensive acrobatics so incredible that the fans never realized that nary a blow was attempted.[1]

Many consider Willie Pep the greatest pure boxer in history. The featherweight danced about the ring—a butterfly decades before Muhammad Ali used the simile to describe his own style—against whom it was virtually impossible to strike a solid punch. Such elusiveness alone could not have placed Pep among the all-time greats. But his career record of 229–11–1 with 65 knockouts certainly does. His prolific schedule alone is impressive. He averaged more than a fight a month for most of his career, battling in 66 bouts in 1941 and 1942 alone.[2]

Pep certainly had pep. The man billed as "The Connecticut Kid" won his first 52 professional fights before becoming—at age twenty—the youngest world champion in forty years with a defeat of Chalky Wright. He inched his consecutive victory total to 63 before losing a nontitle bout against Lou Angott, then winning again just ten days later to start a 73-fight unbeaten streak. Despite continuing his boxing career during World War II, he served in both the army and navy until a perforated eardrum forced him to be discharged. Even a broken leg and back sustained in a near-fatal plane crash in 1947 could not prevent Pep from winning all 43 of his bouts during a three-year stretch after the war.

That ended the peak period for Pep. His second defeat was a knockout in October 1948 to Sandy Saddler. Pep exacted revenge two months later, setting up a battle in September 1950 before forty thousand fans at Yankee Stadium in which he was accused of taking a dive to pay off debts from a gambling habit. Pep never again fought for a title.

Like many boxers of his era, Pep was a son of immigrants—his parents came from Sicily—and grew up in poverty during the Great Depression. Gugliermo Papaleo was born in Middletown, Connecticut, on September 19, 1922. He was often bullied by bigger boys in the neighborhood, who extracted from him the pittance he earned shining shoes. Pep learned to box as a means of self-defense. He recalled with relish a battle with one boy in which his boxing skills allowed him to survive despite a bloody nose and aching stomach. It was the last time anybody tried to pick on Pep.

Soon he was winning the Connecticut amateur flyweight and bantamweight championships. His success motivated him to turn pro at age eighteen. Though Pep showed little knockout power, his elusiveness prevented opponents from registering a knockout for the next eight years.[3]

POINT TOTAL EXPLANATION

Achievements: 33/35

Pep lost only once in his first 137 fights and is arguably the finest defensive boxer ever. Though late in his career he fought largely for the money and was a shadow of his former self, his peak period lasted long enough to place Pep among the all-time greats. He is widely accepted as the best featherweight ever to grace a ring.

Athleticism: 23/25

Pep did not possess the punching power to put foes on the canvas, but he did boast the footwork, quickness, and elusiveness to avoid hard contact. It sometimes requires greater athleticism to fight defensively than offensively, and Pep is certainly a prime example. But though he engaged in many a brawl, particularly in epic bouts against Saddler, he lacked the pure power to consistently register knockouts.[4]

Athletic Requirements of the Sport and Division: 18/20

The sheer number of bouts in which Pep participated adds at least a point to the total in this category. The durability needed to battle in the ring

They Said It

They call Ray Robinson the best fighter pound for pound. I'm the best fighter, ounce for ounce.—Willie Pep

Pep was well loved for his ability. He was the cleverest boxer of the last 40, 50 years. He pulled the damndest trick I've ever seen in a ring. It happened the night he defended the title against Chalky Wright in '44, four years before my first fight with him. Chalky could knock you dead with one punch, but he couldn't lay a glove on Pep, who had taken the title from him. Chalky kept stalking him for one good shot and he finally trapped Pep in a corner. Chalky cocked his right to throw a bomb and Pep ducked through his legs and got away. That's right. Pep ducked right through Chalky's legs.—Sandy Saddler

The best advice I ever got was from a kid in the gym who told me, "When you're in the ring, make believe a cop is chasing you; don't let him catch you."—Willie Pep

monthly and remain viable or more than a decade cannot be underestimated. The lighter divisions also require fighters to be fast on their feet to keep up with the competition.

Clutch Factor/Mental and Emotional Toughness/ Intangibles: 13/15

Pep returned to form after a plane crash nearly took his life. That alone speaks volumes about his worthiness for a strong score here, though he did not rise to the occasion enough against Saddler, a less talented fighter who simply had his number. He also allowed gambling to interfere with his career, which costs him a bit here.

Versatility: 2/5

Like many boxers of his era, Pep grew up poor and had little opportunity to expand his horizons. He concentrated solely on the sport of his choice at an early age, leaving little time to explore any other athletic gifts.

TOTAL POINTS: 89

54

WALTER PAYTON: SWEETNESS

Football

Walter Payton did not boast the power of Jim Brown. He was not blessed with the elusiveness of Gale Sayers or the acceleration of Barry Sanders. But one can argue that no running back aside from Brown was more well-rounded athletically. It is because of that flawlessness Payton retired as the leading ground-gainer in NFL history.

Payton's longevity and annual assault on 2,000 combined yards running and receiving into his thirties is amazing compared to modern-day players at his position, who shine for a few years before fading away. His durability allowed him to play virtually every game throughout his career, making his early passing more painful and shocking.

Playing on mediocre Bears teams with poor quarterbacks until late in his career, Payton thrived despite overwhelming defensive attention. Most impressive among the myriad modern statistics is that he led Chicago in approximate value every year between 1975 and 1986. He exceeded 1,200 yards rushing in ten of eleven years (leaving out his rookie and swan song seasons). The lone exception during that stretch was the strike-shortened 1982 season. He peaked in 1977, leading the league with 1,852 yards and 14 touchdowns. Payton also helped elevate the running back position to one of extensive pass-catching responsibility.[1]

Payton was born on July 25, 1954, in Columbia, Mississippi, two months after the Supreme Court decision in *Brown v. Board of Education* launched the civil rights movement. Integration remained a pipe dream in the heart of Jim Crow territory, and Payton's high school remained segregated until his senior year. But he made the most of his childhood, frolicking, fishing, and hiking in the nearby woods with his siblings. Such healthy physical pursuits aided in his athletic development.

His favorite sport was football. He played three years at Jefferson High School before integration landed him at Columbia High. His vast talents were recognized. Southern schools such as Mississippi and Alabama had begun recruiting African Americans but remained limited in their pursuits. Payton could have traveled north or west to major universities but yearned to stay close to home and selected traditionally black school Jackson State, where his brother Eddie (who would also play in the NFL) had starred.

The younger Payton exceeded 3,500 yards rushing for the Tigers and averaged a whopping 6.1 yards per carry while setting the school's career touchdown record with 65. He established a single-season school mark with 24 rushing scores in 1973 to earn Black College Player of the Year honors. He snagged the award again the following year. He left the school as the all-time leading scorer in NCAA history, with 464 points.

Despite his having competed at a comparatively lower level than many of the premier players entering the 1974 draft, the Bears recognized Payton's talent. Three of the top eight players taken were from traditionally black colleges, including linebacker and Jackson State teammate Robert Brazile, who often joined Payton at Pro Bowls. That Payton emerged as a standout came as little surprise. But few could have predicted that he would retire as the leading career rusher in NFL history.[2]

They Said It

If you ask me how I want to be remembered, it is as a winner. You know what a winner is? A winner is somebody who has given his best effort, who has tried the hardest they possibly can, who has utilized every ounce of energy and strength within them to accomplish something. It doesn't mean that they accomplished it or failed, it means that they've given it their best. That's a winner.—Walter Payton

Walter was an inspiration in everything he did. The tremendous grace and dignity he displayed in his final months reminded us again why "Sweetness" was the perfect nickname.—NFL commissioner Paul Tagliabue

When you're good at something, you'll tell everyone. When you're great at something, they'll tell you.—Walter Payton

POINT TOTAL EXPLANATION

Achievements: 32/35

Payton's tremendous feat of 16,726 rushing yards was due equally to his attributes as a prolific workhorse as to his pure talent. He led the NFL in rushing attempts four consecutive years, but only once in yards per carry. He finished his career with a 4.4 per-rush average, which is quite good, but far from spectacular. He also paced the league in rushing yards and touchdowns just once. Payton accomplished much, no doubt. But a closer examination precludes him from challenging the likes of Jim Brown in this category.[3]

Athleticism: 23/25

What made Payton special was the breadth rather than the depth of his athleticism. He was not the fastest or the strongest back, but he was fast and strong. He was not the most elusive back, nor did he have the greatest acceleration, but he was quite quick. And given the length of his career and his ability to stay on the field for almost every game, his durability is unquestioned.

Athletic Requirements of the Sport and Position: 19/20

The durability of a running back who led the NFL in attempts four straight years and often caught passes out of the backfield results in an extra point here for Payton. Running backs are battered on just about every play—they even pick up onrushing linebackers and linemen to protect the quarterback on pass attempts. Featured backs require a balance of speed, strength, endurance, agility, elusiveness, and coordination along with the ability to take hits and remain effective. The only point lost here is the comparative infrequency of NFL competition.

Clutch Factor/Mental and Emotional Toughness/ Intangibles: 11/15

Payton's toughness in general is unquestioned, but he did not perform as well against premier competition under the brightest spotlights. He averaged just 3.5 yards per carry in nine postseason games and scored two touchdowns—both in the same game. He managed just 61 yards on 22 attempts in his only Super Bowl. Defenses keyed on Payton, but he simply did not rise to the occasion.[4]

Versatility: 4/5

Payton averaged 18 points per game for the newly integrated Columbia High School basketball team as a senior, excelled in track and field (particularly the long jump), and played for the baseball team as well. He even served as a drummer in the school band, which can take a little bit out of you. The only point missing here is that he did not play any other sports beyond high school.

TOTAL POINTS: 89

ALTHEA GIBSON:
THE TENACIOUS ONE

Tennis

Althea Gibson. *Library of Congress*

A cursory examination might lead one to believe that Althea Gibson was the unlikeliest of tennis champions. After all, she was born in the Jim Crow South and raised in Harlem. And tennis, particularly during the time of her youth, was not exactly a sport that opened a shiny, bright path for poor African Americans. But those who figured Althea Gibson had no chance did not know Althea Gibson.

Gibson felt uncomfortable in her role as a pioneer, but she had no choice when she blossomed into a champion. She emerged in 1949 as the first black woman to play in the United States Tennis Association Indoor Championships, falling in three sets in the second round to reigning Wimbledon champion Louise Brough. A year later, Gibson became the first African American to compete at the US Nationals, losing again to Brough in the same round.

She continued to hone her talents while on a full scholarship to Florida A&M, then peaked. A year after playing in a goodwill tour of Asia, she won both the French Open singles crown and teamed with Angela Buxton to snag the French and Wimbledon doubles crowns. Gibson was just warming up. She won the Wimbledon and US Nationals singles championships

They Said It

I always wanted to be somebody. If I made it, it's half because I was game enough to take a lot of punishment along the way and half because there were a lot of people who cared enough to help me.—Althea Gibson

Miss Gibson is over a very cunningly wrought barrel, and I can only hope to loosen a few of its staves with one lone opinion. If tennis is a game for ladies and gentlemen, it's also time we acted a little more like gentlepeople and less like sanctimonious hypocrites. . . . If Althea Gibson represents a challenge to the present crop of women players, it's only fair that they should meet that challenge on the courts.—Alice Marble, arguing in favor of inclusion in *American Lawn Tennis* magazine

in 1957, becoming the first black player to win either event. The result was a ticker tape parade in New York City for the first African American so honored since Jesse Owens in 1936. Gibson then repeated the feat in the same Grand Slam tournaments in 1958. She had earned superstar status, and her photo was splashed across the covers of *Sports Illustrated* and *Time* magazine. Gibson was also named Female Athlete of the Year by the Associated Press in 1957 and 1958. Gibson soon retired from tennis but was not done blazing new trails. She became the first black woman to join the LPGA tour in 1964 at age thirty-seven.[1]

Her journey was indeed amazing given her background. Gibson was born on August 25, 1927, in Silver Creek, South Carolina, but a disastrous harvest prompted her father to move the family in with an aunt in Harlem, where he took a job at a mechanic's garage. Young Althea was not one to sit around. Her love for sports and competition motivated her to compete with the neighborhood boys in myriad athletic activities—even football. Her hand-eye coordination also became evident on the baseball diamond.

All was not peaches and cream for Gibson, who often skipped school, stole candy, and felt the wrath of her father. But her passion and love for sports were positives that outweighed the negatives. She became particularly adept at paddle tennis, winning tournaments sponsored by youth sports programs.

Gibson also thrived at table tennis and eventually took up tennis at the Harlem River Courts. Her tremendous talent earned her a sponsorship that resulted in a move to Wilmington, North Carolina, where she continued her training. She dominated the all-black tournaments to which she was limited due to racial segregation. None other than tennis great Alice Marble eventually stepped in, writing a scathing letter to the powers that be stating her shame that a player as promising as Gibson was not allowed to integrate tournament play. Her words motivated action. Gibson was accepted into the 1950 US Nationals, and the rest is history.[2]

POINT TOTAL EXPLANATION

Achievements: 31/35

Given the obstacles Gibson faced in her rise to greatness, she cannot be punished too severely for her comparatively short period at the top. Gibson ascended to the number one ranking in the world, an incredible feat considering her circumstances.

Athleticism: 23/25

Gibson's length and serve-and-volley game proved intimidating to opponents. She had power strokes, enough mobility to cover the court, and the speed to rush the net and put away points. Her diversity was evident when she won on the clay of Roland Garros despite a serve-and-volley power game that most often cannot survive on the slow surface consistently.[3]

Athletic Requirements of the Sport: 17/20

There are few athletic skills *not* required of tennis players, perhaps more so in a women's game in which so few points are ended quickly by aces. The need for hand-eye coordination on the run is pronounced, as are vertical and lateral quickness, power, endurance, and occasion vertical leaping ability on overheads.

Clutch Factor/Mental and Emotional Toughness/ Intangibles: 14/15

The pressure on Gibson to perform in the face of racism from the white world and expectations from the black world was immense, yet she elevated her game to a championship level. Her downplaying of the race card angered some African Americans, but she refused to give an inch on her insistence of being judged solely on her talent. In short, Althea Gibson had guts.

Versatility: 4/5

That Gibson played so many sports in her youth and won a paddle tennis championship before blossoming into a tennis star earns her a good score here. So do her abilities on the links, which were strong enough to at least compete against the best in the world.

TOTAL POINTS: 89

56

HENRY ARMSTRONG: HOMICIDE HANK

Boxing

It took Henry Armstrong time to blossom. Unlike many historically great boxers, he was not battering a bunch of meatballs early in his career. He lost three of his first four fights and owned a 42–10–6 record after three years in the ring—a fine mark, but not championship level.

Then Armstrong caught fire. He won 56 of his next 57 bouts, including 45 in a row. And he achieved what no other fighter before or since has been able to do: he captured three titles simultaneously. Not bad considering the sport featured just eight weight classes during his era. He hung up his gloves with a 151–21–9 record over fifteen years. Most impressive was that he registered 101 knockouts and was knocked out just twice.[1]

Armstrong was particularly dominant as a welterweight. He defended his title successfully nineteen times in less than two years. But it was his ten-month blitz to a triple crown that gained him the greatest historical notoriety. He first knocked out featherweight Petey Sarron to capture that title in October 1937. He then won fourteen consecutive fights before overwhelming Barney Ross in May 1938 for the welterweight championship. But Armstrong was not finished. He showed amazing grit to wrest the lightweight crown from Lou Ambers three months later. Armstrong was spitting blood from a torn bottom lip. He was warned by the referee that if he spit more blood on the canvas, the fight would be stopped and Ambers declared the winner. So Armstrong swallowed it instead. He nearly passed out in the fifteenth round. But he survived to win a split decision.

He had peaked. Armstrong was overwhelmed by the challenge of defending three titles. He voluntarily relinquished his featherweight championship, then lost to Ambers soon thereafter. Armstrong tried in vain to

They Said It

Henry is able to avoid severe punishment by his continuous rushing tactics in which he gives an opponent little opportunity to think of anything but to protect himself against the murderous assault.—Boxing writer Nat Fleischer

I hit you in the middle, your chin comes down. I hit you in the chin, you go down.—Henry Armstrong

Armstrong is the greatest fighter in many years. Henry doesn't knock these guys out—he paralyzes them. He beats them into submission.—Boxing manager Joe Woodman

take the middleweight crown away from Ceferino Garcia in March 1940, then finally lost his welterweight title later that year. He fought until 1945, losing to Sugar Ray Robinson along the way and winning only six of his last eleven decisions. But he had established his legacy.[2]

That legacy includes an unusual heritage. Armstrong was born Henry Jackson in Columbus, Mississippi, on December 12, 1912, to a half-Cherokee mother and a father who was a mix of Native American, Irish, and African American. The eleventh of fifteen children, Henry moved with his family to St. Louis when he was four years old.

His mother died soon thereafter, and he was raised by his grandmother. He often scrapped with neighborhood kids before quitting his job on the Missouri-Pacific Railroad and embarking on an amateur boxing career under the name Melody Jackson. He soon moved to Los Angeles and continued his amateur career as Henry Armstrong. He turned pro in 1932 after failing to earn a spot on the US Olympic team, and within three years he was among the premier fighters in America.[3]

POINT TOTAL EXPLANATION

Achievements: 33/35

In the early 1930s Armstrong embarked on what would prove to be a prolific career. Though he struggled early and late in that career, he dominated in between. His solo achievement of holding three weight class crowns at one time cemented his legacy as an all-time great.

Athleticism: 23/25

Durability and endurance marked Armstrong's career. He battered opponents with rapid combinations and a looping right hand with the understanding that he would be forced to take hard hits as well, though his quick feet often resulted in him avoiding blows. He boasted a great knockout punch, but also had the stamina and elusiveness to last fifteen rounds and win. He also had the durability to fight every few weeks and stay strong.[4]

Athletic Requirements of the Sport and Division: 18/20

That Armstrong fought and held titles in three separate weight classes translates into a great score here. The featherweight, welterweight, and lightweight divisions require equal parts power and agility.

Clutch Factor/Mental and Emotional Toughness/ Intangibles: 13/15

Armstrong must be credited for his tremendous toughness in the ring, but he was not a particularly strategic fighter. He performed well with titles on the line, largely because of his fearlessness.

Versatility: 2/5

Like many young boxing hopefuls of his era, Armstrong concentrated solely on that sport. But his ability to fight and win up and down various weight classes should count for something here, even if the necessary skills are similar for each.

POINT TOTAL: 89

57

JOE MONTANA: JOE COOL

Football

Another miserable year for the sad-sack San Francisco 49ers was nearing a merciful conclusion. It was November 16, 1980, and Coach Bill Walsh had finally decided to hand over a starting job to third-year quarterback Joe Montana. The team was 3–7. Such struggles were nothing new. The Niners had won just two games in the previous two seasons and had managed only one winning record since 1973.

What was perceived at the time as an insignificant move by Walsh proved to be among the most consequential in NFL history, for it launched arguably the greatest dynasty the sport has ever experienced. Previous starter Steve DeBerg was traded that offseason, and Montana emerged as one of the most prolific quarterbacks of all time. He led San Francisco to eight playoff appearances and four Super Bowl championships in ten years—an incredible feat, considering the team had never even qualified for one before Montana began playing the role of hero.

Montana was simply a winner at what is generally conceded as the most critical single position in team sports. His teams boasted a winning record every full season he played. With the 49ers and the Kansas City Chiefs (in 1993 and 1994), he compiled a regular-season mark of 115–41 and 16–7 in the playoffs. His ball distribution and accuracy were legendary. Montana led the NFL in completion percentage five times, peaking at 70.2 percent in 1989. He also boasted a remarkable talent for hitting receivers in stride for additional yards.

Most impressive was that he elevated his performance in the postseason against tougher competition. His premier efforts were in his four Super Bowl victories. Montana completed 83 of 122 passes for 1,142 yards with

11 touchdowns and no interceptions for a sparkling passer rating of 127.8 in those games. It is no wonder he is considered the greatest Super Bowl quarterback of all time. And it is no wonder that he owns three Super Bowl Most Valuable Player awards.[1]

Not bad for a third-round draft pick out of Notre Dame. But then, Montana did emerge from western Pennsylvania, the cradle of quarterbacks that included Johnny Unitas, Dan Marino, Joe Namath, and Jim Kelly. Montana was born in New Eagle on June 11, 1956, the only child of Joe Sr. and Theresa, and raised in nearby Monongahela. His father urged him to play sports, and play he did—as a pitcher who threw three perfect games in Little League, a basketball player who proved so talented that he landed a scholarship to North Carolina State, and a quarterback who earned All-American status as a high school senior. He picked the latter sport and followed his idol Terry Hanratty—another western Pennsylvania quarterback who played in the NFL—to Notre Dame.

Montana started off with the Fighting Irish just as he would with the 49ers—as an underdog. He was the seventh-string quarterback when he arrived and remained on the sideline into the 1977 season, when he emerged in what appeared destined to be a defeat to Purdue to lead a comeback victory. He threw for 154 yards and a touchdown in the fourth quarter to pull out the victory. So much for Montana coming off the bench.

The Irish did not lose again that year, capturing the national title with a lopsided Cotton Bowl triumph over top-ranked Texas. Montana concluded his college career with an incredible victory over Houston in the 1979

They Said It

Winners, I am convinced, manage their dreams first. They want it with all their heart and expect it to come true. There is, I believe, no other way to live.—Joe Montana

There have been, and will be, much better arms and legs and much better bodies on quarterbacks in the NFL, but if you have to win a game or score a touchdown or win a championship, the only guy to get is Joe Montana.—Teammate Randy Cross

Cotton Bowl in which the sick quarterback threw a touchdown pass with no time remaining after his team had fallen behind by 22 points midway through the fourth quarter. His brilliance down the stretch would prove to be a portent of things to come.[2]

POINT TOTAL EXPLANATION

Achievements: 34/35

Nothing in the regular-season statistics places Montana among the best of the best. Granted, he earned a trip to eight Pro Bowls, but his numbers have been surpassed by others in the pass-happy modern NFL. He never even threw for more than 4,000 yards in a season. But if it's all about winning and hoisting championship trophies, Montana was the best.[3]

Athleticism: 19/25

Montana was not fast, but he was a heady runner who could hurt opponents with his legs. He did not possess a cannon for an arm, but he could bury foes with his passing. He boasted just enough athleticism to keep plays alive. And he had pinpoint accuracy.

Athletic Requirements of the Sport and Position: 17/20

Quarterbacks are like the Scarecrow, Tin Man, and Cowardly Lion: they need a brain, heart, and courage to thrive in the NFL. Powerful arms, quick feet, and strong legs and upper bodies can make quarterbacks who lack the former attributes viable. But those such as Montana and Tom Brady proved that those with little more than moderate athletic talents can still win titles.

Clutch Factor/Mental and Emotional Toughness/ Intangibles: 15/15

No argument here. Only Brady compares to Montana among championship quarterbacks in NFL history in this category. Montana won Super Bowls with his headiness, his grit, and his uncanny ability to rise rather than shrink to the occasion. He led thirty-one fourth-quarter comebacks during his career. Enough said.

Versatility: 4/5

Montana did not play any other sport beyond high school, but his talents as a prep basketball standout and in his earlier days on the baseball diamond earn him all but one point here.

TOTAL POINTS: 89

58

MIKE TYSON: THE BADDEST MAN ON THE PLANET

Boxing

Mike Tyson. © Orlando Ramirez–USA TODAY Sports

Perhaps the greatness of Mike Tyson the boxer would have overshadowed the struggles of Mike Tyson the man in a previous era. But in modern times and beyond, the ear-chomp of Evander Holyfield, rape conviction, and other lawlessness will be remembered with far greater intensity and clarity than anything Tyson achieved in the ring.

And those were some heavy achievements. At his peak Tyson was considered by some to be the most complete heavyweight ever. He was—when in peak mental and physical condition and at the top of his game—a flawless fighter with an underrated strategic acumen, devastating hooks and jabs, and the quickness to avoid debilitating blows. He didn't defeat foes; he pummeled them.

Tyson won his first nineteen fights, all by knockout or technical knockout, then continued his march to the heavyweight championship. He won his next eight fights, then registered a TKO of Trevor Berbick to win the World Boxing Council (WBC) crown. He added World Boxing Association (WBA) and International Boxing Federation (IBF) titles in his next two bouts to become undisputed champion. Tyson was not merely still unbeaten—no foe had even threatened him with defeat.

> ### They Said It
>
> *Everybody thinks this is a tough man's sport. This is not a tough man's sport. This is a thinking man's sport. A tough man is gonna get hurt real bad in this sport.*—Mike Tyson
>
> *He was quick, like a cat. He came in so low to the ground. I was bent over, trying to hit him. But he just came up and bang, bang. He was for real back then.*—Early knockout victim David Jaco
>
> *When you have something in life that you want to accomplish greatly, you have to be willing to give up your happiness. . . . I've lost all my sensitivity as far as being embarrassed, being shy, you just have to lose that.*—Mike Tyson

He ran his record to 37–0 before a knockout loss to James "Buster" Douglas in one of the most stunning upsets in American sports history. This blow five years into his boxing career set Tyson on a road to professional self-destruction from which he never returned. His arrest and conviction for rape led to a jail sentence. He fought his way back into the title picture, winning the WBC and WBA crowns in successive fights in 1995, but his emotional instability got the best of him after one defeat to Holyfield, when he bit his opponent's ear in the rematch and was disqualified.

Tyson lost three of his last four fights, including a title bout against Lennox Lewis. Five of his six career defeats came in his last ten fights. His brilliance in the ring had been overshadowed by his personal problems, but one must find at least some sympathy given the obstacles created by his upbringing.[1]

Michael Gerard Tyson was born in the projects of New York City on June 30, 1966. He was two years old when he was abandoned by his father and sixteen when his mother died. He spoke freely later in life about his emotional pain, which was heightened during his career when his sister died of a heart attack at age twenty-four. Tyson admitted he had let his mother down by running wild in the streets, fighting, and committing petty crimes. He had been arrested thirty-eight times by the age of thirteen.

The only saving grace was that the battles he fought in his neighborhood provided the basis for his skills in the ring. They just had to be honed. This happened after he enrolled at the Tryon School for boys in Johnstown, New York, where he was discovered and trained by former boxer Bobby Stewart. Stewart later turned him over to Cus D'Amato, who became Tyson's legal guardian and turned him into a fighting machine.

Tyson soon emerged as the most promising heavyweight anywhere. He took the anger from his ghetto childhood and transferred it into the ring. It eventually earned him championships and wealth. He squandered both, as well as his reputation, but his greatness as a fighter can never be denied.[2]

POINT TOTAL EXPLANATION

Achievements: 32/35

Mike Tyson the man cost Mike Tyson the boxer a few points here. He lost four years of his career to legal issues and never fully recovered. But his 37 consecutive victories and his undisputed heavyweight championships are a tremendous accomplishment. And he must be credited as well for regaining the title after spending three years in jail. One can argue that the heavyweight division was not as loaded with talent during his heyday run as in other eras, but his knockout rate proved his dominance.

Athleticism: 24/25

Tyson boasted a crazy combination of strength, speed, elusiveness, and coordination with the punching power of an elite fighter. If he had maintained those attributes, he would have earned all the points here. But he was as unbeatable as any heavyweight in history at his peak. He landed his hooks and jabs with great precision, causing maximum damage and resulting in an incredible run of knockouts.[3]

Athletic Requirements of the Sport and Division: 18/20

Some have claimed that boxers are the finest athletes to walk the planet. They should be judged individually, but that contention holds some merit. Heavyweights do not need the same level of quickness and movement that those in lighter divisions require, but they must be able to handle more devastating punches. They fight far less often than other athletes compete, which costs them a bit in this category. But a boxer who doesn't remain in great shape will be on the canvas at the end of his next battle.

Clutch Factor/Mental and Emotional Toughness/ Intangibles: 12/15

Are we talking the peak Tyson here, or the Tyson who lost so much control that he chomped on Evander Holyfield's ear? Tyson used his intensity and strategic strength to dominate during his run to the undisputed championship and beyond. But his focus disappeared inside and outside the ring thereafter, destroying his career.

Versatility: 2/5

Tyson was certainly versatile enough as a fighter to pick up a couple points in this category, but was too busy in his youth getting into trouble to learn another sport. His dedication to boxing was certainly admirable, however.

TOTAL POINTS: 88

DICK BUTKUS: THE MAESTRO OF MAYHEM

Football

Dick Butkus worked up an anger before every game. If there was nothing to be angry about, he manufactured it with his imagination. If he saw an opponent chuckling during warmups, he would pretend that player was laughing at him and his Chicago Bears.

It worked. Butkus played angry, and he performed like a man possessed. Most of his hits in the 1960s or 1970s would draw unnecessary roughness penalties in the modern NFL. Teammates loved him. Players and coaches respected him. Opposing ball carriers feared him. He was the quintessential nasty middle linebacker who dished out punishment.

But Butkus was no goon. He covered the field and made plays. He was a sure and fierce tackler. He was voted onto seven All-Pro and eight Pro Bowl teams. Those totals would have been higher had knee injuries not forced him to retire after just nine seasons in 1973 at age thirty-one. Unlike many linebackers of his era, he thrived on pass defense, pressuring quarterbacks, blanketing potential receivers, and sensing where passes were headed well enough to record 22 interceptions. He also recovered a then-NFL record 25 opponent fumbles, many of which he caused with brutal hits. He was downright mean. And he was the star of a Bears defense that earned the moniker "Monsters of the Midway." It is no wonder that NFL coaches selected Butkus as the player they would most likely want to start a team with in 1970.[1]

Butkus was a blue-collar player from a blue-collar family playing in his blue-collar hometown city. Born on the south side of Chicago on December 9, 1942, he had made his life goal clear by the fifth grade: he yearned to play in the NFL. His work ethic and toughness were already pronounced.

Every decision he made was driven by the desire to compete on the gridiron. He traveled farther to attend Chicago Vocational High School because its football program was run by former all-state fullback and Notre Dame graduate Bernie O'Brien. Butkus proved to be a terror at the prep level and particularly effective stripping runners of the ball while bringing them down.

He chose the University of Illinois because he believed coach Pete Elliott was developing a fine program. Butkus indeed helped turn around its fortunes. The Illini improved markedly, from 0–9 in 1962 to 8–1–1 the following season to earn a Rose Bowl appearance in which they defeated Washington. He finished sixth in the Heisman Trophy balloting that year and third in 1964—no small feat for a defensive player. He made 145 tackles and caused an incredible 10 fumbles. *Sports Illustrated* writer Dan Jenkins described him as a "special kind of brute" whose life's mission was "mashing runners into curious shapes."[2]

The Bears selected Butkus third overall in the 1963 draft and snagged Gale Sayers with their next choice in one of the greatest hauls in NFL history. Butkus quickly destroyed the contention that he was too slow to succeed at the pro level. He emerged as arguably the most feared middle linebacker ever.[3]

POINT TOTAL EXPLANATION

Achievements: 33/35

One can only speculate the number of tackles and sacks Butkus accumulated over a tremendous career played before those statistics were compiled by the NFL. But the fumbles caused and interception totals were remarkable for any linebacker, particularly in that era. Butkus helped change the role of the middle linebacker, and he was thus honored with All-Pro and Pro Bowl recognition virtually every year.

Athleticism: 20/25

Butkus gained greater success with his ferocity than his athleticism. Indeed, he was not particularly fast, but he did boast the quickness and upper-body strength to track down and bring down ball carriers.

Athletic Requirements of the Sport and Position: 18/20

Middle linebackers in the NFL must use their speed and quickness to cover a lot of ground on nearly every play. They are the center fielders

> ### They Said It
>
> *If I was smart enough to be a doctor, I'd be a doctor. I ain't, so I'm a football player.*—Dick Butkus
>
> *If I had a choice, I'd sooner go one-on-one with a grizzly bear. I prayed that I could get up every time Butkus hit me.*—Packers running back MacArthur Lane
>
> *When I played pro football, I never set out to hurt anyone deliberately— unless it was you know, important, like a league game or something.* —Dick Butkus

of the defense. They require almost every athletic attribute. Sheer speed, however, is less important than quickness. That means they need leg strength to quickly react off the snap and drive ball carriers back as well as upper-body power to also halt their progress and bring them down. The only drawback in this category is that they play just sixteen games a year and are in action far less than sixty minutes every week.

Clutch Factor/Mental and Emotional Toughness/ Intangibles: 15/15

Butkus played with incredible raw emotion that drove him to greatness and helped him overcome a lack of pure athleticism. He was unfortunate to have played on weak Chicago teams throughout his career, but he cannot be blamed given that football is a sport in which team success is so greatly dependent on the performances of everyone who plays, particularly the quarterback.

Versatility: 2/5

So intent on playing in the NFL was Butkus that he did not gain much athletic versatility. He did play both fullback and linebacker in high school, so two points seems about right in this category.

TOTAL POINTS: 88

60

TRACY CAULKINS: THE MEDLEY SENSATION

Swimming

That darn Cold War. It not only brought the world to the brink of nuclear annihilation in 1962 and caused geopolitical turmoil for a half century, but it also cost Tracy Caulkins a legacy that could have established her as the greatest female swimmer ever.

Sarcasm aside, the political battles between the Soviet Union and the United States that motivated the latter to boycott the 1980 Summer Olympics following the Russian invasion of Afghanistan prevented Caulkins from displaying her talents on that international stage at her peak. And the subsequent Soviet Bloc boycott of the Games in Los Angeles in 1984 weakened the field and, to an extent, her achievements there.

But Caulkins could race only those who shared the pool, and she beat them all in both the 200-meter and 400-meter individual medley. She clocked in at 2:12.64 in the former to set a new Olympic record. She captured a third gold as a member of the American quartet that won the 400-meter medley relay, and came within one place of taking bronze in the breaststroke.

Yet there will always be something missing. For six years Caulkins had earned the right to be considered the greatest swimmer in the world. She won three individual gold medals at the 1978 World Championships and captured four at the 1979 Pan American Games. Caulkins added three more golds at the Universiade that same year. She became the youngest recipient of the AAU James E. Sullivan Award as the finest American amateur athlete, then, while swimming for the University of Florida in 1982, landed the Broderick Cup as the premier female collegiate athlete.

They Said It

I suppose I could be over the hill in 1984. I don't worry about it, but I'm aware it could happen.—Tracy Caulkins in 1980

Some people, including her father, expected Tracy to set a new world record every time she jumped into the pool. It's not that easy.—Swimming coach Don Talbot

The East German girls were dominating prior to 1978, but the younger American swimmers who hadn't been around in '76 weren't afraid and just went out and swam our best. To a lot of people it was a really big surprise, the way I swam, but I guess I knew it was coming.—Tracy Caulkins on her dominance at the 1978 World Championships

Caulkins won forty-eight US championships and set sixty-three American marks, both of which were records at the time.[1]

She had toiled tirelessly for that success. Born on January 11, 1963, in Winona, Minnesota, before moving to Iowa and then Nashville, Tennessee, she began swimming at age eight and developed her talents rapidly under the tutelage of her father. She at first could only swim the backstroke because of her aversion to getting her face wet. Caulkins also hated the cold water, but the encouragement of her parents led to expanded horizons and comfort in the pool. She blossomed over the next two years and was ranked among the top ten nationally in various events.

Caulkins competed in the Olympic trials at age thirteen for the 1976 Games. She did not qualify, but by that time had already won several national titles and an international reputation. She won her first AAU crowns in 1977, taking the 100- and 200-meter short course breaststroke and the 200- and 400-meter long course individual medleys. She also snagged the 100-meter breaststroke at the US Indoor National Championships that year. Her status as a potential Olympic champion was established when she defeated Andrea Pollock of Germany, who had earned gold in the 1976 games in the 200-meter butterfly. Caulkins continued to train hard, swimming up to ten miles a day and lifting weights three times a week. Her time for Olympic glory would come, but it would have to wait until 1984.[2]

POINT TOTAL EXPLANATION

Achievements: 32/35

It's not her fault that she was a victim of the 1980 boycott, but Caulkins cannot receive points she did not earn. She was, however, quite dominant throughout her career aside from a bit of a slump in 1982 and 1983. Caulkins deserves a strong score here.

Athleticism: 23/25

Caulkins established the consistent durability, body control, timing, leverage, and agility to glide through the water and kick better than the competition. Her long arms and wingspan were ideal for swimming, but that takes nothing away from her athleticism, which she used to thrive in myriad medley events.[3]

Athletic Requirements of the Sport and Events: 17/20

The individual medley is the most athletically challenging of the events because it forces swimmers to switch on the fly and change the physical motions both seamlessly and effectively. They are the decathletes of the pool. Swimmers in general must be balanced, highly coordinated, quick in their movements, and strong enough to push through the water at a fast pace.

Clutch Factor/Mental and Emotional Toughness/ Intangibles: 14/15

The level of concentration Caulkins reached in winning race after race while switching strokes should not be judged lightly. The pressure on her to win gold medals at the 1984 Games after slumping the previous two years—and knowing it would be her last chance—was tremendous, yet she rose to the occasion to win three gold medals. She was ambitious and disciplined in her pursuit of greatness and was eventually rewarded.

Versatility: 2/5

Her focus on swimming precluded the exploration of other athletic endeavors, but Caulkins must be credited for the versatility needed to win individual medley competitions at the highest level.

TOTAL POINTS: 88

61

MICHAEL JOHNSON: THE DUCK
Track and Field

Michael Johnson ran funny for a sprinter. His friends told him that as a kid, and he showed it as an adult. He had short strides and a straight-up-and-down style that earned him his rather unflattering but affectionate nickname. One would not think he would get where he was going too quickly with that style—but he reached the tape in the 200 meters and 400 meters faster than anyone on earth until Usain Bolt came along.[1]

Johnson was the most dominant middle-distance sprinter of his generation in the world. The records he broke in those two events seemed destined to last further into the new millennium, and Johnson expressed shock that Bolt broke them so quickly. But that did not detract from Johnson's achievements before and after the 1996 Olympics in Atlanta. Johnson shattered the world mark in the 200 at those Summer Games with a blurry-fast time of 19.32 and set an Olympic record in the 400 at 43.49. He participated only in the 400 at the 2000 Olympics in Sydney and earned yet another gold. By that time, he had established another world record in the 400, having burned the track in Spain at 43.19 in 1999.

Most amazing is that Johnson had just turned thirty-three years old when he won at Sydney. Misfortunate had prevented him from maximizing his gold-medal talent early in his career, so he made up for it later. A stress fracture in his leg before the Olympic Trials knocked him out in 1988. He was the favorite to take the 200 meters at the Barcelona Games in 1992 after winning it in the 1991 World Championships, but food poisoning caused him to lose weight and strength. After placing first and second in the first two heats, respectively, he finished sixth in the third and failed to reach the finals. Johnson was ready for the 1996 Olympics. He had won the

200 and 400 meters at the 1995 World Championships. Age was creeping up on him, but it seemed that Johnson got better with age.[2]

His buddies growing up would never have considered him a threat to break any records. Johnson, who was born on September 13, 1967, in Dallas, was the youngest of five children of a truck-driving dad and teacher mom. His parents set high standards for their kids but encouraged them to blaze their own trails in life. Johnson realized later in life that he shared the same characteristics as his father—hardworking, demanding, and honest.

A talent for speed despite his odd running style motivated him to start racing competitively at age ten. He continued to improve and managed to place second in the 200 at the 1986 Texas High School Championships with a time of 21.30. His hard work and dedication to this craft helped him knock nearly a second off that time in his first 200 at Baylor University. But a pulled hamstring and broken leg while at Baylor prevented him from displaying his gold-medal potential there. It would not be until 1990 that he earned a number-one ranking in the 200 and 400. And it would not be until six years later that he proved himself worthy of it in Olympic competition.[3]

POINT TOTAL EXPLANATION

Achievements: 34/35

Johnson is considered by many the greatest middle-distance runner ever. He was all but unbeatable when healthy for nearly a decade. One can only speculate how many medals and championships Johnson would have won had he remained healthy early in his career.

Athleticism: 22/25

Obviously, Johnson boasted tremendous speed. His leg strength carried him to victory with short, powerful strides. His score would be higher here had he also run the hurdles, as other premier sprinters and middle-distance runners did.

Athletic Requirements of the Sport and Events: 16/20

Sprinters need speed, acceleration off the blocks, lower-body strength, and balance. One issue with any of these can turn a gold-medal performance

> ### *They Said It*
>
> *Life is often compared to a marathon, but I think it is more like being a sprinter; long stretches of hard work punctuated by brief moments in which we are given the opportunity to perform at our best.*—Michael Johnson
>
> *I knew [at the 100 mark] that he was going to run fast, but when I saw that 19.32, I looked twice. . . . Skipping the 19.50s and the 19.40s? That was unbelievable.*—Johnson's track coach Clyde Hart after his student's world-record performance in the 200 meters at the 1996 Oympics
>
> *The mind is absolutely instrumental in achieving results, even for athletes. Sports psychology is a very small part, but it is extremely important when you're winning and losing races by hundredths and even thousandths of a second.*—Michael Johnson

into absence from the pedestal. But sprinters do not require a wide range of athletic attributes.[4]

Clutch Factor/Mental and Emotional Toughness/ Intangibles: 14/15

Johnson could have chucked it all after misfortune cost him opportunities to medal in 1988 and 1992, but he showed perseverance and determination. The burden on him to prove his Olympic capabilities grew tremendously by 1996, and he rose to the occasion. Johnson deserves credit for that in this category. He was quite the cerebral athlete, which allowed him to overcome the obstacles of age and pressure.

Versatility: 2/5

Johnson did not like contact sports, so he concentrated solely on track. He gets two points here for excelling in both the 200 and 400, but certainly does not deserve a higher score.

TOTAL POINTS: 88

62

BOB BEAMON:
LEAP OF A LIFETIME

Track and Field

No athlete in American history is so linked with one moment in time as Bob Beamon. Those aware of his feat can replay it in their minds: October 18, 1968, Estadio Olimpico Universitario in Mexico City, the Summer Olympics. Beamon racing down the track in his first attempt, his long strides picking up speed, hitting the board with perfect timing, soaring through the air higher and longer than any long jumper in history, and landing, feet forward, in the sand.

The event was over in six seconds. In that time, he had erased all doubt that he had captured the gold. What became known as the Leap of the Century was measured at 29 feet, 2.5 inches, breaking the previous world record by nearly two feet. Officials were forced to bring out special measuring equipment to determine the length of the leap, which caused an overwhelmed Beamon to collapse when he was informed. The mark remained unbroken for twenty-three years, a short time compared to the prediction that nobody could shatter it until the next millennium. Beamon had achieved arguably the greatest single feat in Olympic history.[1]

Athough Beamon will be forever tied to that incredible accomplishment, the memory of his career should not be limited to it. Beamon had set a national high school triple jump record in 1965 before winning the AAU indoor long jump and taking silver in the same event in 1967. He placed first in both the AAU and NCAA indoor long jump and triple jump in 1968. He also won the AAU long jump crown that year.

Injuries prevented Beamon from recapturing the form that brought him fame in Mexico City. He played basketball briefly for the University of Texas–El Paso (UTEP) and was even selected by the Phoenix Suns in the fifteenth round of the 1969 draft before his graduation in 1970, then tried

They Said It

There is no answer for the performance. But everything was just perfect for it, the runway, my takeoff—I went six feet in the air when usually I'd go about five—and my concentration was perfect. It never happened quite that way before. I blocked out everything in the world, except my focus on the jump.—Bob Beamon on his record-setting leap at the 1968 Summer Olympics

Compared to this jump, we are as children.—Soviet jumper Igor Ter-Ovanesyan

unsuccessfully to launch a professional track and field career in 1973. He later made his mark in the fields of art and social work.[2]

Beamon was forced to overcome much on the path to greatness. Born on August 29, 1946, in Jamaica, Queens, he lost his mother to tuberculosis at eight months old and was raised by his maternal grandmother after his father was jailed. The neighborhood in which Beamon grew up was beset by violence, gangs, and drugs. He succumbed to the culture at a young age, striking a teacher in school and getting expelled.

The incident served as a turning point in his life. Beamon was dispatched to a juvenile detention center, then to an alternative school for delinquents in New York. It was there that he gained a sense of discipline and turned away from the street culture that had been holding him back. He turned his anger into positive energy and goal setting. He explored his athletic talents and proved himself in track and field. He broke local and state records before enrolling at North Carolina A&T to stay close to his ailing grandmother. Her death prompted him to transfer to UTEP, which boasted a premier reputation in his sport.

Beamon had become socially aware during the turbulent times of the civil rights and black power movements. Four months before the 1968 Olympics, he refused to compete for UTEP against Brigham Young University, a Mormon college with racist policies. Beamon was suspended for his actions, but he continued to work on his craft. And he would soon be flying through the air in Mexico City.[3]

POINT TOTAL EXPLANATION

Achievements: 30/35

Beamon's accomplishments center basically on two events—the long jump and triple jump. The greatest leap of all time does not qualify him for a perfect score. But given the dominance of his performances in those two events at various venues before he was weakened by injuries, he deserves a strong score in this category.

Athleticism: 23/25

Beamon boasted tremendous speed, acceleration, balance, agility, coordination, and leg strength. His long, powerful strides and ideal timing were keys to his success. His athletic attributes were perfect for the events in which he competed.

Athletic Requirements of the Sport and Event: 17/20

Excelling in the long jump and triple jump requires every athletic talent Beamon had in abundance, but his concentration on just the long jump in the Olympics costs him a bit here. And there are some athletic skills not needed in the long jump, including the arm and upper-body strength of shot putters and discus throwers.

Clutch Factor/Mental and Emotional Toughness/ Intangibles: 14/15

Beamon proved his mettle—clutch factor and toughness—in those six seconds that made history in Mexico City. He rose to the occasion on the biggest stage. The concentration and emotional strength that allowed Beamon to fly where no man had ever flown must be rewarded in this category.

Versatility: 4/5

Beamon was a talented enough basketball player to be drafted by the Suns. And though he did not participate in a wide array of track and field events, that talent in hoops earns him some points here.

TOTAL POINTS: 88

63

OSCAR ROBERTSON: THE BIG O

Basketball

That Oscar Robertson revolutionized the point guard position, paving the road at 6-foot-5 for taller players, ranks a distant second in his impact on the sport. He was the first Magic Johnson and the first LeBron James as a complete talent. And he did what neither of them did: he averaged a triple-double for an entire season. It was more than a half century before that achievement would be matched when Russell Westbrook managed to reach double figures in points, rebounds, and assists.

Celtics coaching legend Red Auerbach exclaimed that Robertson was the most complete player in NBA history. Such praise from no less a source than Auerbach speaks of the consistently brilliant numbers Robertson compiled despite a lack of help most of the year from a mediocre supporting cast (aside from Jerry Lucas, Jack Twyman, and Wayne Embry) with the Cincinnati Royals. Robertson averaged at least 28.2 points per game in each of his first eight pro seasons. He led the league in assists in seven of his first nine years and yanked down double figures in rebounds in each of his first three. He was even among the top foul shooters in the NBA.

Robertson did not have championship-level talent around him, but his own greatness consistently pushed the Royals into the playoffs. His skills were waning when he was dealt in a stunning trade to Milwaukee in 1970, but the swap allowed him to join forces with Lew Alcindor and win a championship before retiring. Playing alongside the future Kareem Abdul-Jabbar resulted in fewer shots, but Robertson remained an all-star.[1]

He took an unlikely path to stardom. Robertson was born on November 24, 1938, in Charlotte, Tennessee, but was raised in the housing projects of

Indianapolis, where his family struggled to make ends meet. He preferred basketball to baseball but could not afford the equipment, so he learned to shoot by tossing a tennis ball and rags bound with rubber bands into a peach basket behind his home.

The makeshift ball and hoop proved adequate enough to land Robertson a spot on the all-black Crispus Attucks High School team. His talent was so pronounced that it motivated teams from white schools to schedule games against Crispus Attucks. Robertson embraced learning the fundamentals while showing off his natural ability and instincts for the game. His team won sixty-one of sixty-two games during one two-year stretch, including a state-record forty-five in a row, as Robertson was named the first black "Mr. Basketball" ever in that hoops-crazed state. He led the first run of an all-black team to the state championship.

Robertson proved even more dominant at the University of Cincinnati. He had developed a one-handed shot that defenders could not block and averaged 33.8 points per game for the Bearcats. He won three nationals scoring titles, was once named College Player of the Year, and established fourteen NCAA records. Among them was a career scoring mark that remained in the books until Pete Maravich broke it in 1970. Robertson achieved all of this despite being forced to stay in dorms rather than hotels as the only black player on the team. It was an injustice that embittered Robertson throughout his life.

They Said It

Just how good was Robertson? He was so great he scares me.—Celtics coach Red Auerbach

It's like all guys want to do is make a dunk, grab their shirt and yell out and scream—they could be down 30 points but that's what they do. Okay, so you made a dunk. Get back down the floor on defense!—Oscar Robertson on the modern game

If you give him a 12-foot shot, he'll work on you until he's got a 10-foot shot. Give him 6, he wants 4. Give him 2 feet and you know what he wants? That's right, man, a layup.—Knicks guard Dick Barnett

The respect he had gained, however, earned him a cocaptain designation on the 1960 Olympic team that won the gold medal. Robertson was soon celebrating a Rookie of the Year award in the NBA. One of the greatest pro basketball careers in history had begun.[2]

POINT TOTAL EXPLANATION

Achievements: 33/35

A comparatively short career and an inability to maximize the playoff potential of his teams results in a few lost points here. Robertson performed well in the postseason but could not get the Royals past the second round. His numbers, however, cannot be overlooked or underappreciated here. The first player to average a triple-double (and he nearly did it a second time) deserves pretty close to a full score, especially considering his consistent stat-stuffing throughout his career.[3]

Athleticism: 21/25

A lack of speed and quickness in comparison to other point guards makes his accomplishments even more impressive. Robertson used his strength and durability to maintain his effectiveness from the first tick of the game clock to the last. He was certainly not slow as a ball handler and defender, but it was his fundamentals that made him great.

Athletic Requirements of the Sport and Position: 19/20

The point guard arguably requires the most athleticism of any player on a basketball court. He needs enough speed and elusiveness to shake defenders and get to the hole or pass to an open teammate. But he also must boast the strength to dribble inside among taller and heavier frontcourt players and maintain balance.

Clutch Factor/Mental and Emotional Toughness/ Intangibles: 12/15

Robertson was not the ideal teammate. He was a perfectionist who demanded perfection from others. One reason for the trade to Milwaukee was that he had worn out his welcome in Cincinnati. He simply did not raise the performance level of his teammates, which tainted his reputation a bit. But there is no evidence to suggest he was not a clutch player.[4]

Versatility: 2/5

Robertson's versatility was limited to the basketball court, but he was as versatile a player as any of his generation. He deserves a decent score here despite his lack of participation in other sports beyond the youth level.

TOTAL POINTS: 87

64

MIKE SCHMIDT: IRON MIKE

Baseball

Mike Schmidt is among the most historically underrated players in baseball history. He performed brilliantly without tooting his own horn or creating media attention. Yet one glance at his yearly and career statistics prove his all-around greatness.

The Philadelphia Phillies third baseman led the National League in home runs eight times and slugging percentage five times, but he was not all about power. He topped everyone in RBI and walks four times. He ranked number one in on-base percentage three years in a row at his peak and reached double figures on stolen bases eight times. Completing the picture was that Schmidt established himself as one of the premier defensive players in his generation and beyond. A Gold Glove presentation was an annual event—he won it nine consecutive years from 1976 through 1984. It was no wonder that he earned the National League Most Valuable Player award three times, including back-to-back seasons.

Struggles with strikeouts, particularly early in his career, prevented Schmidt from posting higher batting averages. But he tamed that problem in his later years with the Phillies, for whom he played his entire eighteen-year career. He consistently batted over .275 from 1980 forward. By that year, he was already ticketed for the Hall of Fame.[1]

Such was not always the case. Schmidt, who was born on September 27, 1949, in Dayton, Ohio, did not seemed destined for greatness as an athlete. He certainly embraced a wide array of sports as a child, including football, basketball, baseball, and golf. He eventually concentrated in baseball and basketball. His performances at the high school and college levels were far from extraordinary, but he had established a scientific approach to hitting that would eventually transform him into a beast with a bat.

They Said It

If you could equate the amount of time and effort put in mentally and physically into succeeding on the baseball field and measured it by the dirt on your uniform, mine would have been black.—Mike Schmidt

Mike Schmidt is the best player in the National League today. There's no question about that. He honestly doesn't realize how much ability he has.—Pete Rose

You're trying your damndest, you strike out and they boo you. I act like it doesn't bother me, like I don't hear anything the fans say, but the truth is I hear every word of it and it kills me.—Mike Schmidt on playing for the notoriously brutal Philadelphia fans

Schmidt focused solely on baseball after a knee injury ended his basketball career. He took a more serious approach to the sport before his sophomore year, playing for a Dayton Summer League team and impressing the coach enough to prompt calls to Ohio University and the California Angels about Schmidt's talents. Schmidt emerged as a standout for the Bobcats at the plate and in the field. He even led the team to the College World Series in 1970 and earned two All-American nods as a shortstop. He had raised his career average at that level to .330, with 27 home runs.

His performance motivated the Phillies to snag him in the second round of the 1971 draft. Schmidt spent little time in the minor leagues. He debuted with Philadelphia a year later and in 1974 led the National League in home runs for the first of three consecutive seasons. A Hall of Fame career had begun.[2]

POINT TOTAL EXPLANATION

Achievements: 33/35

Few players in baseball history can place more wide-ranging accomplishments on their résumés. Schmidt proved himself to be among the best ever as a power hitter and defender, and even a stolen-base threat. He slugged more than 500 home runs—a benchmark for most Hall of Famers—and was tremendously consistent in his production year to year. He scored and drove in 100-plus runs in six separate seasons. Only his comparatively low average and high strikeout totals are drawbacks here, but his improvement in those areas prevents the loss of too many points.[3]

Athleticism: 23/25

Quickness of foot in the field and on the bases and with his hands to generate bat speed was among the many athletic attributes Schmidt possessed. He boasted plenty of raw power as well. An agile defender with exceptional reflexes for a 6-foot-2 third baseman, Schmidt can be considered one of the most athletic players ever at the hot corner.

Athletic Requirements of the Sport and Position: 16/20

Great reflexes are required to play third base, but quickness and range are not essential. Though baseball players need durability to survive a 162-game schedule, that cannot be put into the category of endurance. Unlike football and basketball players, they are not forced to endure hard contact, and they can go entire games with little movement. But the hand-eye coordination needed to hit like Mike Schmidt cannot be questioned.

Clutch Factor/Mental and Emotional Toughness/ Intangibles: 12/15

Schmidt was exceptionally hardworking and dedicated to his craft, but he did not rise to the occasion in postseason play aside from a wonderful World Series in 1980 that resulted in an MVP. He batted .236, hit 4 home runs, and had just 15 walks in 158 plate appearances. He managed just one hit in 20 at-bats in the 1983 Fall Classic.

Versatility: 3/5

Schmidt played basketball in high school and was among the most versatile standouts ever in baseball. He earns a few points in this category.

TOTAL POINTS: 87

65

LARRY BIRD: THE HICK FROM FRENCH LICK

Basketball

Larry Bird never led the NBA in any major statistical categories, but he was productive in all of them—day after day, year after year. He rebounded well, he shot well, he dished out assists, he stole the ball. And perhaps most importantly, he served as an inspirational leader to a championship-level team—day after day, year after year.

Bird established himself as one of the premier players in basketball history with his consistent production. His impact on the Celtics, the most storied franchise in American sports that did not play their home games at Yankee Stadium, was immediate and profound. The team had hit rock-bottom, falling to 29–53 before he was snagged with the sixth overall pick in the 1978 draft. His all-around talent and fundamentals played the most significant role in Boston's winning 32 more games his rookie year and reaching the Eastern Conference Finals. Bird averaged 21.3 points and 10.4 rebounds per game that season.

Then he kept getting incrementally better. His shooting percentage continued to rise. So did his assists, three-point accuracy, blocked shots, and free-throw marksmanship. Bird was not a flawless player—there is no such thing—but he was without weakness. He even made up for his most glaring athletic defect—a distinct lack of speed—with his hustle, knowledge of the game, and understanding of opponent tendencies.

Bird eventually emerged as one of the best scorers in the league. His per-game average peaked at 29.9 during the 1997–1998 season. Most notable were his epic battles against archrival and eventual friend Magic Johnson in NBA Finals matchups against the Los Angeles Lakers, a rivalry launched famously in the 1978 NCAA Championship between

Bird's upstart Indiana State team and Johnson's Michigan State. Bird led Boston to three NBA titles, including a defeat of the Lakers in 1984. He became only the third player and first non-center to earn three straight Most Valuable Player awards. He also landed on the All-NBA first team nine times.[1]

His circumstances growing up did not lend themselves to basketball destiny, even if he was from basketball-crazed Indiana. Bird was born in the tiny corn country town of French Lick on December 7, 1956, far from the big-city playgrounds that spawned so many superstars. He spent much of his childhood shooting hoops, at least when he wasn't working at the grocery store that was connected to the restaurant in which his mother toiled as a cook.

Bird began receiving attention for his basketball talent as a junior at Springs Valley High School. A six-inch growth spurt pushed his height to 6-foot-7, but it was his absurd averages of 31 points and 21 rebounds per game as a senior that had scouts flocking to French Lick. Bird even totaled 55 and 38 rebounds in one game. Yet he received few accolades—Bird was not merely passed over for 1974 Mr. Basketball honors in Indiana, his rela-

---

They Said It

Practice habits were crucial to my development in basketball. I didn't play against the toughest competition in high school, but one reason I was able to do well in college was that I mastered the fundamentals. You've got to have them down before you can even think about playing.—Larry Bird

Larry and I sat down for lunch, and I tell you, we figured out we're so much alike. We're both from the Midwest, we grew up poor, our families [are] everything to us, basketball is everything to us. So that changed my whole outlook on Larry Bird.—Magic Johnson on his evolved relationship with Bird

Leadership is diving for a loose ball, getting the crowd involved, getting other players involved. It's being able to take it as well as dish it out. That's the only way you're going to get respect from the players.—Larry Bird

tive obscurity as a player from a town with a population of two thousand landed him on the third team!

That did not deter Indiana and Louisville from offering college scholarships. He accepted the former, but the culture shock of living on a huge campus in the city of Bloomington proved overwhelming and Bird hitchhiked back to French Lick before basketball practice had even begun. His mother was so angry that she refused to speak with him for two months. Bird enrolled at tiny Northwood Institute, dropped out, then hit rock-bottom when his father and fishing friend committed suicide. The distraught Bird began working for the municipality of French Lick cutting grass, painting benches, and driving a truck.

Bird eventually came to the realization that he was wasting his enormous talent. He landed at Indiana State, a smaller school that competed in the relative anonymity of the Missouri Valley Conference. Bird averaged more than 30 points and 11 rebounds per game in each of his first two seasons, motivating *Sports Illustrated* to splash his picture on its cover in November 1977. Bird had earned stardom. He would soon take that stardom to another level.[2]

POINT TOTAL EXPLANATION

Achievements: 34/35

Others have scored more points, pulled down more rebounds, and dished out more assists. Bird's accomplishments revolve around the totality of his game and his ability to raise the performance level of his teammates, which became evident immediately when he stepped onto the court at Boston Garden. The greatness of those who wore that legendary green uniform alongside him—such as Kevin McHale and Robert Parish—certainly helped. But Bird was the proverbial straw that stirred the drink.

Athleticism: 18/25

Bird possessed no standout characteristics athletically. He was among the slowest players in the league, and he was neither particularly quick nor powerful. He was far from agile. He receives a relatively low score here, but perhaps that makes his Hall of Fame career even more impressive. It was more about his determination and basketball IQ than athleticism.

Athletic Requirements of the Sport and Position: 18/20

Playing 100 or so games every year on an NBA playoff team requires tremendous durability. The power forward and small forward spot occupied by Bird generally requires a wide range of athletic gifts that Bird did not possess. But again, that proves the value of intangibles.

Clutch Factor/Mental and Emotional Toughness/ Intangibles: 15/15

Bird was among the most cerebral and hustling superstars in NBA history. He understood the value of floor spacing, always boxed out for rebounds, played the passing lanes for steals, and studied opponent tendencies. He was not only a perfectionist but also a great clutch player who performed his best with the most on the line. Bird was particularly brilliant in the 1984 Finals, when he averaged 27.4 points and 14 rebounds per game to win MVP honors.[3]

Versatility: 2/5

Bird was a gym rat who never explored other sports at the high school level or beyond. But his versatility on the basketball floor earns him a couple points here.

TOTAL POINTS: 87

66

LINDSEY VONN: KILDON

Skiing

Lindsey Vonn. © Sergei Belski–*USA TODAY Sports*

In sports-crazed America, skiing is close to invisible until the Winter Games roll around. What is odd is that the greatest American skier ever owns just one Olympic gold medal. Yet she is easily the biggest star of her sport in the United States.

Why? Because that skier—Lindsey Vonn—is also the best skier in American history. Devastating injuries have prevented Vonn from maximizing her Olympic opportunities, but her dominance of other international competitions, particularly the FIS World Cup, is unparalleled among US skiers. Her fifty-nine race victories and four overall titles in that event speak for themselves.

One can only speculate about the extent of Vonn's dominance if not for the accidents on the slopes that cost her the 2014 Olympics and other events. She began her career in style, becoming the first American female to win the slalom at the 1999 Trofeo Topolino in Italy at age fourteen. She placed second twice in successive Nor-Am Cup races in Canada that same year, then earned her first World Cup gold in 2000 in the giant slalom. Vonn soon began competing against the premier youth skiers in Europe.

Vonn made her Olympic debut in 2002 in Salt Lake City, placing sixth in the women's combined. Her 2006 Games proved disappointing, but she was ready four years later in Vancouver, where she captured gold in the downhill and bronze in the Super G. By that time she had won gold in those same events in the World Championships. But it was her World

> ### They Said It
>
> *I'm willing to risk everything. I'm slightly crazy and I don't get scared.*
> *If the weather is bad or if there are a lot of big jumps, it makes a lot of*
> *women nervous. But it doesn't affect me. If the light is flat, I know I can*
> *count out half the field because they're scared.*—Lindsey Vonn
>
> *I don't think there's ever been an American skier as dominant.*—US skiing
> standout Bode Miller on Vonn

Cup performances that have proven most impressive. She finished first in the overall standings in 2008, 2009, 2010, 2012, and 2013. That ranks her first among all Americans and second in the world. Vonn placed fourth or better in the FIS World Cup every year from 2005 through 2017 (except 2014, during which she was sidelined by injury).[1]

Vonn, who was born on October 18, 1984, in St. Paul, Minnesota, but raised in nearby Burnsville, credits her paternal grandfather for her career. He was an avid skier who first instructed her on the slopes at age two. Vonn emerged as the star of an athletic family. Her father grew quite demanding after she began taking lessons. She trained for two years in Europe, then gained further inspiration from a meeting with skiing superstar Picabo Street.

The talents of the young skier quickly emerged. She caused older kids to cry when she beat them down the hills. That ability motivated her father to move Lindsey and his wife to Vail, Colorado, the skiing capital of America, where she could hone her skills. Vonn grew homesick, but rather than returning her and her mother to Minnesota, the rest of her family joined her. It was then she began to appreciate the lengths her loved ones would go to provide her the ultimate opportunity to forge a successful skiing career. Their faith in her would soon be justified.[2]

POINT TOTAL EXPLANATION

Achievements: 32/35

Fate and Olympic hills have not been particularly kind to Vonn, whose crashes on the slopes have cost her dearly. But she has remained healthy enough in other international events to prove herself as one of the premier female skiers of all time, and certainly the best among Americans.

Athleticism: 23/25

Vonn transitioned from skinny and weak as a younger skier to bulked up and strong, which allows her to maintain a lower position on the slopes. That strength allows her to use men's skis, which are stiffer and harder but allow her to attack more aggressively.[3]

Athletic Requirements of the Sport: 16/20

Skiers work sporadically, spending most of their time practicing for events. But the sport itself requires tremendous agility, timing, balance, and lower-body strength. On the other hand, it is not a contact sport, and competition occurs far less frequently for skiers than for baseball or basketball players.

Clutch Factor/Mental and Emotional Toughness/ Intangibles: 14/15

Vonn must be credited greatly for remaining active and motivated despite the myriad serious injuries she has suffered both on and off the slopes, including one that might have cost her a medal in the 2006 Winter Games and another that prevented her from participating at all in 2014. She has not always otherwise risen to the occasion in the Olympics, but her performances outside that event have placed her among the greatest skiers of any generation. That she has stated a strong desire to race against the premier male skiers also shows her grittiness.

Versatility: 2/5

Vonn has not competed at a high level outside of skiing, but she has developed her talents, particularly in tennis and golf. She gets a little credit for that.

TOTAL POINTS: 87

KARL MALONE: THE MAILMAN

Basketball

The name does not have the same cachet as his fellow NBA legends: Karl Malone. It just doesn't stack up with Chamberlain or Russell or Jordan or James. After all, Malone never won a title.

But dig deeper. Understand that Malone and brilliant Utah Jazz point guard John Stockton were never provided with a championship-level supporting cast. Then dig even deeper. Examine the numbers. Malone is the second-leading scorer ever behind Kareem Abdul-Jabbar, yet he was no chucker. He shot nearly 52 percent for his career. His offensive talents and aggressiveness close to the basket resulted in his making and taking more foul shots than any player in NBA history, leading the league in that department nine times.

Longevity certainly contributed to his historical greatness statistically. But so did remarkable consistency. Malone played nineteen years in the league, all but one (his final season) with Utah, and exceeded 20 points per game in each but his first and last. He averaged at least 25 points per game every year from 1987 to 1997. He pulled down at least 8.9 rebounds in each of his first fifteen seasons. And he drained more than half his shots in twelve of nineteen years. But Malone was not all about offense. He was voted onto the NBA All-Defensive team four times. It's no wonder he earned first-team all-NBA status eleven consecutive seasons and won league MVP honors in 1997 and 1999.[1]

The claim that his legendary work ethic was the result of a lifelong yearning for respect based on a tough childhood was refuted by Malone, who cited instead a fear of failure. Born July 24, 1963, in tiny Summerfield, Louisiana, during the tail end of the Jim Crow period, Malone was the youngest boy of nine children and raised on the family farm. He spent much of his time living a country lifestyle—hunting, fishing, baling hay, and chopping trees. His mother ran a forklift and held down two or three jobs at a time to provide for the family. Malone revealed later in life that when he was fourteen years old, his father committed suicide. It was that tragic event that motivated him toward a life of hard work and dedication.

Malone led Summerfield High School to the 1979, 1980, and 1981 Class C state championships before taking his talents to Louisiana Tech. His greatness was immediately evident—he won Southland Conference Player of the Year honors as a mere freshman and averaged 20.9 points and 10.3 rebounds per game that season. He established his consistency at the college level, and it never waned. He was taken thirteenth overall by Utah in the 1985 NBA draft. Though some players selected before him succeeded—especially top pick Patrick Ewing—Malone emerged as the gem of that lottery.[2]

POINT TOTAL EXPLANATION

Achievements: 33/35

Though longevity certainly played a role in Malone's finishing his career as the second-leading scorer in NBA history, thriving for nineteen seasons given the rigors of playing power forward in that league must be embraced as a tremendous accomplishment. He loses a bit because he never won a championship, but that is not a disqualifier for greatness. Ty Cobb and Dick Butkus learned all about that.

> ### *They Said It*
>
> *I like to think I have some finesse to my game, but inside the paint is where men are made. If you can't play there, you should be home with your mama.*—Karl Malone
>
> *Karl had everything that makes a champion—he was physically and mentally tough and he had a great work ethic, always trying to make himself better. He had God-given talent. I had never seen an athlete who was so big, so strong and so fast.*—Jazz coach Frank Layden

Athleticism: 23/25

Malone's athleticism revolved mostly around his brute strength, conditioning, and durability. He also had quick feet, and it was that, along with his powerful legs and upper body, that resulted in great box-outs, dunks, putbacks, and defensive stands on post-ups. Malone's success, however, was based greatly on the old adage "Where there's a will, there's a way."

Athletic Requirements of the Sport and Position: 17/20

Times have since changed, with even power forwards often stepping behind the three-point line, but defensive and mobility were not significant prerequisites at that position in Malone's heyday. Good footwork close to the basket was, however, and so was strength from head to toe.

Clutch Factor/Mental and Emotional Toughness/ Intangibles: 12/15

A higher level of competition in the playoffs certainly contributed, but it must be noted that Malone's shooting percentage was significantly weakened when the light shone brightest. And some complained that he had a penchant for making poor decisions under pressure with big games on the line. But Malone's toughness in general cannot be questioned.[3]

Versatility: 2/5

It has been speculated that Malone could have played pro football or chosen a boxing career, but he never explored his talents in those sports. He did, however, display enough versatility on the hardwood to earn two points here.

TOTAL POINTS: 87

MIKE TROUT:
THE MILLVILLE METEOR

Baseball

Mike Trout. © Orlando Ramirez–USA TODAY Sports

It is not true that twenty-four major-league general managers were kicking themselves for bypassing Mike Trout in the first round of the 2009 draft—but that is only because people do not literally kick themselves. It is guaranteed that all those GMs were doing so figuratively.

Several solid players were selected before Trout, including oft-injured all-star pitcher Stephen Strasburg and outfielder A. J. Pollock. But none approached Trout's level of productivity. He simply emerged as the greatest position player in the sport and among the best of all time.

Trout established himself as the Mickey Mantle of his generation. He exhibited a rare combination of speed and power that placed fear in the hearts and minds of pitchers, resulting in two American League Most Valuable Player awards in his first six seasons. Trout finished first or second in that voting every year from 2012 to 2016. Not bad considering his Los Angeles Angels of Anaheim teammates provided little protection in the lineup and the team's annual struggles did not place him in an advantageous position to win MVPs.

The unassuming outfielder, who felt more comfortable returning home to his beloved Millville, New Jersey, in the offseason than cultivating big-name relationships around Hollywood, paced the American League in at least two major statistical categories every full season. He led the AL in runs scored four times, on-base percentage twice, slugging percentage

They Said It

He's one of those guys who, when you're done playing, you're going to say, "I played with Mike Trout. I was there when he got started."—Angels teammate Vernon Wells

It's tough, you know you got the fans, the reporters, and everybody on you. For me, it's getting the negative out of your head. . . . [Y]ou're gonna fail 70 percent of the time, you got to stay positive.—Mike Trout

He is something different. He is a throwback, there's no question about it. What I'm probably most proud of with Mike is his modesty. His character. He understands he's a man playing a kid's game. He's doing what he's wanted to do all his life. And loving it.—Millville mayor Tim Shannon

twice, and stolen bases once in six years. The consistency of his production has been remarkable—and he had yet to reach his twenty-seventh birthday heading into the 2018 season.[1]

Michael Nelson Trout, who was born on August 7, 1991, in Vineland, New Jersey, and raised by two former school teachers in his cherished Millville, seemed destined for an athletic career. Father Jeff taught world history at the high school while coaching baseball and football. He had played four seasons in the Minnesota Twins organization without reaching the big leagues. He fostered a tight-knit family with high moral standards. His son benefited from that, remaining humble and down-to-earth even after gaining fame and fortune.

The younger Trout began his baseball career as a pitcher and shortstop. His brilliance was apparent from the start at Millville High School, where he batted .457 and struck out seventy-nine batters in just fifty-four innings as a mere sophomore. He threw four shutouts the following year, including a no-hitter, and raised his average to .530 while leading the team in home runs and runs batted in. Scouts began to besiege the ballpark—more showed up than fans in the stands.

Trout's burgeoning power particularly excited Angels scout Greg Morhardt, a former teammate of Jeff's in the minors. Morhardt demanded that his team draft Trout. He even hoped that Trout would fail more often as a senior so the scouts from teams drafting ahead of the Angels would sour on him. No such luck; Trout continued to rake. So much for the scholarship offer he had accepted from East Carolina. There was no point in going through with it when he was destined to be drafted in the first round.[2]

Morhardt and the Angels got lucky. Teams shied away from Trout because he played in New Jersey, where the weather and level of competition did not generally produce superstars. Scouts generally recommended seasoned college players or standouts in such states as Florida, California, Arizona, and Texas. Trout did not qualify. And that is why—at least figuratively—general managers from around baseball spent much time kicking themselves in 2009 and beyond. Trout spent little time in the minor leagues and won American League Rookie of the Year honors by 2012.[3]

POINT TOTAL EXPLANATION

Achievements: 31/35

There should be an asterisk here since Trout's career is presumably less than half over through 2017. But a huge majority of players would give a couple years' paychecks to have accomplished in a baseball lifetime what Trout did in his first six full seasons. Trout could easily have won four consecutive Most Valuable Player awards.

Athleticism: 24/25

That Mays- and Mantle-like combination of speed and power is only part of it. Trout boasts the quickness to get a great jump in the outfield and off leads at first base for steals. His only drawback is an average arm. But that is nit-picking.

Athletic Requirements of the Sport and Position: 17/20

Baseball is not greatly challenging athletically, but the grind of playing 162 regular-season games should not be dismissed. And no position on the field is more demanding than center and shortstop. Center fielders must cover more ground defensively than anyone else.

Clutch Factor/Mental and Emotional Toughness/ Intangibles: 11/15

Trout has been criticized, with some justification, for his hitting in the clutch. Though he possessed a fine .320 batting average with runners in scoring position through 2017, it was just .271 with two outs and runners in scoring position, with 6 home runs in 292 at-bats. And he managed just one hit in three postseason games, which contributed negatively to a sweep by Kansas City. A lack of protection in the lineup and his dangerous bat combined to motivate hurlers to pitch around Trout in clutch situations, but first returns in this category are certainly negative.[4]

Versatility: 4/5

Trout was a double-double machine on the basketball court in high school and played a mean game of football. He competed in hoops mostly to stay in shape for baseball season. But add it all up, along with his tremendous versatility as a baseball player, and he earns as good score here.

TOTAL POINTS: 87

69

CHERYL MILLER: BIG SISTER

Basketball

Female athletes in a sports-crazed America that is most passionate about the NFL, NBA, and Major League Baseball often receive little attention and even less credit for their achievements. Those with athletically accomplished male siblings can be pushed outside the spotlight. The women in question must rise above the pedestals on which their male counterparts are placed to gain the acclaim they deserve.

Among those whose greatness could not be ignored, even in comparison to the brilliant careers of two brothers, was Cheryl Miller. Her triumphs on the basketball court did not overshadow those of brother Reggie, who is a Hall of Famer and one of the greatest pure shooters in NBA history, but time and reflection have landed both on the same level. And that is saying something.

Cheryl Miller is arguably the greatest female basketball player of all time. She was certainly the most dominant on the college hardwood. Playing for the University of Southern California from 1982 to 1986, she boasted career averages of 23.6 points and 11.9 rebounds and was named NCAA Player of the Year three times while leading her team to two national championships.[1]

Miller proved equally impressive in international competition. She led the US team to the Olympic gold medal in 1984, averaging 16.5 points and 7 rebounds in six games, despite playing limited minutes, as the Americans destroyed every opponent through the title game. Miller managed a double-double with 16 points and 11 rebounds in the gold-medal dismantling of South Korea. She had already helped American teams win gold in the 1983 Pan American Games and would do so again in the 1986 World

They Said It

Cheryl enlarged her aura by creating an identity at the defensive end. She seems to search for those opportunities to hit the deck for a tie-up, dive into the crowd for a save, leap back over the press table for a loose ball. Everything and anything to turn the game her way.—USC coach Stan Morrison

There are so many things that have happened in my life in which I've been the beneficiary of the advancement of women's rights. . . . My parents didn't have to sit on the back of a bus, but my grandmother and grandfather, they did. So we were brought up with that knowledge and history so we would never take anything for granted. Like I said I'm one of many who have benefited from the efforts and contributions of so many in our history and it's not just women's basketball.—Cheryl Miller on the Civil Rights Act of 1964

Of course Cheryl has revolutionized the game. She's taught young girls to play hard all the time and to be physical. . . . The flamboyance is her bread-and-butter. She sees those cameras and she seizes the moment. Sure, it's all Hollywood, but that's O.K., too. . . . I think Cheryl is the best thing that could have happened to the game.—Women's basketball star Nancy Lieberman

Championships and Goodwill Games. Knee injuries prevented her from continuing her playing career.[2]

Athletic brilliance was not handed down in the family, but a competitive drive certainly was. Miller was born on January 3, 1964, in Riverside, California. Her jazz saxophonist father, who later forged careers in the military and in computers, was a taskmaster who demanded peak performance in school and in sports. The approach to parenting paid off, especially in athletics: Reggie and Cheryl developed into basketball stars, Darrell played for the California Angels as a catcher, and Tammy excelled in college volleyball.

The sports talents and desires of her siblings inspired Cheryl. Pickup basketball games in the backyard were not merely for fun; they were far more competitive than what she experienced with friends. Her brothers were all tremendous athletes. Competing against them allowed her to hone her skills—and growing to 6-foot-2 did not hurt. She simply destroyed opposing high school players while at Riverside Polytechnic, scoring 37 points a game. She finished her high school career with a state-record 3,405 points, including 105 in one memorable performance. It was no wonder that her team won four consecutive state championships with her on the court. And though the feat remains unconfirmed, according to legend she registered the first two dunks by a woman in organized competition.[3]

Her knee injuries forced Miller to retire well before the establishment of the Women's National Basketball Association. She was thirty-two years old when it was launched, and it is intriguing to think about how well she would have competed against the best players of the younger generation had she stayed healthy.

POINT TOTAL EXPLANATION

Achievements: 31/35

It is not Miller's fault that her career was so short. Athough she packed in plenty of accomplishments over that brief time, she cannot receive the same point total of those who competed at a high level for a decade or longer. That she could be considered the greatest women's basketball player of all time despite her short time in the spotlight, however, is quite impressive.

Athleticism: 25/25

Miller dominated the competition with her athleticism. She was simply bigger, stronger, quicker, and faster than those who sought in vain to contain her. She boasted the agility and power to establish herself as the greatest offensive rebounder in the history of women's college basketball.[4]

Athletic Requirements of the Sport and Position: 15/20

Miller never played professional basketball, nor did she compete against premier talent even at the international level—the US team pretty much destroyed one and all. The sport itself requires a high level and wide array of athletic attributes, but Miller was never given the opportunity to fully explore the depth of her talent.

Clutch Factor/Mental and Emotional Toughness/ Intangibles: 14/15

Miller was a polarizing figure on the court. She was a fierce competitor and supremely confident. Her conditioning allowed her to maximize performance. She hustled on the court at all times. But her flamboyance pushed her into the realm of prima donna in the thoughts of many. Her theatrics on the court were often criticized. She loses only one point here, however, because none of her shortcomings cost her team games—the Trojans lost only four during her college career—and her intensity certainly helped capture national championships and gold medals.[5]

Versatility: 2/5

Her tremendous versatility as a basketball player scores her two points here. Miller was a fine all-around athlete as a youth, but her concentration on basketball precludes her from earning more in this category.

TOTAL POINTS: 87

MARK SPITZ: MARK THE SHARK

Swimming

How did one know that Mark Spitz was going to win a gold medal at the 1972 Summer Games in Munich? He was in the water.

Spitz was the most dominant swimmer in Olympic history until Michael Phelps swam along. His 1972 performance lifted the gorilla off his back that had weighed him down after a disappointing effort four years earlier in Mexico City, where he managed to win just a silver and bronze in individual events after boasting he would win six gold medals.

His greatness in Munich proved legendary. Spitz set a world record in the 100-meter freestyle at 51:22 to earn the first of seven gold medals. He established another world mark in the 200-meter freestyle, clocking in at 1:52.78. After helping the American team snag gold in two relays, he broke another world record in the 100-meter butterfly with a time of 54:27. He shattered the 200-meter butterfly mark at 2:00.70 before grabbing his seventh gold in the 100-meter medley relay.

That was more like it. Much was expected but little was delivered from Spitz in 1968, a year after he had won five gold medals at the Pan American Games. His focus on 1972 was evident in 1971, when he set three records and became the first swimmer to win four individual AAU titles in one meet. He then won all four events in a meet in East Germany, setting world records in all of them. His performances earned him the 1971 Sullivan Award as the premier amateur athlete in the United States.[1]

It seemed Spitz was destined to swim. He was born on February 10, 1950, in Modesto, California, but moved with his family to Hawaii at age two. It was there that his father taught him how to swim. When he was six, the family returned to California, where he swam and began competition

They Said It

Swimming isn't everything—winning is.—Mark Spitz

What greater thing could I leave to the sport than to inspire somebody to have the desire to do what I did and take it a step further?—Mark Spitz on the success of Michael Phelps

at the YMCA in Sacramento. His talent became so evident that he began training under renowned instructor Sherm Chavoor, who would become a lifelong mentor.

The relationship quickly paid off. The young Spitz owned a slew of age-group records at age ten and was named the world's best ten-and-under swimmer. The family moved to Santa Clara four years later so Spitz could train at its famous Swim Club. It mattered not to his father that he was forced to commute more than eighty miles a day to work. He encouraged his son to maximize his potential.

Spitz worked particularly hard on the butterfly, which does not come naturally to most swimmers. He won the 100-meter butterfly at age sixteen at the National AAU Championships. It would be the first of his twenty-four AAU titles. Spitz, who also won eight NCAA crowns at the University of Indiana, set thirty-two world records during his career. Though his attempt at a comeback in 1991 with the intent of qualifying for the Olympic team failed, he remains a swimming legend.[2]

POINT TOTAL EXPLANATION

Achievements: 32/35

The comparative shortness of Spitz's career and his disappointing performance at the 1968 Games cost him a bit here. He was retired by age twenty-two. But aside from his effort in Mexico City, his accomplishments in the pool were nothing short of amazing. It seems he shattered another world record with every race. His dominance of the competition of his era earns him nearly every point in this category.

Athleticism: 22/25

Spitz specialized only in short distances, but his strength, coordination, and rhythm surpassed those same attributes in his competition. His late speed allowed him to separate from other swimmers down the stretch.

Athletic Requirements of the Sport and Events: 17/20

Swimmers compete infrequently compared to athletes in sports such as baseball and basketball, which costs them a bit here, but their athletic requirements rank near the top. Swimmers must be strong and balanced, with equal parts of quickness and rhythm that must remain in sync. Both upper- and lower-body power help the best separate themselves from the others. Strength is also important, even in short races, because one letdown can turn a gold medal into no medal at all.

Clutch Factor/Mental and Emotional Toughness/ Intangibles: 14/15

The lone point lost here is the letdown in Mexico City. Spitz otherwise rose to the occasion in every big event, not only winning gold medals but setting world records. The mental and emotional strength he needed to channel his intensity and concentration into besting the competition in every race is remarkable.

Versatility: 2/5

Spitz was a great athlete, but was one-dimensional in every aspect of his career. He did not swim longer distances or compete in other sports. That he won gold in the butterfly, which tests the athletic abilities of swimmers, prevents him from losing too many points in this category.

TOTAL POINTS: 87

TONY HAWK: THE BIRD MAN
Skateboarding

In a 2015 interview with *Time* magazine, Tony Hawk expressed his hope that skateboarding would be accepted as a Summer Olympics event by 2020.[1] His desire was understandable. He is not only arguably the greatest skateboarder of all time, but he played the most significant role in bringing the very challenging sport into the public consciousness.

Hawk had emerged as one of the premier skateboarders in the world by age sixteen. He won more than seventy events during his seventeen-year career, including gold medals in the X Games in 1995 and 1997. Though impressive, such achievements in competition proved no more intriguing than the tricks he invented with his incredible talent as he thrust himself into the spotlight as the most well-known skateboarder in the world. His stunts fueled his popularity. He was the first to accomplish the midair 900—two and a half turns (900 degrees). He showed off that maneuver at the 1999 X Games before retiring from competition.[2]

Hawk was born in San Diego on May 12, 1968, when skateboarding had waned from its 1950s popularity and was little more than a fun mode of short-distance transportation for kids. Hawk received his first skateboard—a blue fiberglass beauty—from his brother at age nine. His first recollection of skateboarding was reaching the end of the driveway and asking his brother which way he should turn.

Hawk's high-strung, hyperactive nature motivated him to embrace the fast-paced activity. He practiced at the Oasis Skatepark and began attracting attention with his ability to create maneuvers that required skills far beyond the level of his peers. He began winning amateur contests throughout California by age twelve and turned professional two years later. He was widely considered the premier skateboarder in the world at sixteen. He continued to compete at an amazing level, winning 73 of 103 events by age twenty-five and finishing second in 19 of them. He won the vertical skating world championship an absurd twelve consecutive years.

Hawk was earning more than his teachers by his senior year, particularly through royalties from sponsor Powell-Peralta. He bought a home before he graduated high school. He continued to compete and gave skating exhibitions around the world throughout the 1980s. But the popularity of skateboarding suddenly died around 1991, taking Hawk and his income down with it.[3]

Hawk proved resilient. He accurately predicted a rebound for the sport and launched a skateboard company he cleverly named Birdhouse Projects. It made little money at first, but his forecast was accurate. The return to popularity of skateboarding resulted in tremendous growth for his company. Coupled with the launching of the X Games he dominated, his business acumen helped Hawk gain wealth and fame.[4]

POINT TOTAL EXPLANATION

Achievements: 32/35

Hawk cannot receive the same consideration here as gold medalists at the Olympics, which present a greater level of international competition. But his thorough dominance of the X Games and other events throughout his career is nonetheless quite impressive. He deserves a strong score here.

They Said It

I think that the board is a lot more intuitive than people assume. You get on it and all you have to do is put one foot on the tail and one foot on the nose and rock it up and down and that will get you into the tricks or wheelies or manuals. It's not about the balance so much as it is about the timing.—Tony Hawk

He's the Michael Jordan of skateboarding. He's the guy with all the talent, creativity and competitive drive.—Skateboarder Tommy Guerrero

Athleticism: 23/25

Premier skateboarders are like gymnasts on wheels. They require tremendous leg strength, balance, timing, and agility. Hawk simply boasted a higher level of those attributes than the competition. He rose higher, twisted longer, and leaped farther than all others, which explained his dominance.

Athletic Requirements of the Sport: 17/20

Skateboarding requires an array of athletic skills, though just a moderate level of endurance and durability compared to other sports.

Clutch Factor/Mental and Emotional Toughness/ Intangibles: 14/15

That Hawk won or placed second in nearly every event in which he participated speaks volumes about his toughness. He cultivated his drive to be the best. One lapse of concentration in a skateboarding maneuver can lead to defeat and even serious injury. Hawk proved himself worthy of a near-perfect score in this category.

Versatility: 1/5

Hawk never proved himself in any athletic endeavor beyond skateboarding. While the sport itself features an array of events, they all test the same athletic attributes. Hawk only deserves one point here.

TOTAL POINTS: 87

JOE DIMAGGIO:
THE YANKEE CLIPPER

Baseball

Joe DiMaggio. *Library of Congress*

"**J**oltin' Joe has left and gone away," sang Paul Simon more than a decade after DiMaggio retired. But he never really went away in the hearts and minds of those who witnessed his greatness.

The debate raged throughout their careers. Who was the better ballplayer: DiMaggio or Ted Williams? Adding fuel to the fire was that they were the central figures in the greatest rivalry in American sports history. That the latter was a superior pure hitter and more productive offensive player was undeniable. But many believe that DiMaggio was a more well-rounded athlete. He was certainly a more accomplished fielder and base runner. And even Williams admitted to believing that DiMaggio was a better all-around player.[1]

DiMaggio was not too shabby as a hitter either, as his 56-game hitting streak in 1941 attests. That record might stand forever, given the modern propensity for batters to swing for the parking lots, streets, or oceans beyond the ballpark fences. A DiMaggio strikeout might not have prompted a parade in the pitcher's hometown, but it was certainly rare. For instance, he fanned 13 times in 622 plate appearances in 1941, averaging 28 strikeouts per season over his career.

DiMaggio would have approached 3,000 career hits had he not lost three prime years to World War II and half of his 1949 season to a

They Said It

I wish everybody had the drive he had. He never did anything wrong on the field. I'd never seen him dive for a ball, everything was a chest-high catch, and he never walked off the field.—Yankees teammate Yogi Berra

There is always some kid who may be seeing me for the first or last time. I owe him my best.—Joe DiMaggio

I have always felt I was a better hitter than Joe, but I have to say that he was the greatest baseball player of our time. He could do it all.—Ted Williams

painful heel injury that nearly forced him to retire. He replaced the recently retired Babe Ruth in the lineup in 1936 and embarked on a phenomenal seven-year run before military service interrupted. He averaged 31 home runs and 134 RBI during that stretch while twice leading the league in batting. DiMaggio peaked early, batting .346 with career highs of 46 home runs and 167 RBI in 1937, yet he finished second in the Most Valuable Player voting. No problem—he would win it three times, including in 1941, when Williams became the last hitter to break the .400 mark. DiMaggio's all-around talent had been rewarded. He remained highly productive after the war, bouncing back from a subpar season the year he returned. He led the league with 39 home runs and 155 RBI in 1948.[2]

The son of Sicilian immigrants was born on November 25, 1914, in Martinez, a California town just northeast of San Francisco. The son of a fisherman was the eighth of nine children; his brothers Vince and Dom joined him as major-league players. (Dom was a seven-time all-star with the archrival Red Sox.) His brothers helped their dad on the fishing boat, but not Joe. He spent his time playing for several amateur and semipro teams in San Francisco.

Vince, who by that time had hooked up with the San Francisco Seals of the Pacific Coast League, convinced Joe that he too had the talent to play professional baseball. The older brother placed a bug in the ear of his manager, who was looking for a shortstop. He got one at the end of the

1932 season in Joe, who played three games before signing a contract for $225 a month to play in 1933. DiMaggio certainly earned that money, and then some. Moved to the outfield, he batted .340 and set a league record by hitting safely in sixty-one consecutive games. A knee injury prevented a more rapid rise to the majors, but the Yankees wasted no more time after DiMaggio hit .398 with 34 home runs and 154 RBI for the Seals in 1935. By that time, Ruth was finishing his career with the Boston Braves, and the Bronx Bombers were looking for another Bomber. DiMaggio did not let them down.[3]

POINT TOTAL EXPLANATION

Achievements: 33/35

DiMaggio did not play as long as some other superstars and lost three years to the war. He faded a bit at the end of his career. But he played the most significant role in the Yankees' leaving the Ruth era behind and maintaining their legendary dynasty. Most telling was that DiMaggio finished in the top ten in MVP voting in ten of the thirteen years in which he played, winning it in 1939, 1941, and 1947.[4]

Athleticism: 23/25

DiMaggio was no burner, but he always got a good jump in the outfield and on the bases. He also boasted tremendous bat speed that generated a long and strong swing. His power came not from a burly physique, but from his ability to square up the ball consistently and drive it with his slightly uppercut swing.[5]

Athletic Requirements of the Sport and Position: 16/20

The durability required to play the exhibition season, 162 regular-season games, and (for the Yankees) the usual World Series cannot be underappreciated. And playing in the massive center field expanse of Yankee Stadium was challenging. Though baseball does not require great athleticism, there are certainly attributes such as speed, quickness, power, agility, and hand-eye coordination that come into play—just not as often as they do in other sports.

Clutch Factor/Mental and Emotional Toughness/ Intangibles: 12/15

DiMaggio had a calm exterior and an outwardly colorless personality. He did his job calmly, without flamboyance or bluster. He was a steadying influence on his teammates and rarely slumped at the plate. He did, however, struggle in World Series competition compared to his regular-season efforts. His teams won nine of ten Fall Classics in which he participated, but he batted just .271 in 199 at-bats, with just 8 home runs and 30 RBI.[6]

Versatility: 2/5

DiMaggio was raised in an era in which baseball was king among team sports. But his versatility in the sport of his choosing warrants a couple points here.

POINT TOTAL: 86

PEGGY FLEMING: THE STEEL-NERVED SKATER FROM SAN JOSE

Figure Skating

Peggy Fleming had yet to reach her teenage years when a tragic event changed her life forever. And it occurred thousands of miles from her California home. The February 1961 plane crash in Belgium that killed the entire US figure skating team not only took the life of her coach, William Kipp, but it began a mad scramble to groom replacements on the ice. The timetable for Fleming had suddenly sped up.[1]

Not that Fleming didn't already have promising credentials. After all, she had won the 1959 Bay Area Juvenile Championships and the 1960 Pacific Championships. But she was just a kid then. She would now be thrust into a spotlight generally reserved for more experienced and accomplished figure skaters. She continued to win medals at home, but folks wondered how she would perform against the best of the best in international competition. They got their answer in 1964 when the sixteen-year-old Fleming placed sixth in the Winter Games at Innsbruck, Austria, and seventh in the World Figure Skating Championships.[2]

Fleming had emerged as a medal contender, but it was coach Bob Paul who transformed her into a champion. Fleming used her steely nerves and focus on and off the ice in her drive to the top. She developed a style that had style, unlike European skaters who concentrated on technical merit at the expense of choreography. Fleming was unafraid to explore. Among her most impressive moves was a double axel sandwiched between two spread eagles. It was a tough combination to master but proved awe inspiring when performed flawlessly.

And Fleming began to perform as close to flawlessly as any skater in history. She won every gold medal at the US Figure Skating Championships

> ### They Said It
>
> *When I was on the ice, in the lights, with the music and the motion, there was a certain kind of flirtation that gave great energy and expressiveness to my performance.*—Peggy Fleming
>
> *Peggy has no weaknesses. . . . Peggy lands softly and everything she does is connected. It's pure ballerina.*—East German figure skater Gabriele Seyfert
>
> *The first thing is to love your sport. Never do it to please someone else. It has to be yours.*—Peggy Fleming

from 1964 to 1968. She did the same at the World Figure Skating Championships in the last three of those years. She was named ABC's *Wide World of Sports* Athlete of the Year in 1967, the first female so honored.

When the 1968 Winter Olympics in Grenoble, France, rolled around, Fleming was ready. She thoroughly dominated the Games, winning both the compulsory figures and free skating competition to earn the overall gold medal. She placed first on every judge's card but one throughout the event. It was not only among the most impressive performances in the history of the sport, but it proved to be the only American gold medal of the Winter Olympics that year. Her effort in Grenoble ended an incredible run. Fleming had not been defeated since 1965.[3]

Not bad considering she started skating comparatively late in life. Born near San Jose on July 27, 1948, Fleming did not take up the sport until age nine, when she lived in Cleveland for a short time. In 1960 the family returned to California. Fleming began to display her talents under the tutelage of coach Carlo Fassi. It would not be long before a tragedy turned into opportunity for one of the greatest figure skaters of all time.[4]

POINT TOTAL EXPLANATION

Achievements: 32/35

Had the 1968 Olympics been a singular accomplishment for Fleming, it could have been written off as a bit of an anomaly. But that performance was the culmination of a four-year run of dominance. Her early retirement at age nineteen (though she did tour with skating shows such as the Ice Follies) precludes her from earning a higher score in this category, but she competed long enough to be credited strongly. In addition, she helped transform figure skating into an art form as a profoundly influential skater.[5]

Athleticism: 23/25

Fleming was not merely a figure skater. She was a dancer, an artist on the ice. She used her balance, agility, and athletic precision to nail routines that must be performed as close to perfectly as possible to earn a place on the top step of the podium.

Athletic Requirements of the Sport: 16/20

Figure skaters require wide-ranging athletic talents and skills, including flexibility, coordination, balance, agility, stamina, and lower-body strength. Only their comparatively infrequent competitions—they practice far more than they compete—prevents the sport from earning a higher score.

Clutch Factor/Mental and Emotional Toughness/ Intangibles: 14/15

Fleming was known for her steely nerves, determination, and high level of concentration. No figure skater who consistently earns gold medals can be short in these attributes, because one lapse in any of them can cause a fall that destroys any chance at victory. Figure skating is a do-or-die proposition.

Versatility: 1/5

Fleming focused so intently on figure skating at such a young age that she did not delve into other athletic endeavors, aside from a bit of surfing. Though brilliant, her career was one-dimensional.

TOTAL POINTS: 86

WALTER JOHNSON: THE BIG TRAIN

Baseball

Walter Johnson. *Library of Congress*

The website Baseball Reference places in bold statistics of individual players that led the league in a certain category in a particular year. The pages of premier players are dotted with bold numbers.

Not Walter Johnson. His page is inundated with them. So dominant was the Washington right-hander that it seemed he led baseball in everything every season. This is an exaggeration, of course, but it can be argued that the career performance of the Big Train outdistanced that of all other players in history in comparison to their contemporaries—and that includes Babe Ruth.

Granted, Johnson never pitched against black players, who were shamefully barred from the game during his era. But his achievements are staggering. He compiled a sub-2.00 earned run average in eleven of his first thirteen seasons. He won at least twenty games in ten consecutive years. He hurled 110 career shutouts, a major-league record. In a period in which batters took far more pride in making contact than they do in modern baseball, Johnson twice exceeded 300 strikeouts and led the league in that category twelve times, including every year from 1912 to 1919. His 1913 season has been deemed by many the greatest ever for a major-league pitcher. Johnson finished with a 36–7 record and

1.14 ERA, the best by a starting pitcher until Bob Gibson posted a 1.12 mark in 1968.

Those who cite the greater insight and depth of modern statistics cannot be dissuaded that Johnson put together the most dominant career of any pitcher in the history of the sport. He led the league nine times in fielding independent pitching (FIP) and seven times in walks and hits to innings pitched (WHIP).[1]

One major reason for that dominance is that Johnson simply threw harder than anyone else in his generation, aside (possibly) from Smoky Joe Wood—hence the nickname. But his development of a curveball in the early 1910s prevented hitters from timing up his fastball and transformed him into a virtually unhittable pitcher.[2]

Who would have thought such a thing from the son of a Kansas farmer who did not even play the sport as a young child? Born on November 6, 1887, in Allen County, Johnson spent much of his early years hunting, fishing, and helping his parents till the soil. Droughts forced the family to move to Southern California around the turn of the century, but work on the farm had filled out Johnson's frame.

Now a strapping teenager, he began pitching for a sandlot team, then on a semipro nine sponsored by a local oil company, for which he proved quite impressive. Johnson barnstormed year-round with the team and continued to hone his skills. But they needed little refinement—he was proving his natural talent. He later stated that it seemed a baseball belonged in his

---

They Said It

He's got a gun concealed about his person. They can't tell me he throws them balls with his arm.—Sportswriter Ring Lardner

From the first time I held a ball, it settled in the palm of my right hand as though it belonged there and, when I threw it, ball, hand and wrist, and arm and shoulder and back seemed to all work together.—Walter Johnson

Just speed, raw speed, blinding speed, too much speed.—Ty Cobb on Johnson's fastball

palm. He developed a short windup and sidearm delivery that whipped the ball to the plate in quite a hurry.

The stepping-stone to the majors began with Weiser of the semipro Southern Idaho League. Johnson won seven of eight decisions for that team in 1906 and went 14–2 the following year with an absurd 0.55 ERA to earn the nickname "The Weiser Wonder" as big-league scouts took notice. He had thrown seventy-seven consecutive shutout innings when the Senators came calling. He proved so dominant in his debut that opposing pitcher Billy Donovan of the Detroit Tigers marveled that he was the best raw pitcher he had ever seen. Donovan knew talent when he saw it—and soon the rest of the baseball world would see it as well.[3]

POINT TOTAL EXPLANATION

Achievements: 35/35

No pitcher can earn a perfect score here if Johnson does not. His accomplishments in what some perceive as the ultimate individual sport surpass or at least equal that of any hurler in the history of the game. His career WAR ranks third among all players and second among all pitchers.

Athleticism: 21/25

Johnson was a superior athlete to many pitchers. He not only owned a power arm but was a fine hitter for a hurler and even displayed enough speed and quickness to steal some bases.

Athletic Requirements of the Sport: 15/20

Pitchers can sometimes be out of shape, but it was wise to stay in decent condition in Johnson's day. Top starters completed most of their games back then, sometimes approaching 400 innings in a season and throwing well over 150 pitches in most outings. That required a strong arm and endurance. Pitchers also need good balance and coordination.

Clutch Factor/Mental and Emotional Toughness/
Intangibles: 13/15

Johnson performed decently in only two World Series, but one must understand that he was in his late thirties by then. He did pitch four shutout innings in relief in the ninth inning of Game 7 in 1924 to clinch the only World Series victory in franchise history. And that he won so consistently despite pitching for a usually poor Washington team is a plus in this category.

Versatility: 2/5

Non-Olympic athletes of his era rarely excelled in more than one sport on an organized level. But that Johnson was versatile enough to hit well and steal some bags earns him a couple points in this category.

TOTAL POINTS: 86

75

BARRY SANDERS:
THE LITTLE FELLA

Football

In the mostly sad-sack history of the Detroit Lions following the departure of Hall of Fame quarterback Bobby Layne, the team managed one era in which it was a consistent playoff participant—and that was when Barry Sanders scampered around football fields as the most feared running back in the NFL.

Sanders was the Gale Sayers of his era. He zoomed through the smallest of holes created by his blockers and was gone if he reached the second level and juked or simply raced his way into the open field. Granted, he went down easily if corralled. He was sometimes swatted down in the backfield. But that was the catch—he was so hard to catch. He managed 5.0 yards per carry during a brilliant career that was shortened by an early retirement.

The 5-foot-8 dynamo led the league in rushing four times, peaking in his second-to-last season by exceeding 2,000 yards on the ground and averaging a Jim Brown–like 6.1 yards per attempt. He scored 10 touchdowns per season and averaged more than 100 yards per game in 1991, 1993, 1994, and 1997. He was a dangerous enough receiver to put defenders on notice.

Sanders stunned the football world when he called it quits after rushing for 1,491 yards in 1998. Many believed he would return to the game, but that anticipation waned as he remained sidelined and awaited his inevitable Hall of Fame induction.[1]

It all started on July 16, 1968, when Sanders was born in Wichita, Kansas, into a family that eventually had eleven children. Sanders proved to be an overachiever his entire life. His parents nurtured a strong work ethic; his father, William, taught him the tools of the roofing trade at an early age.

The younger Sanders toiled and sweat in the summer sun, but he dared not complain lest he risk a beating.

Sanders overcame his diminutive size to excel in sports. He was particularly fond of basketball, but 5-foot-8 hoop stars are rare, so his father urged him to try to land a college scholarship in football. That seemed unlikely, given his lack of playing time, until his senior year at North High School. That is when he exploded for 1,417 yards, nearly breaking a Wichita record. He earned all-state honors, but most Division I programs noted his comparative inexperience and offered scholarships elsewhere. Oklahoma State took a chance and Sanders jumped on the opportunity—not just for the school's football program, but for its business school.

The rigors of playing football fifty to sixty hours a week while attending school weakened his academic performance, and he received little opportunity to play in the backfield, though he did lead the nation in kickoff and punt returns as a sophomore. He finally landed a starting role his junior year and set thirteen NCAA rushing records, including 2,628 yards and 19 touchdowns from scrimmage. He ran away with the Heisman Trophy balloting as only the eighth junior to capture the honor.

Those achievements convinced Sanders to skip his senior season and make himself eligible for the NFL draft. That decision paid off—literally—when he was selected third by the Lions and offered one of the largest rookie contracts ever. He would go on to earn every penny.[2]

They Said It

Too often we are scared. Scared of what we might not be able to do. Scared of what people might think if we tried. We let fears stand in the way of our hopes. We say no when we want to say yes. We sit quietly when we want to scream. And we shout with the others when we should keep our mouths shut. Why? After all, we do only go around once. There's really no time to be afraid. Just do it!—Barry Sanders

In work ethic, character, discipline, in every way, he sets a standard for each and every one on this team.—Teammate Jerry Ball

POINT TOTAL EXPLANATION

Achievements: 31/35

Sanders should not be blamed for the lack of supporting talent during his ten seasons, particularly at a revolving-door quarterback position that weakened the passing game and focused defensive attention squarely on him. He loses points for his comparatively poor postseason performance after his first two playoff games and for his penchant for getting caught behind the line of scrimmage. But his overall numbers and his raising the level of the Lions' overall play during his career must be rewarded.

Athleticism: 22/25

Few backs in the history of the NFL could match his acceleration and elusiveness. Sanders could turn a short gain into a touchdown with one move that left defenders grasping at air. But unlike Jim Brown or Eric Dickerson, he did not boast a combination of speed and power. His strengths were so pronounced that he earns a high total here.

Athletic Requirements of the Sport and Position: 18/20

Running backs are as challenged athletically as any position on the gridiron. The best boast all athletic attributes, including speed, quickness, acceleration, and both upper- and lower-body strength. Running backs take a pounding on most carries and must not allow that to sap their strength at any point during a game or season. It is no wonder that most premier backs stay on top for only a few years. Sanders remained a premier back throughout his career.

Clutch Factor/Mental and Emotional Toughness/ Intangibles: 12/15

Sanders must be credited for thriving in a game of 300-pound linemen and onrushing 220-pound linebackers. Not many his size could take the pounding for ten years. He was also an inspirational figure to teammates. But after fine postseason performances in 1991 and 1993, he was a nonfactor in the playoffs. He rushed for minus-1 yard on 13 carries in a 1994 first-round defeat to Green Bay and finished his career with a mediocre postseason average of 4.2 yards per carry and just one touchdown in five games.

Versatility: 3/5

Sanders was a fine athlete in his youth and considered basketball for his future. He focused on football in high school and beyond but deserves a few points here.

TOTAL POINTS: 86

TY COBB: THE GEORGIA PEACH

Baseball

Ty Cobb. *Library of Congress*

Ty Cobb was an irascible, mean-spirited, racist, foul-mouthed, cheating jerk. He slid into infielders with spikes high. He charged into the stands to beat a heckler who had been disabled in a printing press accident. He hated women and children. He was even charged with attempted murder. But he was the best darn baseball player of his generation—arguably of all time.[1]

Cobb was certainly the premier hitter of the dead-ball era. That he would lead the league in hitting was nearly as sure a bet as the sun rising in the east. He missed out just once from 1907 to 1919. His career .366 batting mark remains the highest in baseball history. But the Detroit Tigers star was far more than simply a high-average hitter. He managed triple figures in RBI four times, leading the league in each of those seasons, exceeded 100 runs scored eleven times, managed the highest on-base percentage seven times during one ten-year stretch, and finished his career with 897 stolen bases to rank fourth all-time.

By the time Babe Ruth launched the live-ball era, Cobb was nearing the end of his career. But Cobb was no Punch-and-Judy hitter. He was among the greatest gap hitters in the sport and used his speed to maximize hits. He paced the American League in triples four times and slammed ten or more in thirteen consecutive seasons. He even led the league in slugging percentage eight times, including every year from 1907 to 1912.[2]

The story of this colorful figure began when he was born on December 18, 1886, in The Narrows, Georgia, to school teacher William and his fifteen-year-old wife, Amanda. He was the oldest of three children. The boy developed a passion for baseball and exhibited enough talent to land on the Royston, Georgia, town team by age fourteen. He soon emerged as a standout, but his focus on the sport displeased his father, a scholar who preferred that his son pursue a career in law or medicine. Though Ty idolized his dad, his strong will and stubbornness were already pronounced. He vastly preferred the ball diamond to the library, and continued his athletic pursuits.

Cobb was just seventeen when he began contacting teams in the newly formed South Atlantic League. He was offered a contract to join Augusta in spring training for $50 a month if he made the team, but he would have to pay his own expenses. He spoke of his opportunity with his father, who had relented with the threat that his son could not return as a failure. Ty was inspired—and he did not let his dad down. He soon landed a deal with a semipro team in Anniston, Alabama.

Fate smiled upon Cobb in 1905. He had played well enough for Anniston to earn another shot with Augusta, playing in the same town where the Detroit Tigers trained. He impressed the big-league team with his talent and aggressive style of play. He emerged as the premier hitter in the league under the tutelage of Augusta manager George Leidy.

Cobb was forced to overcome tragedy in the summer of 1905 before he could refocus on his career. Believing his wife was having an affair, Cobb's father approached the house one night with a pistol. The details of what happened next are sketchy, but Amanda Cobb shot twice and killed him as he climbed to the porch and neared the window. She claimed that she believed he was a burglar but was arrested for manslaughter and eventually acquitted.

This traumatic experience stunned Cobb, but he was more determined than ever to justify his father's faith in him. He soon debuted with the Tigers, but he struggled both on the field and as a teammate. He became embittered at the hazing he received from his fellow players. That anger, combined with the grief he still felt, made Cobb resentful. Though that does not validate his mistreatment of others throughout his career, it does offer something of an explanation.

> ### *They Said It*
>
> *I had to fight all my life to survive. They were all against me . . . but I beat the bastards and left them in the ditch.*—Ty Cobb
>
> *Ty Cobb is a prick. But he sure can hit. God Almighty, that man can hit.*—Babe Ruth
>
> *Baseball is a red-blooded sport for red-blooded men. It's no pink tea and mollycoddles had better stay out. It's a struggle for supremacy, a survival of the fittest.*—Ty Cobb

Cobb's terrible relationships made him miserable. It took two seasons for him to clear his head enough to show his remarkable talent. He batted .316 in his second year and won the batting title in 1907. One of the greatest careers in sports history was about to take off.[3]

POINT TOTAL EXPLANATION

Achievements: 34/35

Baseball players are the athletes least blameworthy for team failures, so the punishment here is light for Cobb's never having won a World Series. The Tigers qualified three straight years starting in 1907. Baseball is the most individual of the major team sports, and Cobb individually was as dominant in his era as any player in its history.

Athleticism: 21/25

Cobb's brilliance was based more on his headiness and aggression than on his athletic gifts. He boasted very good speed, but his penchant for extra-base hits was the result of consistently barreling up the ball more than it was of raw power. He had tremendous hand-eye coordination as well.

Athletic Requirements of the Sport and Position: 17/20

The daily rigors of playing baseball and the athleticism required to track down balls in the outfield result in a decent score here. The speed and quickness needed to become a premier base stealer has also been considered here.

Clutch Factor/Mental and Emotional Toughness/ Intangibles: 12/15

There are certainly powerful positives and negatives here. Cobb was a fierce competitor. He was also a student of the game. It has been said that he outthought his opponents. His aggressive and even reckless baserunning caused fear in pitchers and fielders that resulted in errors. But Cobb was also disliked by his teammates, which caused friction. More good than bad here, but it also must be noted that Cobb did not hit well in the three World Series in which his Tigers participated. His postseason batting average of .262 is more than 100 points lower than his career mark.[4]

Versatility: 2/5

There was certainly a lack of options for athletes in the infancy of the twentieth century. One could not have expected Cobb to have been involved in a variety of sports. His versatility as an offensive standout earns him a couple points in this category.

TOTAL POINTS: 86

BONNIE BLAIR: THE BLUR

Speed Skating

Bonnie Blair was the Carl Lewis of American speed skaters. She was a super sprinter on ice—perhaps the greatest short-distance speed skater in Olympic history.

Blair is the only three-time gold medalist in the 500 meters, as well as the lone back-to-back champion and three-time medalist in the 1000 meters. She won the former in 1988, 1992, and 1994 and the latter in 1992 and 1994. And despite her third-place finish overall in 1988, she set an Olympic record along the way. Her crowning achievement was a world record that year in the 500 meters, becoming the first skater ever to break the 39-second barrier. She even showed her endurance by placing fourth in the 1500 meters in 1988 and 1994.

Her brilliance was not limited to the Olympics. She proved dominant in other international competitions, including the World Championships. Blair set four world records in the 500 meters at the World Short-Track Championships in 1986 and World Sprints in 1989, 1994, and 1995.[1]

Speed skating was a Blair tradition. Her siblings were passionate skaters before she was born on March 18, 1964, in Cornwall, New York. Her father, Charlie, dropped off mother Eleanor at the hospital to give birth to Bonnie before hauling his other kids to a speed skating competition.

The young Blair was raised in Champaign, Illinois. She too embraced speed skating as a youth but did not boast the confidence of her father that she could blossom into a champion. He predicted it when Bonnie was twelve years old. It was not until four years later that she came to believe it herself.

It did not take Blair long after that to prove it. She performed well enough to join the national skating team following high school graduation

> ### They Said It
>
> *Winning doesn't always mean being first. Winning means you're doing better than you've ever done before.*—Bonnie Blair
>
> *She's not like other skaters. She holds up to it. Bonnie is as hard as nails.*—Assistant US speed skating coach Dan Immerfall on Blair's handling pressure during the 1988 Winter Olympics

and qualified for the 1984 Winter Games in Sarajevo at the age of nineteen. She exhibited her potential by placing eighth in the 500 meters. Four years later she was a world-record holder and gold medalist. And she was merely rounding into her prime.

Blair was named Sportswoman of the Year by *Sports Illustrated* in 1994 and inducted into the United States Olympic Hall of Fame ten years later. She remains the most decorated American female athlete in Winter Olympic history.[2]

POINT TOTAL EXPLANATION

Achievements: 34/35

Blair competed in four Olympics and captured gold in three of them. She overwhelmed the competition in other international events as well, proving dominant in both the 500 and 1000 meters. She set several world records. Blair deserves nearly a perfect score in this category.

Athleticism: 21/25

Leg strength, agility, balance, and coordination were physical tools Blair boasted in abundance in her runs to gold medals. She was among the most technically sound athletes ever to lace up a pair of skates.[3]

Athletic Requirements of the Sport and Events: 15/20

Speed skaters, particularly those who excel in short distances, are much like sprinters in that they must be strong in bursts. They need coordination and balance to maintain a rhythm in their movements. But they do not re-quire the same level of endurance and upper-body power of other athletes, and the fact that their events last only a minute or two at a time makes their events far less taxing than those such as tennis, boxing, and football, which force athletes to maintain a top level of performance for hours.

Clutch Factor/Mental and Emotional Toughness/ Intangibles: 14/15

What makes speed skating less grueling long-term makes it more chal-lenging short-term mentally and emotionally. One slip-up—one fall in an event—destroys all hopes. Blair proved her mettle and her ability to rise to the occasion time and again in world championship and Olympic competition. Her gold medals in events that last a minute or two speak for themselves.

Versatility: 2/5

Blair was not a well-rounded athlete who dabbled in many sports, but that she placed fourth in the 1500 meters at two Olympic Games while earning gold medals in short distances results in a couple points here.

TOTAL POINTS: 86

SECRETARIAT: BIG RED

Horse Racing

Television viewers who happened to click on the 1973 Belmont Stakes as it was winding down might have thought their eyes were deceiving them. The cameras were panned far enough away, but there was only one horse in the picture. That horse was Secretariat.

Was he racing alone? Did the competition pull out because their owners knew they had no chance to win? No, they were back there. They were just so far behind Secretariat that they had fallen out of the camera's frame.

Secretariat won the race by an absurd 31 lengths, destroying the record of 25 set in 1943 by Count Fleet. The horse among ponies completed the Belmont in 2:24 flat, which broke the previous mark by more than two seconds. He was clocked at 37.5 miles per hour for the entire 1½ miles. Remarkably, that record still stands forty-four years later.

The margin of victory was shocking, but his completion of the first Triple Crown in twenty-five years was anything but. Secretariat bolted from the starting gate against four hapless competitors with 1–10 odds of winning the Belmont. He had exploded into the American consciousness as one of its biggest celebrities. His picture had been splashed on the covers of *Time*, *Newsweek*, and *Sports Illustrated*.[1]

His literal and figurative run of greatness began in earnest at the Kentucky Derby, where he started slowly before winning by 2½ lengths with a track record of 1:59.24 that also remains intact. Secretariat ran each quarter mile faster than the previous one. No other horse broke the two-minute mark at the Derby until 2001. He followed that with another come-from-behind performance at the Preakness Stakes. He bolted from last to first along the first turn and was never again challenged. Though

They Said It

*You carry an ideal around in your head, and boy, I thought, "This is it."
I never saw perfection before. I absolutely could not fault him in any way.
And neither could the rest of them and that was the amazing thing about
it. The body and the head and the eye and the general attitude. It was
just incredible. I couldn't believe my eyes, frankly.*—Veteran sportswriter
Charles Hatton

*Two twenty-four flat! I don't believe it. Impossible. But I saw it. I can't
breathe. He won by a sixteenth of a mile! I saw it. I have to believe it.*
—*Blood Horse* editor Kent Hollingsworth

his final time has been disputed, the *Daily Racing Form* clocked him in
at a track-record 1:53.4.

The chestnut colt came from powerful bloodlines. He was sired by
1957 Preakness winner Bold Ruler and bred by Somethingroyal, who was
the daughter of French and Irish long-distance standout Princequillo.
Secretariat was born on March 30, 1970, and ridden mostly by Canadian
jockey Ron Turcotte. He won five consecutive races as a two-year-old,
including the Futurity Stakes at Belmont and an eight-length victory in
the Laurel Futurity. He began his third-year season by wiping out the
field in the Bay Shore Stakes, then led wire-to-wire for the first time in
his career in the Gotham Stakes, setting the tone for his dominant stretch
for the Triple Crown.

Secretariat was far from done. He captured the prestigious Arlington
Invitational and Marlboro Cup and finished his racing career with a victory
in the Canadian International Stakes. In a surprise that ranks up there with
the sun setting in the west, he was named Horse of the Year. Secretariat
won sixteen of the twenty-one races in which he competed.[2]

Whether he should be included among humans when ranking the
greatest American athletes is open for debate. But that Secretariat was an
incredible athlete is undeniable. ESPN placed him thirty-fifth on its list of
the top American athletes of the twentieth century. And he was voted into
the Horse Racing Hall of Fame in 1974.[3]

POINT TOTAL EXPLANATION

Achievements: 32/35

The comparatively short career of a racehorse limits his potential point total in this category. But Secretariat proved himself, especially given the era in which he competed, the fastest horse of all time. His records still stand after nearly a half century, which is not something human record-holders of that time can still claim.

Athleticism: 24/25

Secretariat boasted the speed, acceleration, balance, and power necessary to win the Triple Crown. He proved himself far superior to the competition in those athletic traits.

Athletic Requirements of the Sport: 15/20

Racehorses simply do not compete often enough to deserve anything close to full point totals here. Secretariat, for instance, totaled twenty-one races. But the best must be fast, strong, and agile to beat the competition.

Clutch Factor/Mental and Emotional Toughness: 14/15

Granted, it's tough to get inside the head of any horse aside from Mr. Ed. But Secretariat performed his best in the biggest races, including the Kentucky Derby, Belmont to secure the Triple Crown, and Arlington Invitational. Even a horse requires focus to achieve maximum speed and Secretariat certainly deserves credit for that.

Versatility: 1/5

Can you blame a horse for not running for touchdowns in the NFL or slam-dunking a basketball? No—but you also can't shower Secretariat with points for versatility. He did boast an array of skill sets that allowed him to thrive, so he cannot be shut out here.

TOTAL POINTS: 86

79

ROCKY MARCIANO: THE BROCKTON BLOCKBUSTER

Boxing

It's odd how a boxer can remain undefeated throughout his career and not be considered among the best. Rocky Marciano won all forty-nine of his fights—forty-three by knockout—yet most boxing experts do not place him in the same league as Muhammad Ali, Joe Louis, Jack Dempsey, and other heavyweights who tasted multiple defeats.

Granted, Marciano did not face the level of competition that the aforementioned fighters did. He defeated Louis, whose skills had all but deteriorated. He twice knocked out Jersey Joe Walcott and ended his career with victories over Ezzard Charles and Archie Moore. Yet he has been criticized for his skills and the heavyweight ranks at the time he fought.

All Marciano did was win. He won his first sixteen fights before defeating Walcott in 1952 to snag the heavyweight crown. He defended his title six times before retiring in 1956. His professional career lasted a mere eight years.[1]

Rocco Francis Marchegiano was born to Italian immigrants on September 1, 1923, in Brockton, Massachusetts. He barely survived to become a toddler—pneumonia almost killed him at the age of eighteen months. But he lived to become an avid athlete, landing a spot on the high school baseball and football teams before dropping out of school following his sophomore year. He had already honed his boxing skills, practicing his punching on a stuffed mailbag hung from a tree.

Marciano toiled to help his family make ends meet during the waning years of the Depression and before the US entry into World War II. He worked on delivery trucks and as a ditchdigger, railroad layer, and shoemaker. He served for two years in the army during the war before launching his boxing career.

As an amateur he showed little of the potential that would launch him to greatness, compiling an 8–4 record, but he won the 1946 Armed Forces Tournament. He still had not decided to make boxing his career. A love for baseball motivated Marciano to try out for a Cubs farm team in Fayetteville, North Carolina. He failed to land a spot, forcing him back to Brockton, where he began working with local boxing trainers.

Among his handicaps was age. Marciano was approaching his midtwenties and was quite raw. And he was not a natural. He boasted plenty of passion but struggled to prove himself ready to fight as a professional. Meanwhile, funds were running out. The mayor of Brockton stepped in to keep his training going.

Marciano finally fought for money on July 12, 1948, in Providence, Rhode Island. He knocked out Harry Bilazarian in the first round, then did the same a week later to John Edwards. Marciano was on his way. He was still awkward and poor mechanically—he telegraphed a looping right hand—but his knockout power was established. It would remain with him for the rest of his career, sending nearly every foe to the canvas.[2]

POINT TOTAL EXPLANATION

Achievements: 33/35

How does an undefeated fighter lose two points here? With a short career and comparatively weak competition. But Marciano could only battle the boxer in the same ring with him, and he beat them all.

They Said It

Why waltz with a guy for ten rounds when you can knock him out in one?—Rocky Marciano

Sixty percent of them guys Marciano licked didn't know from nothing. They got a call to go up and fight. They went. They got knocked out. Nobody got locked up and a lot of guys got paid off.—A fight manager of the era on Marciano's early career

What could be better than walking down any street in any city and knowing you're the heavyweight champion of the world?—Rocky Marciano

Athleticism: 18/25

Marciano boasted plenty of punching power and was famous for his endurance, durability, and ability to take a punch. He often swung wildly, and his blows sometimes lacked accuracy, but it often didn't matter. If they landed anywhere, they hurt. Marciano was a bit awkward and not a polished fighter. His style was no thing of beauty. He simply pummeled opponents into submission. He compares unfavorably to other greats of the division as a pure athlete.[3]

Athletic Requirements of the Sport and Division: 17/20

The heavyweight division had weakened since Louis was in his prime. And the need for speed and agility that was more prominent in earlier years (and again later when Ali emerged) was also not pronounced during Marciano's heyday. But there is something to be said for the power, durability, and endurance required in the battles waged during that time.

Clutch Factor/Mental and Emotional Toughness/ Intangibles: 14/15

The fact that Marciano began his career late and was forced to overcome a distinct lack of athleticism—especially quickness—results in a strong score in this category. He remained in excellent condition and simply gutted out many fights that did not end in early knockouts. His reputation as nothing more than a brawler belies the fact that many considered him a strong tactician and smart fighter.[4]

Versatility: 3/5

Marciano receives some credit here for his athletic endeavors in high school and beyond. That he played organized football and earned a tryout with a Cubs farm team is certainly worth something, despite his rather one-dimensional fighting style.

TOTAL POINTS: 85

80

RED GRANGE:
THE GALLOPING GHOST

Football

Red Grange. *Library of Congress*

It was October 18, 1924. University of Illinois star Red Grange gathered in the pigskin on the opening kickoff against defending Western Conference champion Michigan. Grange evaded defender after defender, sprinting 95 yards for the touchdown. Perhaps the greatest performance in the history of college sports had begun.[1]

Grange had gained a reputation for long-distance scores, but he outdid himself on this afternoon. He added touchdowns of 67, 56, and 44 yards in the first quarter alone. He did not even play the second quarter, then added a fifth running touchdown and a scoring pass in the second half. His elusiveness had grown legendary in a 39–14 triumph. It was no wonder he had been nicknamed "The Galloping Ghost."

Sportswriters covering teams in the east remained skeptical. They believed that those from Midwest schools could not compete with the cream of their region. Grange proved their folly in 1925 against national power Pennsylvania, scoring three touchdowns and totaling 363 yards in a 24–2 victory. Grange had been universally accepted as the greatest football player of all time.[2]

That can certainly be perceived as faint praise given that pro football was in its infancy, but the college game had been firmly established by the mid-1920s. Grange had become such a star that Chicago Bears owner George Halas believed he could alter the fate of his team, and the National Football League as well. So he signed Grange to a contract that scheduled the Galloping Ghost to kick off his professional career a mere ten days after his last college game.

The strategy worked. The Grange-led Bears packed stadiums. He continued to score touchdown as a pro, but a crippling knee injury in 1927 destroyed his elusiveness. He emerged as a more effective defensive back than running back. Though his impact on the field proved to be limited, his mere presence grew the popularity of the NFL.

Grange was born the son of a lumber camp foreman in the tiny Pennsylvania village of Forksville on June 13, 1903. His mother died when he was five, and the family moved to Wheaton, Illinois, soon thereafter. They lived with various relatives until they could afford a place of their own. Grange played football and basketball with neighborhood friends. Sports emerged as a motivating force in his life despite a heart murmur diagnosis.

His family remained poor even after his father landed a job as a police officer. Harold delivered ice in the summer to help out, but still found time to hone his athletic skills. He excelled in football, baseball, basketball, and track at Wheaton High School. His football team won all but one game his senior year—and that was the one in which he was knocked unconscious and remained out for two days.

Grange found it difficult to speak when he awoke, but the traumatic experience did not deter him from remaining on the path to gridiron greatness. Convinced to try out for the football team when he arrived at Illinois, he was a bit intimidated by the size of the competition but managed to earn a starting spot. The football world would be forever grateful for his persistence.[3]

POINT TOTAL EXPLANATION

Achievements: 27/35

Grange's talent surpassed his accomplishments, greatly because he played in an era during which there were limited avenues for that talent. But one cannot place him at the same level as his contemporary Jim Thorpe, who did maximize his opportunities as an Olympian and baseball player. Grange might have become as dominant in pro football as he was in the college game, but the knee injury wiped out that possibility.

Athleticism: 23/25

Grange's elusiveness, shiftiness, and acceleration as he bolted through the line of scrimmage remains legendary nearly a century after he exploded

---

They Said It

I played football the only way I knew. If you have the football and 11 guys are after you—if you're smart, you'll run. It was no big deal.—Red Grange

I'll just use one word—humble—the most humble person I've ever met. He'd make you feel at home, no matter who you were, and he never bragged.—University of Illinois classmate Seely Johnston

---

onto the scene at Illinois. Grange was clearly far superior than the competition of his era, which is how these categories are judged.

Athletic Requirements of the Sport and Position: 18/20

Grange excelled at both running back and defensive back, which earns him some points here. Two-way players remained common in the NFL into the 1950s. Grange must be credited for excelling on both sides of the ball. Quickness, speed, and a powerful vertical leap are needed to play defensive back, while the first two attributes were particularly necessary for tailbacks of his generation.

Clutch Factor/Mental and Emotional Toughness/ Intangibles: 14/15

Grange was known for his toughness and ability to rise to the occasion. He performed his best against premier competition with defenses keying on him—his effort against highly lauded Pennsylvania being a perfect example. That he thrived at a mere 170 pounds is astounding. That he continued his career for many years after a debilitating knee injury also speaks volumes.

Versatility: 3/5

Grange not only played various sports in high school, but he excelled at two positions on the football field and served as a quarterback and kicker at times. Versatility was a necessary component of college and pro players in his day, but Grange went beyond the call of duty.

TOTAL POINTS: 85

CHRIS CHELIOS: THE GODFATHER OF USA HOCKEY

Ice Hockey

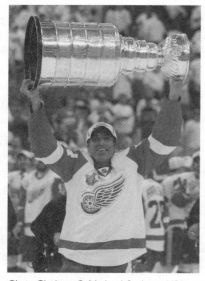

Chris Chelios. © Michael Sackett–USA TODAY Sports

He rode a stationary bike in the sauna. He played in the Olympics with a broken foot. The work ethic of Chris Chelios was legendary. In a league dominated by Canadians, particularly before the influx of European standouts, Chelios is considered by many to be the greatest American-born player of all time.[1]

Chelios played a remarkable twenty-six seasons, matching Gordie Howe for the most in NHL history, and played 1,651 games, the most of any defenseman ever. He was awarded the Norris Trophy as the finest defenseman in the league three times and played a significant role on three Stanley Cup champion teams. He was a five-time, first team all-NHL selection.

Defensemen who can score like Chelios are a rare commodity. His offensive skills resulted in him tallying more than 70 points three times and reaching double figures in goals scored eight times. He slipped the puck past goaltenders twenty times for Montreal in the 1987–88 season.[2]

Those who perceived Chelios as a goon were badly mistaken. He was fanatical in his preparation and conditioning and perhaps the toughest player in the league, but he was also among its most respected. So dedicated was Chelios to his craft that he refused to say goodbye well after his peak skills had waned. He could not bring himself to retire even in his midforties after leaving the Red Wings following the 2008–2009 season, so he played forty-six games with his hometown Chicago team of the American Hockey League and seven games with the NHL Atlanta Thrashers before finally hanging up the skates.[3]

He retired at age forty-eight. His career proved quite incredible considering he was raised in a neighborhood in which kids did not embrace hockey. Born Christos Tselios on January 25, 1962, in Chicago, he began playing in nearby Evergreen Park, but his opportunities to grow as a hockey player dissipated when the family moved to Poway, California, when he was fifteen years old.

Chelios showed his determination after losing spots on his college team and two Junior B teams in Canada. He returned to Southern California, worked to get stronger, and landed on the Moose Jaw Canucks of the Saskatchewan Junior Hockey League. He performed well enough to be drafted by the Montreal Canadiens in 1981. He honed his skills at the University of Wisconsin and was chosen to play for the United States team at the IIHF Ice Hockey World Junior Championships. He helped his college team win the NCAA title in 1983. He soon made his debut with Montreal. And thirty years later he was making his induction speech at the Hockey Hall of Fame.[4]

POINT TOTAL EXPLANATION

Achievements: 33/35

Chelios was no Bobby Orr among scoring defenders in NHL history, but he did compile enough points to preclude him from being considered a one-dimensional defenseman. Some place him among the greatest defensemen ever, and his longevity is certainly a plus here as well.

They Said It

He didn't look good doing it. He wasn't graceful. He wasn't the Paul Coffey type, the smooth-skating defenseman who stood out. He had a choppy look. He wasn't fluid. But he always got there. He was always in position. He was always frustrating to play against. He always hurt you in some way.—Blackhawks teammate Jeremy Roenick

Athleticism: 18/25

Chelios was a bit awkward in his puck-handling and shooting. He was not the most fluid of skaters. His quickness and speed on the ice was lacking. All he did was get the job done. This is not the category for intelligence and perseverance, however.

Athletic Requirements of the Sport and Position: 17/20

Like basketball players, those in the NHL play a brutal schedule of as many as 100 games a season. Defensemen should be agile, balanced, and strong in both the upper and lower body. They do not require a great of mobility, as they spend most of their time on one side of the ice, but they must possess the dexterity to skate backward effectively and with precision.

Clutch Factor/Mental and Emotional Toughness/ Intangibles: 15/15

No other player of his generation worked harder at his craft. Chelios was considered the ultimate ice warrior by teammates and opponents. His determination to rise above his circumstances as a Southern Californian and his hockey-related rejections to become a Hall of Famer helped him earn a perfect score here.[5]

Versatility: 2/5

Chelios dedicated his professional life to hockey, so other athletic endeavors were out of the picture. But that he was a threat as a scorer as well as a premier defenseman results in a couple points here.

TOTAL POINTS: 85

CHRIS EVERT: THE ICE MAIDEN

Tennis

When Chris Evert exploded onto the scene, the heyday of tennis was still a mere twinkle in the eyes of Billie Jean King and Bobby Riggs, whose epic Battle of the Sexes in 1973 launched the sport into an era of unparalleled popularity. The graceful Evert and her girl-next-door persona looked timid at first glance. But make no mistake about it—she was an assassin. She roamed the baseline coolly, spraying passing shots within inches of the line and past those who dared to rush the net. And it often seemed like an unforced error warranted a news bulletin.

Christine Marie Evert was born on December 21, 1954, in Fort Lauderdale, Florida. She began her tennis training under her father and coach, Jimmy Evert, at age five. Her tiny frame required a two-handed backhand that was rare at the professional level at that time. It remained so when she took the sport by storm in her first professional event in 1971, when she reached the US Open semifinals before falling to King. Her methodical, flawless form and clean, precise strokes were well established before she reached her teenage years.

Her stoic nature served to maintain poise from first point to last. But it could not be mistaken for a lack of passion. Evert was among the fiercest, most relentless competitors in the history of tennis. Her determination grew as she smelled victory. Her dominance coincided with the blossoming of tennis's popularity, which was no coincidence. Not only had fans embraced her style and talent, but her brief romance with brash young tennis star Jimmy Connors proved to be fine tabloid fodder.

Evert emerged as the premier player in the world in the mid-1970s despite tremendous competition from the likes of King, Martina Navratilova, and Evonne Goolagong. She won seven Grand Slam titles between 1974

They Said It

If you can react the same way to winning and losing that's a big accomplishment. That quality is important because it stays with you the rest of your life and there's going to be life after tennis that's a lot longer than your tennis life.—Chris Evert

She concentrates to the last point. It makes her a champion.—Tennis star Margaret Court

and 1977. She even captured Wimbledon twice, no small feat considering its grass surface generally benefited hard hitters and serve-and-volley players. Evert simply drilled forehands and backhands past them.

Age eventually took a toll, but Evert won eleven more Grand Slam championships between 1978 and 1986, establishing a particularly heated rivalry with Navratilova. Evert was never beaten in the first or second round of a major event, reaching the semifinals in 52 of 56 in which she competed and compiling a stunning record of 103–7. She finished seven seasons ranked number one in the world and performed quite well in her later years against such young superstars as Steffi Graf and Monica Seles.

Though not staunchly political in the storied fight to gain financial equality for female players, Evert did serve as president of the Women's Tennis Association for nine years. President George H. W. Bush called her "the role model for our nation's young women" and attended her induction into the International Tennis Hall of Fame in 1995.[1]

POINT TOTAL EXPLANATION

Achievements: 32/35

Evert captured at least one major singles title for a record thirteen consecutive years and ranks third all-time with eighteen Grand Slam singles championships. Among her achievements were seven French Open titles—its slow clay surface proved ideal for her baseline weaponry. She enjoyed nine stints as the top-ranked player in the world from 1975 to 1985, spending a whopping 260 weeks at that position. Only Navratilova, Graf, and Serena Williams held down the top spot longer. The first male or female player to reach 1,000 career singles victories, Evert finished with 1,309, ranking behind only

Navratilova. She also became the first player to top the 150-championship mark, finishing with 157. And her .900 winning percentage (1,309–148) is the best ever for a professional tennis player. It's no wonder she became the first female to surpass $1 million in career prize money.[2]

Athleticism: 19/25

Evert was not particularly strong or fast or quick, but she reached the balls she needed to and her hand-eye coordination was among the best in American sports history. She timed baseline forehands and backhands as well as any tennis player ever, which allowed her to hit passing shots and service returns with incredible precision. An admirable level of endurance kept her fresh and strong during long three-setters against the premier competition in the world, resulting in title after title. Evert rarely rushed the net, thereby conserving her energy. But it also provides her fewer points here with regard to athleticism, particularly in comparison to the likes of the stronger, more forceful Navratilova and Williams.

Athletic Requirements of the Sport: 18/20

Tennis at the highest level requires quickness, speed, endurance, and constant movement. It is among the most taxing sports in which to excel, particularly on those hot summer days on scorching surfaces.

Clutch Factor/Mental and Emotional Toughness/ Intangibles: 15/15

The icy Evert rarely beat herself. She was overcome at times, especially later in her career, by players boasting superior power and athleticism, but nobody in the history of tennis performed with greater mental or emotional strength. It was indeed those qualities that placed her among the finest players ever to lace up a pair of sneakers.

Versatility: 1/5

Evert was raised in an era in which girls simply did not compete in many organized sports. And her concentration on maximizing her talents on the court left her little time for other athletic endeavors. She was also not particularly versatile on the court as strictly a baseliner. The result is a rather low score in this category.

TOTAL POINTS: 85

83

AL OERTER: HE-MAN HEAVE MAN

Track and Field

The greatest discus throwers the world could muster had to gain a sense of confidence when they saw American Al Oerter at the 1964 Summer Games in Tokyo. The two-time Olympic gold medalist was wearing a neck brace, courtesy of a pinched cervical nerve. He was also attempting to throw with torn rib muscles.

No sweat, right? Someone was bound to beat him. The pain forced him to be carried off the field after his fifth throw. There was just one problem for his rivals: that toss traveled 61 meters, an Olympic record. Gold medal number three. Olympic record number three.[1]

Oerter finished his career with four Olympic gold medals in four tries. Most amazing is that he set a new mark in each of them. He won at Melbourne in 1956 with a heave of 56.36, in Rome with a 59.18, broke that one in Tokyo, then destroyed it Mexico City four years later with a toss of 64.78. And he was *still* not done. He returned in 1977 after an eight-year retirement and established a personal best of 67.46. And at age forty-three, he placed fourth in the 1980 Olympic Trials with a career-best 69.47.

This remarkable quarter-century run began in earnest in 1957 with an NCAA championship and the first of six AAU crowns. Oerter also won the Pan American Games in 1959. He did not set a world record in the discus until 1962, when he launched one 61.10 meters. He finished his career having set three more world records.[2]

Oerter, who was born on September 19, 1936, in Queens, was always more inspired by competition than by setting records. But he set them anyway. The depth of his athletic talent became evident at Sewanhaka High School, where he thrived as both a discus thrower and a sprinter.

His fascination with the discus began when one landed at his feet and he threw it back so far that his coach immediately placed him into that event. He shattered a prep record in the discus before landing at the University of Kansas, where his classmate was Wilt Chamberlain. Oerter won two NCAA titles with the Jayhawks and had already snagged gold at Melbourne by the time he graduated. He was on his way.[3]

POINT TOTAL EXPLANATION

Achievements: 33/35

Four Olympic gold medals in four attempts is amazing, but it does not quite stack up against those who excelled in more than one event. Oerter's records have since been shattered, but he was the most dominant discus thrower ever of any one era.

Athleticism: 19/25

Oerter was not simply stronger than the competition. His superiority was also based on the balance and agility needed to make the spin that provides the body momentum and timing to launch the discus a long way. But because he focused on only the discus, some of what he accomplished later in his career can be attributed to muscle memory.[4]

They Said It

I don't think the discus will ever attract any interest until they let us start throwing them at each other.—Al Oerter

In the opinion of many of us, he is the greatest field-event athlete of the century. There's a magic about him when he's competing. He's nervous before the meet. He doesn't eat well and his hands shake. But once the event is about to start, a calmness settles over him. The other athletes see it, and it intimidates them. They watch him, and they are afraid of what he might do.—American hammer thrower Harold Connolly

These are the Olympics. You die before you quit.—Al Oerter on competing injured at the 1964 Games

Athletic Requirements of the Sport and Event: 15/20

The discus requires a wider range of athletic attributes than the shot put, which is greatly an exercise of brute strength in the arm and lower and upper body. The spin for discus throwers requires a higher level of movement and body control.

Clutch Factor/Mental and Emotional Toughness/ Intangibles: 15/15

Oerter always saved his best for the Olympics and other significant international competitions. Amazingly, he never won the Olympic Trials, yet he took gold in all four Olympics in which he competed. It is no wonder he is considered by many the greatest field competitor in the history of the event.

Versatility: 3/5

Oerter not only sprinted and threw the discus for his high school team, he also played football. He deserves a few points here despite having concentrated on only one event beyond the prep level.

TOTAL POINTS: 85

84

MARY T. MEAGHER: MADAME BUTTERFLY

Swimming

Her name rarely arises when folks reminisce about great American Olympic athletes, perhaps because the Soviet Bloc boycott weakened the competition. But the performance of Mary Meagher at the 1984 Summer Games in Los Angeles is certainly worth talking about.

Meagher was a specialist. She swam the butterfly and only the butterfly in major meets. But—like Edwin Moses in the 200-meter dash, though not for the same length of time—Meagher was dominant in that one event. She would likely have won gold in the 1980 Moscow Games had the Americans participated. But she definitely made up for it four years later, winning the 100- and 200-meter butterfly in Los Angeles. She also butterflied in the 400-meter relay to help the US quartet take gold.

The greatest butterfly swimmer ever until Michael Phelps swam along established two world records in the 100 and five in the 200 starting in 1979. But no one effort could compare to her mind-boggling performance at the 1981 US Nationals, during which the sixteen-year-old shattered the world mark in the 100-meter butterfly by a ridiculous 1.33 seconds and broke the world record in the 200 with a time of 2:05.96. Neither clocking would be bettered for the next fifteen years. Though her butterfly times were slower in 1984, she still established Olympic records in both events. Closing in on twenty-four at the 1988 Games in Seoul, Meagher finally succumbed a bit to the wear and tear of competition. But she was still fast enough to win bronze in the 200-meter butterfly and help the 400-relay team take silver.[1]

It was not all about swimming for Meagher growing up. Born October 22, 1964, in Louisville, Kentucky, her backyard was connected to the

They Said It

Winning the gold medals in '84 was really a nice accomplishment. '84 was just full exhilaration. It was the highlight of my career and I'm glad some things came together—emotionally and physically.—Mary T. Meagher

She never seems to be satisfied. A normal person who has done what she has done might tend to be satisfied. But she has a burning desire to improve. Obviously, she is racing other people, but she is really racing the clock.—Swimming coach Mark Schubert

schoolyard, where she played myriad sports and games, including kickball and sardines in a can, with friends and ten siblings. She was often driven to the River Road Country Club during the summer to swim, play tennis, and golf. It was her second home between school years. And though she competed in many athletic activities, it was swimming at which she had the most talent. She was particularly inspired after watching an older girl swim the butterfly; her brother then taught her the proper technique in that stroke.[2]

Meagher took to the butterfly like, well, a duck takes to water. She set her first world record—in the 200 meters—at age fourteen. She later won World Cup and Pan American Games championships. She was also a Sullivan Award finalist for the premier amateur athlete in the United States in 1981, 1982, and 1983. And though she slumped a bit following her incredible US Nationals performance in 1981, she was ready for Los Angeles. She captured that butterfly.[3]

POINT TOTAL EXPLANATION

Achievements: 31/35

Meagher was like Edwin Moses in that she dominated one Olympic event. Though she did not control the butterfly for as long as Moses did the 400-meter hurdles, she did set more world and Olympic records, and her performance at the 1981 US Nationals was among the best any athlete has ever enjoyed. Her inconsistency, however, costs her a few points here.

Athleticism: 22/25

The butterfly is the most athletically challenging of the Olympic swimming events, and Meagher remains among the best in history. Her strong legs, flexibility, timing, acceleration off the blocks, and speed endurance catapulted her to the top.[4]

Athletic Requirements of the Sport and Event: 17/20

There is no time to lose one's ideal stroke in short-distance swimming. The coordination must remain perfect throughout a race to maintain any opportunity for a gold medal. And that is particularly difficult to master in the butterfly because there are so many critical moving parts.

Clutch Factor/Mental and Emotional Toughness/ Intangibles: 14/15

Meagher was known for her drive to greatness. She perceived competitive swimming as a race against the clock, not her competition. That personal reality allowed her to focus strictly on her own performance, which in turn resulted in world records and the ability to rise to the occasion for the biggest events, such as the 1984 Olympics.

Versatility: 1/5

Playing kickball in the schoolyard as a child does not translate into long-term versatility. Neither does concentrating solely on one event throughout a career.

TOTAL POINTS: 85

LISA LESLIE: SMOOTH

Basketball

Lisa Leslie. © Bob Donnan–*USA TODAY Sports*

It was July 30, 2002. The Los Angeles Sparks were hosting the Miami Sol in a WNBA game. Sparks center Lisa Leslie had broken from the pack and grabbed a feed downcourt. There was nothing but court between her and the basket. She leaped skyward and slammed the ball through the basket with her right hand.

Dunks such as that occur many times a game in the NBA. But never had one been achieved in the WNBA. The enormity of the accomplishment was not lost upon Leslie or her teammates, who celebrated the triumph despite trailing badly. The 6-foot-5 center had broken through the barrier.[1]

If anyone seemed destined to pull it off, it was Leslie. She had already won the first of her three Most Valuable Player awards after arguably the most dominant college career of any woman in the history of her sport. Few doubted Leslie was capable of dunking—she was simply waiting for the right opportunity.

That one moment could not, however, encapsulate the greatness of Lisa Leslie. By the time she threw down that dunk, she had already established career conference records in points, rebounds, and blocked shots for the University of Southern California. The three-time All-American won multiple national Player of the Year honors in 1994. She had also starred for the American team that won two Olympic gold medals. Leslie had performed her best against the toughest competition in 1996, compiling 35 points and 8 rebounds in a rare close call against Japan and tallying 29 in the championship defeat of Brazil.[2]

Leslie was just warming up. She helped launch the inaugural season of the WNBA in 1997 and emerged as its premier player. She retired twelve years later as the league's all-time leader in career points and rebounds and was one of just two players to record at least 800 blocked shots.[3]

The height that helped Leslie become the first dunker in the WNBA was not always a comfort to her. Born July 7, 1972, in Los Angeles, she had grown to 5-foot-2 by second grade. Leslie was already taller than her teacher, which motivated classmates to tease her, even calling her Olive Oyl after the character from the *Popeye* cartoons. That added to a difficult childhood that was worsened by her upbringing in a poor family that resided in the tough Compton neighborhood. After her father deserted the family when she was young, her mother learned to drive a truck to make ends meet and was gone on long-distance hauls for weeks at a time.[4]

Leslie was perceived with wonderment when people discovered she did not play basketball as a young child. Her acceptance of the encouragement of middle school friends who insisted she join the team proved a turning point in her life. Though she played with little enthusiasm at first, she displayed enough talent to help the team win all its games. Leslie played

They Said It

I don't think I would have been able to stick with it and been proud of who I am and be feminine out on the court. I think I would have folded to the peer pressure if I didn't have my mom to encourage me to be me and be proud of how tall I am.—Lisa Leslie

Mobility in her feet [makes] her very difficult to defend. And then defensively, she can throw a shot into the third row and set the complete tempo for you defensively. So she's just dominating on both ends.—Seattle Storm coach Anne Donovan in 2006

on the all-boys team in eighth grade and eventually gained the respect of her teammates. Her dedication to the sport grew when she arrived at high school. She moved in with an aunt and began honing her skills with an older male cousin who provided mentoring. Her skills blossomed when a move to Inglewood placed her at Morningside High School. She gained fame as a senior when she scored 101 points in one half of a game in which her teammates fed her the ball to maximize her total. She would have broken the national record for points in game had the opponent not forfeited at halftime. Leslie finished her senior season with averages of 27.3 points and 15 rebounds, prompting *Sports Illustrated* to proclaim her the top high school player in the country. But the best was yet to come.[5]

POINT TOTAL EXPLANATION

Achievements: 32/35

The records Leslie set in the WNBA were as much the result of longevity as talent. She played every year of the league's existence through 2009. Leslie compiled fine numbers in Olympic and professional competition, but nothing overwhelming after college. She did lead the Sparks to two championships and was named Finals MVP in both.

Athleticism: 23/25

Leslie's mobility for her size is perhaps her most impressive athletic attribute. But she was also quite strong in both her upper and lower body, which made her particularly tough to control with her back to the basket.

Athletic Requirements of the Sport and Position: 14/20

The WNBA schedule is a mere thirty-four games a season, and each game consists of two twenty-minute halves. The result is that it requires far less durability and energy from its players. The play is also less physical than what NBA players experience.

Clutch Factor/Mental and Emotional Toughness/ Intangibles: 13/15

Leslie performed well enough in the 2001 and 2002 championships series to win MVP honors both times. She was particularly dominant in the former, racking up 48 points, 22 rebounds, and 10 assists in the two-game sweep. But her career postseason numbers were quite similar to those she compiled in the regular season.

Versatility: 3/5

Leslie was a bit of a late bloomer in sports, which provided her just enough time to blossom in basketball. But she also played volleyball and ran track in high school. She was also a state qualifier in both the 400-meter run and long jump.

TOTAL POINTS: 85

86

O. J. SIMPSON: THE JUICE

Football

It takes great imagination and mind control to remember O. J. Simpson only as a great athlete. To forget the Bronco chase and the trial and the glove that didn't fit and the jail sentence. To recall only the combination of power and speed, the first 2,000-yard-rushing season, the first superstar running back following the retirement of Jim Brown. Remember that O. J. Simpson—the one so revered that he was hired to run through airports for Hertz and play alongside Leslie Nielsen in those absurd *Naked Gun* movies?

When Simpson gained eligibility for the NFL draft following a brilliant career at the University of Southern California, he was the most coveted rookie running back in league history. Poor production his first three seasons can be blamed greatly on coaching philosophy. His first head coach, John Rauch, insisted that no offense should revolve around one running back. Simpson managed to lead the Buffalo Bills in rushing with mediocre totals of 697, 488, and 742 yards in his first three years in the NFL.

The Bills floundered with a record of 8–32–2 during that period. Simpson was not enjoying his professional career. With business interests in California calling, he declared that he would retire after five seasons. But new head coach Lou Saban changed everything. He made Simpson the centerpiece of the offense. Simpson signed a multiyear extension upon his first glance at the playbook. He had 292 carries in 1972, after averaging just 161 the previous three years. He rushed for 1,251 yards to lead the NFL, then exploded for his epic seasons in which he broke the 2,000-yard barrier and scored a league-high 12 touchdowns. He again led the NFL in rushing in 1975 and scored 23 touchdowns, including seven through the air. He played his last two seasons with San Francisco and finished his career with 11,236 yards rushing.[1]

Little could anyone imagine that the man Bills owner Ralph Wilson described as "a better person than he is a football player" would notoriously land in jail on murder and robbery charges. But his early life was hardly a bed of roses. Orenthal James Simpson was born on July 9, 1947, in San Francisco. He was raised in the housing projects of the tough Potrero Hill neighborhood by single mother Eunice. He was a sickly child, having contracted the muscle and bone disease rickets at age two and being forced to wear leg braces for three years. He joined a gang at age thirteen and soon began spending his weekends battering those he claimed deserved it. A conversation with immortal Giants centerfielder Willie Mays helped turn his life around. Mays suggested that Simpson turn away from gang-banging and set positive goals for himself.

Simpson played football at Galileo High School, but his poor grades precluded him from landing a scholarship. He finally attracted recruiters while shattering records in junior college and landed at USC, the only school for which he yearned to play. It was there that he emerged as a superstar. He won the Heisman Trophy as a senior, setting NCAA records with 1,709 yards on the ground. In two seasons with the Trojans, he rushed for 3,423 yards.[2]

Simpson's pro career did not take off immediately, but soon he was starring on the football field and launching an acting career. Then all the good public relations he had cultivated over a quarter century ended in one fateful and horrifying night on June 12, 1994.

POINT TOTAL EXPLANATION

Achievements: 29/35

Simpson simply did not perform at a top level for long enough to warrant a wonderful score in this category. He managed five 1,000-yard totals in eleven seasons, though limited rushing opportunities played a role. He led the NFL in yards per carry only once and compiled a rushing average of 4.4 yards or less eight times. He averaged 6.0 in his 2,003-yard season, but his career was marked with inconsistency.[3]

Athleticism: 23/25

Simpson boasted a combination of power and speed at his peak that few backs have displayed. His leg strength and balance allowed him to

> ### They Said It
>
> *Fear of losing is what makes competitors so great. Show me a gracious loser and I'll show you a permanent loser.*—O. J. Simpson
>
> *You'll never be able to hear O. J. Simpson's name or even watch the great vintage footage of O. J. Simpson as one of the very greatest players who ever lived without thinking of this tragedy.*—Sportscaster Bob Costas

accelerate through holes and elude tacklers. Teammates claim he could reach top speed in two strides.[4]

Athletic Requirements of the Sport and Position: 18/20

The comparative lack of games played in the NFL precludes a higher score here, but the athletic requirements of an NFL featured back are as pronounced as those of any position on the field. One must have either tremendous quickness to gain yards and avoid debilitating hits or tremendous power to absorb them. It's no wonder that in the modern age the average period of greatness among premier backs is like the life span of your average housefly.

Clutch Factor/Mental and Emotional Toughness/ Intangibles: 11/15

Simpson averaged just 3 yards per carry in his only postseason game. He even faded down the stretch that year as the Bills sought to reach the playoffs. He did perform his best with the eyes of the football world upon him as he broke the 2,000-yard barrier, but nothing indicates he played better in clutch situations. After all, the Bills made the playoffs only once during his career.

Versatility: 3/5

Simpson was at least somewhat a pass-catching threat and was certainly a well-rounded back. He helped USC shatter a world record in the 440-meter relay at the 1967 NCAA Track and Field Meet. Though he concentrated almost entirely on football throughout his professional career, he deserves a few points in this category.[5]

TOTAL POINTS: 84

BILLIE JEAN KING: THE MALE CHAUVINIST PIG TAMER

Tennis

Billie Jean King. © Manny Rubio—*USA TODAY Sports*

One can understand the dominant image most Americans conjure up of Billie Jean King: coolly hitting ground strokes to all corners of the court, exposing Bobby Riggs, the man she labeled a male chauvinist pig, as an aging huckster who could not compete at her level. It was the legendary Battle of the Sexes of 1973, the most famous single tennis event in American history. And King, who understood the importance of the clash to the burgeoning women's movement, won it in straight sets.

But King should not be remembered solely for her dominance of Riggs that fateful night at the Houston Astrodome. That she was ranked number one in the world at the time should alone prove that her accomplishments extended far beyond that triumph. King was no longer at her peak when she defeated Riggs, though she was coming off a Wimbledon singles championship and would complete her run of twelve Grand Slam singles titles by winning the US Open in 1974 and Wimbledon again the following year.

King proved most dominant in those two majors, though she accomplished a career Slam when she defeated Evonne Goolagong in the 1972 French Open final. She won 129 singles titles in all. And her impact on women's tennis as an advocate for the players, particularly in fighting for equal pay, remains immeasurable.[1]

Her journey began as Billie Jean Moffitt on November 22, 1943, in Long Beach, California. She was raised in a sports-crazed home—her firefighter father played basketball in the navy and earned an NBA tryout invitation that he rejected, and her brother Randy was a standout major-league reliever. King grew up as a tomboy who played softball and touch football with the neighborhood boys.

Unlike other tennis stars, King was not force-fed the sport starting as a toddler. She began to play at age eleven. Her softball coach Clyde Walker, who doubled as a tennis instructor, gave free lessons once a week. He made the sport fun for King. So taken with tennis was King that she proclaimed to her mother in all seriousness that she would someday be the top-ranked player in the world. Her parents could not have imagined that such a dream would become reality, but they encouraged her and felt a sense of pride that their daughter was pushing toward her goals. Her father even placed a porch light in the backyard so she could practice at night.[2]

King was shunned by the tennis establishment even at that age. While working at the Los Angeles Tennis Club, she was told to butt out of a picture by the president of the Southern California Lawn Tennis Association because she was wearing tennis shorts rather than a dress or skirt. She came to resent the haughty attitudes of those in charge.

She also came to greatness in the sport. Her parents drove her forty miles and dropped her off so she could spend entire weekends taking lessons from tennis legend Alice Marble. Though that relationship eventually

They Said It

Natural talent only determines the limits of your athletic potential. It's dedication and a willingness to discipline your life that makes you great.—Billie Jean King

She has prominently affected the way 50 percent of society thinks and feels about itself in the vast area of physical exercise. Moreover, like [Arnold] Palmer, she had made a whole sports boom because of the singular force of her presence.—Sports Illustrated *writer Frank Deford*

soured, King had improved enough to land a spot on the Junior Wightman Cup team at age fifteen. She earned enough money to afford the travel necessary to compete in prestigious youth events. King performed well enough to skyrocket to number four in the rankings of all American female tennis players in 1960. A year later King and partner Karen Hantze were winning the Wimbledon doubles championship. She was on her way to becoming one of the most legendary and accomplished tennis players of all-time.[3]

POINT TOTAL EXPLANATION

Achievements: 30/35

Other players, including Serena Williams, Margaret Court, Chris Evert, and Martina Navratilova, won more Grand Slam singles titles. But King also thrived in women's doubles and mixed doubles. The span between her first and last Slam title was nineteen years, which speaks volumes about her longevity.

Athleticism: 21/25

King covered the court quite well with her quickness and displayed enough power to serve-and-volley or rush the net off ground strokes for winners. She also boasted a deft touch to put opponents away with drop shots.

Athletic Requirements of the Sport: 18/20

The speed, agility, and endurance required of premier tennis players such as King cannot be underestimated. The sport can be especially tiring for women, whose rallies are most often lengthier than those of men, who end points quickly with aces. The hand-eye coordination necessary to blast passing shots within a foot of the line while running full-tilt is incredible. And that is just one example of the athleticism required of tennis players at that level of competition.

Clutch Factor/Mental and Emotional Toughness/ Intangibles: 13/15

One must note how King rose to the occasion under the weight of tremendous pressure to beat Riggs. She believed the entire women's movement would suffer a huge setback if she lost. But King also failed in many attempts to advance beyond the quarterfinals or semifinals in

Grand Slam tournaments. Though she is widely accepted as a tenacious player, she often failed to come through with her finest performances with championships on the line.

Versatility: 2/5

King was certainly not one-dimensional on the court. It should be noted also that few opportunities in organized team sports were afforded female youth of her era.

TOTAL POINTS: 84

WILMA RUDOLPH: THE TORNADO

Track and Field

The story of Wilma Rudolph is not merely one of an Olympic gold medal sprinter. It is one of heart and determination, overcoming physical debilitation and numbing Jim Crowism. Wilma Rudolph was a hero, admirable far beyond her physical talents.

Rudolph was indeed a tremendous athlete. She proved it well before the 1960 Games in Rome, having gotten her feet wet by winning bronze in the 100-meter relay four years earlier in Melbourne at the tender age of sixteen—some mean feat considering polio left her unable to walk until she was nine. And she was sure running in Rome. Rudolph buried the competition in the 100 and 200 meters and earned a third gold in the 100-meter relay while setting two world records and an Olympic record along the way. She was the first American woman to win three gold medals in track and field in a single Summer Olympics. Rudolph won the 1961 Sullivan Award as the nation's premier amateur athlete.

She took her momentum and ran with it—literally. Rudolph, who had first established her greatness at the 1959 Pan American Games with a gold in the 400-meter relay and silver in the 100 meters, had become one of the most dominant track stars in the world. She won the AAU 100-meter dash in four consecutive years. She added the 200 meters in 1960 and won that three successive times.[1]

That she could even walk stunned her doctor. Rudolph weighed a mere four and a half pounds when she was born in Saint Bethlehem, Tennessee, on June 23, 1940. She was stricken with many illnesses as a child, including pneumonia and scarlet fever as well as polio, which weakened her left leg and forced her to wear metal braces. The lack of care available to African

> ### They Said It
>
> *My doctors told me I would never walk again. My mother told me I would.*
> *I believed my mother.*—Wilma Rudolph
>
> *She was the Jesse Owens of women's track and field, and like Jesse, she*
> *changed the sport for all time. She became the benchmark for little black*
> *girls to aspire.*—Olympic historian Bud Greenspan
>
> *I loved the feeling of freedom in running, the fresh air, the feeling that the*
> *only person I'm competing with is me.*—Wilma Rudolph

Americans in Tennessee during that time prevented Rudolph from receiving the best treatment. But the prognosis in her ability to eventually walk on her own was not promising.

That Rudolph could have gotten lost in the shuffle would not be surprising—she was the twentieth of twenty-two children in an exceedingly poor family. She was tended to by her siblings, who took turns rubbing her leg every night and stopped her from removing her braces. Her mother drove her long distances to find doctors who could provide effective treatments.

The attention and care Rudolph received finally paid off. She shed her leg braces at age nine, allowing her to run and play with other children. In the backyard, her brothers set up a basketball hoop that she used daily, developing her into a tremendous player. She starred on her high school team, scoring 49 points in one game to shatter the state record. Among those who recognized her talent and overall athletic potential was Tennessee State track coach Ed Temple. He asked Ed Gray, her high school basketball coach, to establish a track team as well. Gray complied, and Rudolph dominated in that sport as well.

The rest is history—but Rudolph continued to make history following her Olympic triumphs. Upon her return to Tennessee, old-school governor Buford Ellington planned a segregated parade and banquet for her. She refused to participate until it was integrated, and Ellington was forced to relent. The event was the first integrated celebration ever in her hometown. Rudolph remained active in the fight against segregation until the laws were changed. She later served as an advocate for inner-city youth through the Wilma Rudolph Foundation, which coordinated community-based sports programs.[2]

POINT TOTAL EXPLANATION

Achievements: 30/35

Rudolph concentrated solely on sprinting and won gold in only one Olympic Games. Those facts would normally limit her score even more, but she must be credited here for the achievement of overcoming polio to set world records. That alone is an amazing feat.

Athleticism: 20/25

Rudolph boasted incredible short-distance speed and the quickness to blast off the blocks, which is critical in the sprints.

Athletic Requirements of the Sport and Event: 16/20

Her shortcomings in the first category are the same here since she participated only in the sprints. Sprinters require flat-out speed, quickness, leg strength, and agility. But the upper-body power needed by those in field events and leaping ability required of hurdlers are not prerequisites for sprinters, who are a bit one-dimensional.

Clutch Factor/Mental and Emotional Toughness/ Intangibles: 15/15

Rudolph is as deserving of a full point total in this category as any athlete ever. That she won an Olympic medal seven years after shedding her leg braces is remarkable. Her grit and determination to maximize her athletic potential despite the enormous odds against her must be rewarded.

Versatility: 3/5

The basketball talent that led to her track success was pronounced—Rudolph dominated the high school competition. She twice earned spots on the all-state basketball team. The result is a strong score here.

TOTAL POINTS: 84

89

KELLY SLATER: KING KELLY

Surfing

Kelly Slater appeared in twenty-seven episodes of the TV show *Baywatch* between 1992 and 1996 in the role of Jimmy Slade. He did not luck into it. He landed the spot on the highly popular—if not artistically acclaimed—show by becoming the greatest surfer in American history. He also landed many other acting roles.

Slater is widely accepted as the best of all time. He captured eleven World Surf League championships, including five consecutive titles from 1994 to 1998. He won the Billabong Pipeline Masters in each of those years and eight in all, including one in 2013 at the age of forty-one. He captured World Surf League titles at both the youngest (twenty) and oldest (thirty-nine) age of any surfer ever.[1]

If birthplace means anything—and it should for a surfer—Slater seemed destined for greatness in that sport. He was born on February 11, 1972, in Cocoa Beach, Florida. His father worked as the owner of a bait-and-tackle shop while his mom served as a firefighter and emergency medical technician. Young Kelly began surfing at age five with a bodyboard and fins on the three-foot waves of Cocoa Beach. He received his first custom-made surfboard at age eight, and the rest is history.

Slater spent twelve hours a day at the Third Street North beach as a kid in the 1970s and early 1980s. He became good enough to accomplish three backside 360s on one wave at age nine. He got some of his inspiration from his father, who was not a professional but an accomplished surfer nevertheless. The young Slater traveled to California, where he won his first amateur title in 1982 at the US Junior Championships. He was eventually surviving twenty-foot tubes and even forty-footers while earning crown after crown. It's no wonder that Cocoa Beach city commissioners named the east end of Third Street North "Kelly Slater Way" in November 1999.[2]

POINT TOTAL EXPLANATION

Achievements: 35/35

Slater has been as dominant in his sport as nearly any American athlete ever. He was ranked between first and sixth in the world every year between 1992 to 2014. He topped the rankings eleven times during that stretch despite a three-year hiatus from the sport.

ATHLETICISM: 19/25

Slater earned a reputation as not only one the more technically sound surfers, but perhaps the most athletic one. He owned all the requirements of a premier surfer, including agility, balance, coordination, stamina, and the ability to react swiftly to waves and conditions.

Athletic Requirements of the Sport: 14/20

Surfers need to remain in place, but that does not mean they do not require some athletic attributes. It takes endurance to paddle, strength and stability to pop up, and strong reflexes and balance simply to stay on a

They Said It

For me it's sort of like time slows down. You become hyper aware of a lot of different things—the way the wave is breaking, timing, putting yourself in the right part of the barrel. It takes all of your mental capacity to do it just right.—Kelly Slater

Kelly has changed the way people look at surfing, the way he's so cool. Even if he wasn't a surfer, he'd still be looked upon like he's Steve McQueen.—1960s surfing champion Gary Propper

board while riding waves. Reaction time is immediate as a giant wall of water cascades within inches behind the surfer's body.[3]

Clutch Factor/Mental and Emotional Toughness/ Intangibles: 15/15

The strain—mental and emotional—for surfers is difficult to quantify. One mental or physical mistake destroys all hope. Slater has proven to have an extremely high level of concentration in blossoming into a legendary surfer. That he continued to beat the best year after year against younger competition is a testament to his mental and emotional toughness.

Versatility: 1/5

Surfers must maintain incredible steadiness to succeed, but versatility is not part of the package and, even though Slater golfs a bit, his passion for surfing has precluded him from delving into other competitive sports.

TOTAL POINTS: 84

90

JOHNNY UNITAS: THE GOLDEN ARM

Football

The statistics are like from a later era. Quarterbacks of the late 1950s and 1960s struggled to throw more touchdowns than interceptions—contact rules favored defensive backs, and dump passes to running backs were far less frequent. Yet Johnny Unitas consistently tossed more touchdowns than picks. Twenty touchdowns made for a fine season in his era, and he did it nine times. Heck, Joe Namath threw far more interceptions than touchdowns. Bart Starr never tossed more than 16 touchdown passes in a year. And both landed in the Pro Football Hall of Fame.

Unitas was simply prolific. Other quarterbacks approached his yardage and touchdown totals—Washington gunslinger Sonny Jurgensen comes to mind—but none matched his team accomplishments. Unitas led his Colts to a .500 record or better every year from 1957 to 1970, including two NFL championships, one being an epic triumph against the Giants in 1958 that launched both him and professional football into the American consciousness.

His career statistics no longer rank among the best of all time, but he was undeniably the greatest quarterback of his era. Unitas finished his career with 40,239 yards, a tremendous feat considering the NFL offense in his team generally revolved around the ground game and that he had the luxury of handing off to Hall of Famer Lenny Moore as well as other top backs such as Tom Matte and Alan Ameche. Unitas led the NFL in passing yards in four of his first seven seasons and touchdowns in four of his first five after being stupidly discarded by the Pittsburgh Steelers. But his signature moment occurred in the ballyhooed 1958 title game, the first nationally televised NFL game, when he completed seven straight passes to lead an 86-yard scoring drive to tie the epic battle, then engineered a touchdown march to win it in overtime.[1]

They Said It

Johnny Unitas was the best quarterback ever to play the game. He was better than I was, better than Sammy Baugh, better than anyone.—Hall of Famer Sid Luckman

I always thought I could play pro ball. I had confidence in my ability. You have to. If you don't, who will?—Johnny Unitas

[Unitas was great for] an uncanny instinct for calling the right play at the right time, his icy composure under pressure, his fierce competitiveness and his utter disregard for his own safety.—Colts wide receiver Raymond Berry

Unitas was a product of the Cradle of Quarterbacks—western Pennsylvania. He was born in Pittsburgh on May 7, 1933, and his father died when he was four years old. He played both halfback and quarterback at St. Justin's High School, where he performed well enough to land a scholarship to the University of Pittsburgh. He failed his entrance exam, so instead he landed at Louisville. He played quarterback there throughout and landed a starting job as a freshman but was never considered a premier prospect. He needed four seasons to throw for 3,139 yards and 27 touchdowns. He arrived at 6-foot-1 and 145 pounds, not exactly the strapping size scouts look for in a quarterback. And an injury that limited his senior season did not help. It came as little surprise when he lasted until the ninth round of the 1955 NFL draft and was cut by the Steelers before he took a snap.[2]

Unitas remained persistent. He played semipro football for six dollars a game until Colts coach Weeb Ewbank learned that he was performing exceptionally well. He signed Unitas and placed him as the starter in 1956 when George Shaw was sidelined with an injury. By the following year he was among the premier quarterbacks in the NFL.[3]

POINT TOTAL EXPLANATION

Achievements: 33/35

Had Unitas enjoyed more success in the postseason—his passer rating was under 48.0 in three of his team's playoff runs—he might have earned a near-perfect score here. That is not nit-picking, but it cannot overshadow his career greatness and his overall record of 118–63–4 as a starting quarterback.[4]

Athleticism: 19/25

Unitas was a prototypical pocket passer with little mobility. Though he lacked elusiveness and speed, he had a strong arm, fine footwork, and quick release. And he was not a statue back there—his awareness helped him to escape enough pressure to rush for an average of 152 yards in his first nine seasons and score 10 touchdowns on the ground during that time.[5]

Athletic Requirements of the Sport and Position: 16/20

The quarterback position has evolved, so one must at least take that into some consideration here. Despite the mobility of such quarterbacks as Fran Tarkenton and Bobby Douglass in the 1960s and early 1970s, that athletic attribute is required to a far greater extent in the modern era. Quarterbacks of previous NFL generations were mostly pocket passers who threw less often.

Clutch Factor/Mental and Emotional Toughness/ Intangibles: 13/15

Unitas gained a reputation as a great clutch quarterback with his 1958 title-game performance and strong effort in 1959, but he did not pass well in the playoffs otherwise. He threw for four touchdowns and nine interceptions in seven postseason games from 1964 to 1971. But Unitas impressed his peers with his in-game toughness. He was a tremendous play-caller and leader. And the fact that he overcame a lack of athleticism to break NFL records should account for something here.

Versatility: 2/5

Unitas was versatile enough to play tailback in high school, so he gets a couple points here despite not having competed in other sports at a significant level.

TOTAL POINTS: 83

TED WILLIAMS:
THE SPLENDID SPLINTER

Baseball

Ted Williams. *Photos used with permission of the National Baseball Hall of Fame Museum (Cooperstown, NY).*

Rumor has it that Ted Williams could read the label on a 78 RPM record as it spun on a turntable. It has also been stated that he could see the seams on a baseball from the time it left the pitcher's hand to the moment he made contact. Such claims would be dismissed about anyone else. But one can be convinced of their accuracy, considering the subject.[1]

Another contention is that Williams is the greatest hitter who ever lived. That argument too has merit. It has even gained credence under the microscope of modern statistical analysis. Removing three years of military service, Williams paced the American League in walks, on-base percentage, and slugging percentage for six consecutive seasons. He led the AL in walks in five of them. Most famously, he was the last player to bat .400 in a season, achieving the feat in 1941 after refusing to sit for a year-end doubleheader with a .400 mark and slamming six hits. And he finished the 1957 season with a .388 average at age thirty-nine. So fearful were hurlers of Williams in his day that they walked him more than 2,000 times, resulting in a .482 career on-base percentage that has remained the best ever.[2]

Williams was a child prodigy. Born August 30, 1918, in San Diego, he learned the sport from his uncle, who had played semipro baseball. He tore up opposing pitchers at Herbert Hoover High School, batting .583 as a junior before falling to .406 his senior year, the same average he achieved in 1941 with the Red Sox. But Williams was not merely an offensive standout; he compiled a 16–3 record as a pitcher.

His all-around talent motivated the New York Yankees to offer him a contract, but his mother refused to allow him to move so far from home at age seventeen. He latched on with the Pacific Coast League San Diego Padres instead. The teenager slugged 23 home runs and drove in 98, prompting the Red Sox to sign him and send him to Minneapolis, where he won the 1938 Triple Crown by batting .366 with 43 home runs and 142 RBI.[3]

The Sox could wait no longer. They opened the 1939 season against the archrival Yankees with Williams starting in right field. He slugged four hits and his first major-league home run three days later, really hit his stride in late June, and remained on a tear from that point forward. The only pitch that stopped him was the one made by Uncle Sam, who took three seasons away from him as he trained as a pilot and gunner during World War II, but he never saw active service overseas. He was called upon again during the Korean War, losing most of two seasons as he flew thirty-nine missions for the Marines.[4]

Neither stretch slowed him down. Williams returned to action in 1946 to embark on one of the most dominant periods ever by an American athlete. He won his second Triple Crown in 1947 and Most Valuable Player awards in 1946 and 1949. He earned two batting championships and led the league four times in on-base percentage after returning from Korea. He even batted .316 in 1960 at the age of forty-one.

They Said It

A man has to have goals—for a day, for a lifetime—and that was mine, to have people say, "There goes Ted Williams, the greatest hitter who ever lived."—Ted Williams

Did they tell me how to pitch to Ted Williams? Sure they did. It was great advice, very encouraging. They said he had no weaknesses, won't swing at a bad ball, had the best eyes in the business, and can kill you with one swing. He won't hit anything bad, but don't give him anything good.
—All-star pitcher Bobby Shantz

The time lost to the military prevented Williams from several achievements, including 3,000 career hits. But he ended his career as one of the most productive hitters of all time, as his .634 slugging percentage—which ranks only behind Babe Ruth's—attests.[5]

POINT TOTAL EXPLANATION

Achievements: 34/35

No hitter in baseball history compiled more impressive numbers than Williams, but he managed to lead his team to just one World Series appearance, which costs him a point. Baseball, however, is an individual sport, so he cannot be penalized too greatly if (most often) the Yankees simply boasted superior all-around talent. His dominance as a hitter in both average and power was complete, arguably second only to Ruth in the history of the sport.

Athleticism: 19/25

Williams boasted some athletic traits, such as tremendous hand-eye coordination, quick wrists, and great balance. But his success was his mastery of the science of hitting. He was a line-drive hitter whose power was the result of consistently hitting the ball hard. He boasted average speed, rarely stole a base, and was a mediocre right fielder with no more than a decent arm. But his attributes proved so strong that they dominated his overall performance.

Athletic Requirements of the Sport and Position: 16/20

Playing baseball at a high level requires more athleticism than golf, for instance, but less than most other sports. But the 162-game (in Williams's day 154-game) schedule is demanding. Right fielders such as Williams do not need the speed and mobility that center fielders require nor the quickness of a shortstop.

Clutch Factor/Mental and Emotional Toughness/ Intangibles: 12/15

Williams loses points here as well. Not only was he able to push his team into the World Series just once, but he batted a mere .200 with no home runs and one RBI in the 1946 defeat to St. Louis. His clutch numbers were uniformly lower than his other statistics, though his on-base percentage was higher, suggesting that opposing hurlers pitched around him with runners in scoring position or games on the line.[6]

Versatility: 2/5

Williams embraced baseball at an early age and stuck with it. And why not? When you bat nearly .600 as a high school junior and you're offered contracts by the Yankees and Red Sox as a teenager, you're not about to risk an injury playing quarterback for the football team. Still, his lack of experience in other sports costs him in this category.

TOTAL POINTS: 83

GREG LOUGANIS:
DYNAMITE DIVER

Diving

Greg Louganis. © George Long–USA
TODAY Sports

It's a shame if one recollection, one image of Greg Louganis remains prevalent in the minds of any casual fan anywhere: that of him slamming his head on the diving board in the second-to-last qualifying effort in the springboard event at the 1988 Summer Olympics in Seoul, South Korea. What some might not remember is that Louganis overcame that emotional and physical trauma to win the gold medal.

It was generally no surprise to anyone familiar with his dominance of the sport that Louganis ended up atop the standings. But that he finished first after one of the most shocking accidents in international sports history was a testament to his greatness.[1]

After winning a silver medal in the platform in 1976 at the tender age of sixteen, Louganis appeared primed to snag gold in 1980 until the American boycott of the Moscow Games destroyed that possibility. Based on his performances in various events, he was certainly ready for 1984. He had won the platform in 1978 and both the platform and springboard in 1982 at the World Championships. He also captured both events in the 1979 Pan American Games. By the time his career had concluded, he had established an American record, taking more than thirty national crowns and many in-

ternational titles. Most impressive was his effort at the 1982 World Championships, where he became the first diver in the history of international competition to earn a perfect 10 from all seven judges, courtesy of his perfect 2½
pike. He received the highest score ever for his 3½ pike in the same event.

Louganis was indeed in peak form for the 1984 Games. He placed first
in both events but proved particularly dominating in the platform by becoming the first diver ever to exceed 700 points. To the surprise of no one,
he again captured the platform and springboard competitions at the 1986
World Championships, then repeated the feat at the 1988 Olympics, after
which (thankfully, to his rivals) he announced his retirement.[2]

Those gold medals were a tribute to the fighting spirit that allowed
Louganis to overcome obstacles and adversity throughout his life. Born
on January 29, 1960, and adopted at nine months of age by a couple living
just outside of San Diego, he was often ridiculed and bullied as a child for
the dark skin inherited from his Samoan father. A passion for gymnastics
proved to be a positive outlet for Louganis. He emerged as a talented
enough gymnast to perform for audiences by age nine.

It was at that time his mother accompanied him to diving practice to
prevent him from performing dangerous stunts into his backyard pool.
He embraced the new activity after discovering he had talent. He entered the national Junior Olympics two years later but expressed doubts
to his mother during the event. Her reassurance buoyed his spirit and
performance as he rocketed from twelfth place to second. The comfort he
received from his mother would remain with him forever. There would
be no stopping Louganis—aside from politics—from that point forward.[3]

They Said It

*At first, I was just so embarrassed. I was like, "How do I get out of this pool
without anybody seeing me?" This is the Olympic Games, you are supposed to be a pretty good diver. Good divers don't do stuff like that.*—Greg
Louganis on slamming his head on the board during the 1988 Olympics

*He used to be very introverted, he was in a lot of turmoil. I've seen him
grow to be a very relaxed, confident, comfortable person who can deal with
media, speak in front of crowds and just be happy.*—Coach Ron O'Brien

POINT TOTAL EXPLANATION

Achievements: 34/35

Louganis is widely accepted as the greatest diver ever, though his 1976 Olympic performance in Montreal was considered a disappointment despite his age. Louganis was unstoppable from 1978 to 1988. That longevity is impressive. More impressive would have been his run of gold medals had politics not prevented him from diving in Moscow.

Athleticism: 20/25

Louganis simply displayed more athleticism within the parameters of his sport than his rivals. His flexibility and body control were second to none.

Athletic Requirements of the Sport and Events: 12/20

Diving ranks near the bottom of individual sports in such attributes as speed, quickness, agility, hand-eye coordination, durability, and endurance. Success is greatly based on muscle memory, coordination, and tremendous concentration.[4]

Clutch Factor/Mental and Emotional Toughness/ Intangibles: 15/15

It's all about mental and emotional toughness, clutch performances, and intangibles for a perennial gold medalist such as Louganis. One must be tough mentally and emotionally to concentrate enough to get the body to do what the mind knows it must do, especially with billions of eyes staring at you. Louganis earns every point here.

Versatility: 2/5

Louganis gets a bit of credit here for his talent in gymnastics as a youth before turning his attention to diving.

TOTAL POINTS: 83

93

JOSH GIBSON: THE BLACK BABE RUTH

Baseball

Trying to rank Negro League players among other sports legends cannot be achieved through statistics. Though such records have been compiled from the time when Major League Baseball shamefully excluded black players from their ranks, several factors make comparisons difficult at best. But when examining both the numbers and eyewitness accounts of those fortunate enough to have seen Josh Gibson play, one conclusion is certain: he was among the best hitters to ever grace a diamond.

His statistics cannot be compared. The Negro Leagues had only enough money to schedule about sixty games per season and the records of many of them remain unavailable. Other factors that make comparisons impossible include ballpark differences—some in which Negro League teams played did not even have fences. And since comparison between major-league and Negro League talent is speculative at best, one cannot calculate how Gibson would have performed against the likes of Babe Ruth and Ted Williams. After all, he only averaged 132 plate appearances a year.

What has been recorded is Gibson's 2,528 plate appearances in Negro League and Mexican League competition, which can be translated into five major-league seasons. If he had maintained the same pace of production throughout his career, he would have averaged 30 home runs and a tremendous slash line of .358/.421/.659.

Gibson's consistency cannot be challenged. His numbers were virtually equal at age twenty-three as they were at age thirty-two. He not only survived a coma before spring training in 1943, but he returned to hit a ridiculous .486 with an OPS of 1.351 that year. He even played at a high level with a brain tumor for the rest of his career.[1]

They Said It

Gibson is one of the best catchers that ever caught a ball. Watch him work this pitcher. He's top at that. And boy-oh-boy, can he hit that ball!—Hall of Fame pitcher Dizzy Dean

I played with Willie Mays and against Hank Aaron. They were tremendous players, but they were no Josh Gibson.—Giants slugger Monte Irvin

There is a catcher that any big-league club would like to buy for $200,000. His name is Gibson. He can do everything. He hits the ball a mile. He catches so easy he might as well be in a rocking chair. Throws like a rifle. Too bad this Gibson is a colored fellow.—Hall of Fame pitcher Walter Johnson

It is believed Gibson was born on or about December 21, 1911, in segregated Buena Vista, Georgia, to sharecropper parents. His father moved to Pittsburgh in 1923 to work at a steel mill and sent money back until he could afford to move the family to Pennsylvania after Josh had completed fifth grade. The young Gibson learned the electrical trade at school there but dropped out at age fifteen to work at an air brake manufacturing plant and help the family financially. At 6-foot-1 and 200 pounds, the strapping teen learned he could work as productively as adult men.

Gibson also explored his athletic abilities. Despite his size, he preferred swimming and baseball to football or basketball. He played for an all-black Gimbels Department Store team at age sixteen, moving from catcher to third base. His talent motivated Gimbels to give him a job as an elevator operator so it could keep him on the team. The team eventually competed in an expanded Negro Greater Pittsburgh Industrial League. One team that formed during that time was the dominant Pittsburgh Crawfords. The team's manager was so impressed with Gibson after watching him play that he signed him to a contract.

He played for the Craws in 1929 and 1930 and gained a reputation for his power. Word of his batting prowess reached the Negro League Homestead Grays. They already had two catchers, but they placed Gibson on their radar. Legend has it that the Kansas City Monarchs arrived in

Pittsburgh to play the Grays one day and that the latter lost its catcher to a broken finger, motivating Grays owner to summon Gibson from the stands and replace him. Though the story has never been confirmed, baseball history does show that Gibson played for Homestead that year and batted .338. An incredible career was about to begin.[2]

POINT TOTAL EXPLANATION

Achievements: 30/35

Putting Gibson's career accomplishments into context is difficult, especially considering the short Negro League season and the impossibility of comparing the competition to that of major-league players. But Gibson was certainly among the greatest players and premier power hitters of his generation.

Athleticism: 22/25

Gibson was athletic enough to have played left field and third base as well as catcher. He carried a powerful bat and strong arm with a fast release. His quick hands and compact swing sent balls a long way. His calling card was power. No less an authority than the *Sporting News* once claimed he hit a 580-foot home run at Yankee Stadium that landed two feet from the top of the bleacher wall.[3]

Athletic Requirements of the Sport and Position: 15/20

Catchers must be durable game to game and year to year. Required also defensively are good footwork and sure hands, as well as lower- and upper-body strength. Gibson cannot receive as much credit here due to the significantly shorter schedule he played, though Negro League teams did travel often to play exhibitions.

Clutch Factor/Mental and Emotional Toughness/ Intangibles: 13/15

The path to greatness for a black kid in the 1920s was far rockier than the one enjoyed by the ballplayers of today. Though little is known about Gibson the teammate that cannot be verified statistically, the mere fact that he maintained his drive through all the hardships of life warrants a strong score in this category.

Versatility: 3/5

Gibson not only displayed some ability at other positions besides catcher, he was also an avid swimmer during his youth. He deserves a few points here.

POINT TOTAL: 83

EDWIN MOSES: THE BIONIC MAN

Track and Field

The date was August 26, 1977. The location was West Berlin. American track star Edwin Moses lost a 400-meter hurdles race to Harald Schmid of West Germany.

Fast forward to June 4, 1987. US upstart Danny Harris defeated the thirty-one-year-old Moses in the same event.[1]

Nearly ten years had passed. And between those dates, Moses never lost in the 400-meter hurdles. He had participated in 122 such events, and he had won them all. It is considered among the greatest feats in the history of track and field.

Not that Moses needed to concentrate on any other athletic pursuits. Though he dabbled early in his career in the 400 meters and 110-meter hurdles, he participated only in the 400 meters in Olympic competition. But he won the gold medal in that event in both 1976 and 1984—the American boycott of the 1980 games most assuredly cost Moses a third. Moses was thirty-three years old when he earned the bronze in the 1988 Seoul Olympics.

Moses exploded onto the scene to finish first in 1976. He won US titles in the 400-meter relay in 1977, 1979, 1981, and 1983 and World Cup crowns in 1977, 1979, and 1981. He won a world championship in the event in 1983, earning him the Sullivan Award, which honors the premier American amateur athlete annually. After snagging another Olympic gold, Moses gained a share of the *Sports Illustrated* Sportsman of the Year Award along with gymnast Mary Lou Retton.[2]

Edwin Corley Moses, however, proved to be far more than a great athlete. Born August 31, 1955, in Dayton, Ohio, he learned lessons about the value of education from his teacher parents. He eventually embraced individual over team sports, the result of bad experiences such as getting cut from the basketball team and banished from the football team for fighting. Moses took to gymnastics and track. His intellectualism and priorities motivated Moses to eschew the pursuit of an athletic scholarship to accept an academic one to Morehouse College in Atlanta, where he majored in physics and engineering.

Moses still yearned to maximize his talent as a sprinter and hurdler. Morehouse boasted a track team—but no track. He was forced to train at local high schools, working exclusively on the 400 meters and 110-meter hurdles—the 400-meter hurdles would have to wait. Moses earned the nickname "The Bionic Man" for his grueling workouts and scientific approach to running. He competed just once in the 400-meter hurdles before March 1976, but his talent for that event became immediately evident. His nearly ten-foot strides made him a natural. He would blossom quickly into the best in the world.[3]

POINT TOTAL EXPLANATION

Achievements: 31/35

Winning two gold medals and participating in just one event throughout a career does not measure up to the accomplishments of other American greats. But that Moses won 122 consecutive races certainly deserves credit.

They Said It

I don't really see the hurdles. I sense them like a memory.—Edwin Moses

Edwin is so good it isn't even a story anymore, is it, when he wins or sets a record? After all those races he's still almost invisible. Taken for granted. He can be at 75, 80 percent and still beat everybody else. He's gone past the textbooks now. In an art gallery, do we stand around talking about Van Gogh? Extraordinary talent is obvious. We're in the rarefied presence of an immortal here. Edwin's a crowd unto himself.—US Olympic track coach Dr. Leroy Walker

One suspects that he boasted the potential to capture medals in a wide range of Olympic and other international sprint or hurdle competitions. But we'll never know.

Athleticism: 21/25

Moses used his long strides, powerful legs, speed, leaping ability, and balance to become the most dominant intermediate hurdler in history. The event itself requires tremendous athleticism, but Moses simply did not test himself in other endeavors. That costs him a few points here.[4]

Athletic Requirements of the Sport and Event: 16/20

In the case of Moses, there is nothing to differentiate judgment in this category from his own athletic talents. He basically only competed in one event. The athletic skills Moses possessed were required of 400-meter hurdlers. There is little distinction because Moses was simply the best.

Clutch Factor/Mental and Emotional Toughness/ Intangibles: 13/15

Moses was known for combining science with athletics to create a virtually unbeatable machine—at least in one event. He also rose to the occasion time and again in international events. It matters not here that he focused only on the 400-meter hurdles. That he boasted the mental and emotional toughness to win every race is a testament to far more than just his athleticism.

Versatility: 2/5

Let's be generous here. Though Moses participated generally in one event throughout his career, he did play some football and basketball in high school and trained as a gymnast as well.

TOTAL POINTS: 83

95

JACK NICKLAUS: THE GOLDEN BEAR

Golf

The battle to win the hearts and minds of fans as the greatest male golfer ever morphed in the 2000s as Tortoise vs. Hare II. The Golden Bear had been the tortoise. He slowly, steadily won tournaments over a long career. Included were eighteen majors, easily the most in history. The Hare was Tiger Woods, who captured title after title in a comparatively short period of time, then collapsed under the weight of personal issues and sweet swings he simply could not recapture.

The winner? It is generally conceded that Jack Nicklaus is the finest golfer of all time. Nicklaus won seventy-three events during his storied twenty-five-year career, including at least two every year from his rookie season of 1962 until 1978. He peaked about midway through that period, snagging nineteen titles (including four majors) from 1971 to 1973. Nicklaus is one of two golfers to win the career Grand Slam three times. From the 1970 to the 1978 British Open, he was among the top ten finishers in thirty-one of thirty-three majors. It is a feat that might never be matched.[1]

Nicklaus boasted enough physical talent to dominate events and the psychological ability to compete in and even win tournaments when he was not on top of his game. He rarely beat himself. He tempered explosive shot-making and an aggressive approach with conservative, calculated play, particularly in majors. He changed the sport upon his arrival in 1962 with a powerful upright swing that allowed him to tower the ball with a slight fade. He emerged as the most controlled driver and dominating long-iron player in PGA Tour history. His combination of power, control, and technique allowed him to hit precise shots with length off high grass. Nicklaus's strengths as a golfer were ideal in mastering the narrow fairways, deep rough, and fast greens typical of Grand Slam event courses.[2]

They Said It

I never hit a shot, not even in practice, without having a very sharp, in-focus picture of it in my head.—Jack Nicklaus

If I had to have someone putt a 20-footer for everything I own—my house, my cars, my family—I'd want Nicklaus to putt for me.—Golfer Dave Hill

Confidence is the most important single factor in this game, and no matter how great your natural talent, there is only one way to obtain and sustain it: work.—Jack Nicklaus

Though one can never predict such dominance, his early success certainly boded well for his future. Nicklaus was born on January 21, 1940, in Columbus, Ohio. His pharmacist father cultivated his interest in golf and remained an advocate for many years. Nicklaus, who idolized golf superstar Bobby Jones, continued to hone his skills. He proved to be a prodigy, shooting a 51 over nine holes at the challenging Scioto Country Club at age ten.

It was on that course that Nicklaus trained under club pro Jack Grout. Nicklaus won the Ohio Open at age sixteen and the International Jaycee Junior Golf Tournament a year later. He won the US Amateur crowns in 1959 and 1961 while attending Ohio State University, for which he also snagged the NCAA championship. He had already finished second at the 1960 US Open with an amateur-record score of 282, providing a figurative warning to the rest of the golf world that he was on his way.[3]

POINT TOTAL EXPLANATION

Achievements: 33/35

Nicklaus is arguably the greatest golfer of all time, but the shortcomings of the sport itself as an athletic endeavor preclude even the best from earning every point available here. Granted, that is covered in the next category, but no golfer can earn the highest level of athletic achievement in a sport that requires the lowest level of athleticism.

Athleticism: 23/25

Nicklaus boasted the power to blast drives high and deep, the hand-eye coordination to drop chip shots close to the pin, and the body control to nail tough putts. He also thrived as a shooting guard on his high school basketball team and competed in baseball, tennis, and track and field.[4]

Athletic Requirements of the Sport: 8/20

The lack of athleticism needed even to become a champion in golf keeps this score down. Golfers need not be quick or fast. They can be downright fat and win. The reason golfers can still compete well into their forties and even fifties—unlike those in other individual sports—is that the game requires so little athleticism in comparison to, for instance, tennis and track and field.

Clutch Factor/Mental and Emotional Toughness/ Intangibles: 14/15

One can question the physical attributes required of a championship golfer, but not the mental and emotional toughness. And Nicklaus was known for both. He often came roaring from behind to win tournaments. He was among the premier clutch players of all time.

Versatility: 4/5

Many golfers cannot compete in other sports because they simply do not boast the athletic attributes necessary. Nicklaus cannot be counted among them. He played many sports well in his youth and developed a strong tennis game later in life.

TOTAL POINTS: 82

ROGERS HORNSBY: THE RAJAH

Baseball

While Ty Cobb and then Babe Ruth and Lou Gehrig were dominating the American League, stars from the Senior Circuit were receiving less attention. But one player clearly stood out. And that player was Rogers Hornsby of the St. Louis Cardinals.

Like the Yankees superstars, Hornsby thrived upon the launching of the live-ball era. His ability to make consistent hard contact resulted in league-leading totals in doubles four times between 1920 and 1924, with two home run titles and four RBI crowns during that time. But mostly Hornsby just got on base. He led the National League in batting every year from 1920 to 1925 and in on-base percentage nine times from 1920 to 1931. He also paced one and all in slugging percentage nine times. He finished his career among the best of all time in each of those categories. His numbers would have been even more impressive had foot and leg injuries not limited his playing time and destroyed his production starting in his midthirties. His .424 batting average in 1924 remains the best ever in a single season.

Modern analytical data also smiles upon Hornsby historically. He ranked first in WAR among position players eleven times from 1917 to 1929 and is ninth in that category of all time. His career batting average of .358 ranks only behind Ty Cobb, and his on-base percentage of .434 places him eighth in baseball history.[1]

The Cardinals had the foresight to sign Hornsby in 1915. But their radar failed them when they promoted him to player-manager a decade later. Though Hornsby guided his team to the World Series title in 1926, his irascible, overbearing nature rubbed players and owners the wrong way. Like other superstars (such as Ted Williams) who were handed managerial reins, Hornsby grew frustrated trying to improve players with less talent, which included just about everyone. Hornsby managed six teams and never returned to the World Series. He was fired during the season by the New York Giants, Boston Braves, Chicago Cubs, and St. Louis Browns.

But those shortcomings, as well as his early struggles defensively throughout the infield, could not detract from his brilliance as a hitter. Hornsby, who was born on April 27, 1896, on a farm near the tiny town of Winters, Texas, began showing his talent as a small child. His father died when he was a toddler, prompting his mother to move herself and her five kids to her parents' farm near Austin. It was there that Hornsby displayed the courage and conviction to compete against older kids.

Following another move, this time to a growing Fort Worth, he played on a team that often traveled to games in other neighborhoods by trolley. Hornsby became so adept at the sport that he was sometimes inserted into the lineup of a local adult team at the age of ten. Five years later he was playing alongside grown men for the North Side Athletics of the Fort Worth City League and taking offers from other squads that had caught wind of his talents.

Oddly, however, given his struggles afield in the big leagues, his batting lagged at that time. He played both football and baseball at North Side High School but dropped out to take a job that helped support his family. He played baseball whenever given the opportunity, but his skills had stagnated, particularly at the plate. He landed a tryout with the Class B

They Said It

I don't like to sound egotistical but every time I stepped to the plate with a bat in my hands, I couldn't help but feel sorry for the pitcher.—Rogers Hornsby

Son, when you pitch a strike Mr. Hornsby will let you know.—An umpire in response to a rookie pitcher's complaints about the strike zone with Hornsby at the plate

Dallas Steers, but never emerged from the bench before his release two weeks later.

Hornsby was persistent. He landed spots as a shortstop with Class D Hugo and Denison of the Oklahoma League, then found work with Denison. He made 45 errors in 113 games and batted just .232. His career was going nowhere. But he returned to Denison in 1915 and began finding his batting stroke. Despite remaining error-prone, his talent impressed a Cardinals scout. Less than a year after Hornsby's career appeared doomed, he was signed by St. Louis and playing in major-league games. He committed 8 errors in just 18 games and batted .246. But he raised that mark to .313 in 1916 and was destined for one of the greatest careers in baseball history.[2]

POINT TOTAL EXPLANATION

Achievements: 33/35

Hornsby had the offensive numbers to earn a perfect score here, but his issues defensively, struggles at the plate in World Series competition, and fade late in his career preclude it. Still, he was as accomplished and compete a hitter in National League history over his first fifteen seasons.

Athleticism: 22/25

One of the fastest players of his generation, Hornsby didn't maximize that talent as a base stealer. He boasted tremendous hand-eye coordination at the plate, resulting in gap-to-gap and occasionally over-the-fence power, but he lacked range at shortstop and was forced to move to second base early in his career.[3]

Athletic Requirements of the Sport and Position: 15/20

Hornsby played every infield position and a bit in the outfield, but he cannot be credited here because he mostly struggled defensively. Baseball players require the hand-eye coordination Hornsby certainly had, as well as balance and footwork at the plate and in the field. The lack of constant movement or contact makes athletic attributes less wide-ranging for baseball players as opposed to their counterparts who play sports such as football and basketball.

Clutch Factor/Mental and Emotional Toughness/ Intangibles: 10/15

Poor performances in two World Series opportunities limit the total here. Hornsby batted a mere .245 in the 1926 and 1929 Fall Classics, with just two extra-base hits and nary a homer. He was also intensely disliked by those within his organization after taking over as player-manager. Though he was an intense player, Hornsby alienated his teammates.[4]

Versatility: 2/5

Hornsby receives a bit of credit in this category for playing high school football. Athough he was a wonderful all-around hitter, his poor defense made him somewhat of a one-dimensional player.

TOTAL POINTS: 82

97

FLORENCE GRIFFITH JOYNER:
FLO-JO

Track and Field

Florence Griffith lost one individual Olympic race. Unfortunately for her, it was the finals of the 200 meters in 1984. She finished second to fellow American Valerie Brisco-Hooks by nearly a quarter of a second after placing first in all three qualifiers.

The woman they call Flo-Jo had to live with that for four years. And she did not let it happen again at the 1988 Summer Games in Seoul. She participated in both the 100 and 200 and broke the tape first every step of the way. Not only that, but she set Olympic marks in both, then a world record in the latter at 21.34, shaving nearly a second off her 1984 time. She won all eleven races in South Korea in one of the most dominating performances in international track and field history.[1]

What was the difference? Perhaps her marriage to fellow track standout Al Joyner between those events played a role. After all, she had earned a reputation since early that decade for folding in the big races. Then came 1988, when she shattered the world record in the 100 with a clocking of 10.49 at the US Olympic Trials before blitzing the field in Seoul. Not that her career was a complete washout before 1988. She had won the NCAA championship while at UCLA in both the 200 and 400 in 1982 and 1983, respectively.[2]

The woman with the colorful wardrobe was born on December 21, 1959, in the Watts neighborhood of Los Angeles. She was the seventh of eleven children growing up in the housing projects. Young Florence had a flair for life from the start. She held handstand competitions, wheeled herself around on a unicycle, trained a pet rat, and designed unique clothes for her Barbie doll. Her athletic gifts became evident during a trip to the

> ### They Said It
>
> *I've always overworked in the weight room. I love working with weights. I knew they'd give me the strength I needed.*—Florence Griffith Joyner
>
> *We were dazzled by her speed, humbled by her talent and captivated by her style.*—President Bill Clinton

Mojave Desert when her father challenged the kids to try to catch a jack-rabbit. She did just that. By the age of seven she was competing in track and playing football and basketball with her brothers.

Her talents surfaced quickly. She eventually set prep records in sprints and the long jump before helping Cal State Northridge win a national championship in 1978. The financial burdens of college forced her to drop out and take a job as a bank teller, but her brilliance on the cinders motivated UCLA to provide her with a scholarship. Soon she was winning NCAA titles.[3]

After her track career, Flo-Jo was stricken with a seizure disorder and died tragically young at age thirty-eight in 1998. But her Olympic performance a decade earlier will forever live.

POINT TOTAL EXPLANATION

Achievements: 30/35

One incredible Olympic run does not an incredible career make. But Griffith Joyner does deserve credit for breaking Olympic and world records along the way. Most impressive is that her records still stand thirty years later. Her abrupt retirement four months later did not allow her to take the momentum she gained in 1988 and—literally—run with it.

Athleticism: 22/25

Flo-Jo's muscular legs and long strides allowed her to pull away from the pack, especially in 1988. She did not explode off the blocks, but she took over races with her acceleration and power running. Accusations of performance-enhancing-drug use were never justified—she passed all her drug tests. She was just one strong sprinter.[4]

Athletic Requirements of the Sport and Events: 15/20

Griffith Joyner was strictly a sprinter. Though sprinters require quickness, acceleration, and leg strength, their athletic range is not greatly challenged. Many sprinters are also hurdlers and long jumpers—she did not compete in the latter at a national or international level.

Clutch Factor/Mental and Emotional Toughness/ Intangibles: 12/15

The spectrum was wide for Griffith Joyner in this category. She struggled to rise to the occasion before 1988 but ran above and beyond expectations that year. Her score is limited here, but she would not have earned a place in the top 100 at all had she not exploded in Seoul.

Versatility: 2/5

Griffith Joyner expanded her horizons a bit on the track in high school and set records in the long jump. She deserves a couple points for that here.

POINT TOTAL: 81

98

GABBY DOUGLAS:
THE FLYING SQUIRREL

Gymnastics

Arielle Douglas was ten years old when she knew something about her four-year-old sister, Gabby, that their mother did not know: she had already perfected her cartwheel and was incredibly flexible. So Arielle, the oldest sister in the family and the favored go-between, tried to convince her mom that Gabby belonged in a gymnastics class. Little could anyone have imagined that the suggestion would lead to Olympic gold.

It didn't take long between events. Just twelve years after Gabby Douglas began flipping around her first class, she was winning the horse vault, balance beam, and women's individual all-around at the 2012 Summer Games in London. She became the first US gymnast to capture the all-around and team gold in the same Olympics. The kid nicknamed "The Flying Squirrel" for her acrobatics on the uneven bars not only bested Russia's brilliant Viktoria Komova in a spirited battle for the all-around title but emerged as the first African American woman to achieve it. She finished among the top four in every event, placing third in the uneven bars and fourth in the floor exercises.[1]

Despite the amazing triumphs at age sixteen, Douglas considered retiring with the motivation of exploring life as an ordinary teenager—if that was still possible. She finally dismissed those intentions and helped the US team take all-around gold at the 2015 World Championships in Scotland while winning an individual silver medal behind new wunderkind Simone Biles. Douglas struggled a bit at the 2016 Olympics at Rio de Janeiro, losing out on a chance for individual title to teammates Biles and Aly Raisman, but she played a role in another team championship and placed second in the uneven bars.[2]

And to think the path to greatness began with a homeless family living in a van, then a simple cartwheel. Douglas was born on New Year's Eve in 1995, in Newport News, Virginia. She soon became a gymnastics prodigy, motivating Arielle to suggest that she be moved to West Des Moines, Iowa, to train with noted gymnastics coach Liang Chow. The move was initially traumatic for Douglas, who was forced to pack up and travel twelve hundred miles away from home, saying goodbye to her two beloved dogs and her favorite boogie board for riding waves off Virginia Beach.

The unfamiliarity of living with a white couple, Missy and Travis Parton, in Iowa because she could not afford housing and working with a Chinese coach proved a bit frightening for the fourteen-year-old, but it paid huge dividends. Chow had already coached Olympic gold medalist Shawn Johnson and soon transformed Douglas into one as well. Not bad considering five months earlier, US women's national team coordinator Martha Karolyi considered Douglas too unconfident and unfocused to even qualify for the Olympic team.[3]

POINT TOTAL EXPLANATION

Achievements: 27/35

Douglas barely won her gold in 2012 and did not follow with the same level of performance four years later before taking a break from the sport, which clouded her 2020 Olympic status. The all-around title was impressive, but Douglas simply did not achieve enough or perform long enough to earn a higher score here.

They Said It

You just have to not be afraid and go out there and just dominate. You have to go out there and be a beast. Because if you don't, you're not going to be on the top.—Gabby Douglas after winning all-around gold in 2012

God never took something away without filling the hole, without replacing it with something. And for us he just happened to replace it with a 16-year-old black girl.—Missy Parton, who took in Douglas after Parton's mother died

CHAPTER 98

Athleticism: 21/25

That Douglas placed among the top four in every event at the 2012 Games in a sport that requires nearly every athletic talent proves her worth in this category. But again, she needed to prove it beyond London.

Athletic Requirements of the Sport and Events: 18/20

Times have changed in competitive gymnastics. Routines have become cluttered with demanding skills that leave little room for artistry. Floor routines have grown particularly more challenging athletically. All the events require tremendous timing, balance, agility, quickness, and even speed and strength. There are few athletic attributes not required to blossom into an Olympic gymnast.[4]

Clutch Factor/Mental and Emotional Toughness/ Intangibles: 12/15

If Douglas's performance in 2012 was an anomaly, she must be at least credited for rising to the occasion on the biggest international stage. But her consideration of retirement at age twenty, especially considering her subpar performance in the 2016 games, indicates a lack of passion for the sport and competitive spirit. One wonders, after all, why she would not yearn to prove herself an individual champion once again.

Versatility: 3/5

The sport of gymnastics itself challenges versatility. Though Douglas has not proven herself in other athletic endeavors—unless one includes boogie boarding as a kid—her all-around talents as a gymnast earn her a few points in this category.

TOTAL POINTS: 81

99

LYNETTE WOODARD: THE GLOBETROTTER

Basketball

Lynette Woodard was simply born too early. Her basketball talents blossomed, but she had no outlets for them that would result in the fame and fortune they so richly deserved. Sure, she dominated at the University of Kansas and accepted work in Europe. She won Olympic gold in 1984. And she gained notoriety as the first female player with the legendary Harlem Globetrotters. But she was thirty-eight years old when the WNBA launched. She played one season with the Cleveland Rockers and another with the Detroit Shock, but was not exactly in peak form to shine in that spotlight.

It was too bad. After all, Woodard was the best women's basketball player of her generation—it's just that the next generation reaped benefits that she could not. She reached her zenith wearing a Jayhawks uniform. Woodard dominated college competition, scoring 3,649 points in four seasons before the three-point shot was established. She remains the all-time leading scorer in the history of women's college basketball. Woodard also outscored all her male peers who played at Kansas. She tallied nearly 700 more points than Danny Manning, the school's top men's career scorer. He would have required another full season to match Woodard, whose sophomore season was among the best in the history of college sports. She averaged 31 points, 14.3 rebounds, and 5.1 steals per game while shooting 56 percent from the field.[1]

Woodard, who was born in Wichita, Kansas, on August 12, 1959, honed her skills as a youth against male competition. She was introduced to the sport by her older brother and practiced in her bedroom by shooting rolled-up socks. Among her inspirations was cousin Hubie "Geese" Augbie, who performed with the Globetrotters exhibition team for nearly a quarter century. He taught Woodard ballhanding techniques and tricks that would raise the level of her game.

They Said It

Everyone has a gift; you let it take you as far as it can.—Lynette Woodard

She's one of the all-time greatest athletes in women's sports. I'm not sure there are any greater advocates than guys . . . who played against her. —*Kansas City Star* sportswriter Mechelle Voepel

She used those talents to thrive at Wichita North High School. Though she generally played forward, she boasted the skills to dominate at any position. Her aggressive style and prolific scoring played the most significant role in her team's winning two state championships. She earned All-American status as a highly recruited senior. Her desire to remain close to home motivated her to enroll at Kansas.[2]

The 1980 US boycott of the Moscow Games destroyed an opportunity for Woodard to display her talents at an international level. She led an Italian league in scoring in 1982, but that brought little attention and frustrating struggles with the language. She helped the US team capture a gold medal at the 1983 Pan American Games in Venezuela, then finally got her chance to fulfill an Olympic dream in 1984. She helped the US team win easily, but a Soviet Bloc boycott in Los Angeles put a damper on the accomplishment.[3]

The Globetrotters honored Woodard by inviting her to be their first female player. Performing with a team known not just for its clowning but also for its ballhandling allowed her to display and improve her already immense talents in that area of her game. She played with the legendary group extensively for two years for returning to play in Italy, then Japan, before retirement. The WNBA came calling in 1997 and Woodard answered. But her contributions were minimal as she approached age forty.[4]

POINT TOTAL EXPLANATION

Achievements: 29/35

Woodard might have earned every point available here had she continued to perform at the same level as she did during her peak years at Kansas. She averaged just 10.5 points and 4 rebounds per game in the 1984 Olympics, and not against premier competition otherwise internationally. Woodard was a victim of timing—she might have dominated the WNBA had it existed in her prime.[5]

Athleticism: 21/25

Woodard did not possess one or two standout athletic attributes; it was her all-around talent that allowed her to dominate early in her career. She boasted enough quickness to lose defenders with her ballhandling and a vertical leap that allowed her to yank down rebounds despite playing the small forward and guard positions. She had no flaws in her game fundamentally, but that is not was this category is all about.

Athletic Requirements of the Sport and Position: 16/20

The comparatively low level of competition Woodard faced playing professionally prevents her from receiving a great score in this category. Women's basketball does not require the same level of physicality as the men's game, especially comparing premier college programs and the NBA to the WNBA, which plays shorter games and a much shorter schedule. But Woodard had a long career, which counts for something here.

Clutch Factor/Mental and Emotional Toughness/ Intangibles: 12/15

Woodard was thoroughly outplayed by Cheryl Miller at the 1984 Olympics, the only international spotlight competition in which she participated. She had one of the worst shooting percentages on the team and shot poorly from the line as well.[6]

Versatility: 2/5

Woodard did not play in an era that encouraged versatility from its female athletes. But she was versatile enough as a basketball player to earn a couple points here.

TOTAL POINTS: 80

ELDRICK WOODS: TIGER

Golf

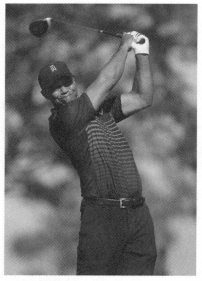

Tiger Woods. © Orlando Ramirez–USA
TODAY Sports

First things first. Tiger Woods played golf. The lack of athleticism required to compete in that sport precludes a high ranking. The good news is that he embarked on a stretch of dominance arguably unmatched in individual sports history that lasted about a decade. The bad news is that, aside from one short stretch thereafter, his personal demons, and to some extent a back problem, caused a complete collapse.

Woods won tournaments as a matter of course—pun intended—an amazing feat given the sheer amount of competition. He won thirty-two of ninety-six—one-third of the events in which he participated—from 1999 to 2003. He proved even more dominant from 2005 to 2009, snagging thirty-one of seventy-five potential championships. He mastered the four majors to such an extent during those eleven years that he seemed destined to overtake Jack Nicklaus as the greatest golfer and big-tournament player of all-time. His fourteen major triumphs all occurred between 1997 and 2008, and they were spread equally. He won the Masters and PGA Championship four times each and the British Open and US Open three times apiece.[1]

The greatness of Woods had served as motivation for African Americans to take up a sport that had rarely attracted them and had, at least at the country club level, often historically excluded them. Simply put, Woods was a phenomenon.

Then came the roller coaster ride. The sex scandals. The divorce. A short rebound that shot him back to number one in the world. Then the back surgery. And, finally, the collapse. Woods dropped out of the top 100 in March 2015, fell from the top 500 a year later, and was ranked 1,005 in July 2017. The implosion was stunning given that he had spent a record 683 weeks as the top-rated player in the sport.[2]

It was all quite shocking for fans who remembered the two-year-old toddler who accompanied his father, Earl, to slam drives down a pretend fairway and putt with Bob Hope on the nationally televised *Mike Douglas Show*. Born Eldrick Woods in Cypress, California, on December 30, 1975, Woods had a club in his hand at nine months, shot 50 over nine holes at age three, and dropped in his first hole in one three years later. Though he later stated that his childhood was a normal one—replete with trips to the mall, addiction to TV wrestling, and rap music—such was certainly not the case given the amount of time he spent on the golf course beating the heck out of the competition. He received subliminal psychological training

They Said It

I love to play golf and that's my arena. And you can characterize it and describe it however you want, but I have a love and a passion for getting that ball in the hole and beating those guys.—Tiger Woods

Nobody could drive it like him, nobody could hit long irons like him, or the wedges and the putter. There wasn't anybody ever who was that good in every department. And then he'd believe he was better prepared for Thursday than anyone else, and it became a pattern.—Golf World writer Jaime Diaz

I stopped living according to my core values. I knew what I was doing was wrong but thought only about myself and thought I could get away with whatever I wanted to.—Tiger Woods

through a series of tapes that reminded him to focus and believe in himself. Rather than resent such methods, Woods embraced them. He played the tapes while swinging a club in front of a mirror or putting on the carpet.

Woods won his first tournament at age ten and had won all thirty junior events in which he played by the next year. He continued to dominate, earning the United States Golf Association National Junior Amateur Championship in 1987, becoming the youngest PGA tournament participant in 1992, and turning pro in August 1996.

He had by then established himself as, well, a tiger on the course. He gained a reputation as an incredible clutch player, slamming tremendous drives, accurate chips, and long-distance putts with titles on the line. His brilliance translated into greatness at Stanford University, where he was voted Pac-10 Player of the Year and was a first-team All-American. Soon he would be burning up the courses on the PGA Tour.

POINT TOTAL EXPLANATION

Achievements: 33/35

Woods would have been worthy of 40 points in this category had he maintained the pace he established from 1999 to 2009. But he loses a couple points because of his epic collapse. Until then, however, he was easily the most accomplished golfer ever.

Athleticism: 20/25

Woods played other sports during his youth, displaying a level of athleticism and array of athletic attributes not required on the golf course. He did possess the power to blast drives, the flexibility to hit wide-ranging shots with accuracy, and tremendous hand-eye coordination.

Athletic Requirements of the Sport: 8/20

A panel of sports scientists and other experts once ranked the most athletically demanding sports based on many components, including endurance, speed, durability, and agility. Boxing, hockey, football, and basketball were rated the top four. Golf was ranked 51 of 60, behind table tennis and horse racing and ahead of fishing and roller skating. Point made about the eight points here.[3]

Clutch Factor/Mental and Emotional Toughness/ Intangibles: 14/15

This is a tough one. No golfer ever displayed the mental and emotional toughness of Tiger Woods on the course during his long peak. His performances with championships hanging in the balance are legendary. But his inability to overcome his personal problems and return to prominence as a golfer costs him a point in this category.

Versatility: 3/5

Woods boasted some talent in other sports growing up, including baseball, basketball, football, and track. His golfing greatness precluded him from greatly exploring his abilities in those sports, but he gets some credit for that here.

TOTAL POINTS: 78

NOTES

Chapter 1

1. The Official Website of Jim Thorpe, https://www.cmgww.com/sports/thorpe/biography.

2. Ibid.

3. "Jim Thorpe," Baseball Reference, https://www.baseball-reference.com/players/t/thorpji01.shtml.

4. "Jim Thorpe," Sports Reference: Olympic Sports, https://www.sports-reference.com/olympics/athletes/th/jim-thorpe-1.html.

Chapter 2

1. "Michael Jordan," Basketball Reference, https://www.basketball-reference.com/players/j/jordami01.html.

2. "NBA Encyclopedia: Michael Jordan," NBA.com, http://www.nba.com/history/players/jordan_bio.html.

3. "How Many Has Michael Made?" Michael Jordan Career Retrospective, NBA.com, http://www.nba.com/jordan/game_winners.html.

4. "Michael Jordan," Basketball Reference.

5. "NBA Encyclopedia: Michael Jordan," NBA.com.

Chapter 3

1. Frank Litsky, "Bob Mathias, 75, Decathlete and Politician, Dies," *New York Times*, September 3, 2006, http://www.nytimes.com/2006/09/03/sports/othersports/03mathias.html.

2. "Bob Mathias," Sports Reference: Olympic Sports, https://www.sports-reference.com/olympics/athletes/ma/bob-mathias-1.html.

3. Frank Litsky, "Bob Mathias, 75, Decathlete and Politician, Dies."

4. "Bob Mathias," California Sports Hall of Fame, http://californiasportshalloffame.org/inductees/bob-mathias.

Chapter 4

1. Larry Schwartz, "Jim Brown Was Hard to Bring Down," ESPN Classic, http://www.espn.com/classic/biography/s/Brown_Jim.html.

2. Marty Gitlin, *Jim Brown: Football Great & Actor* (North Mankato, MN: ABDO, 2014), 48.

3. "Jim Brown," Pro Football Reference, https://www.pro-football-reference .com/players/B/BrowJi00.htm.

4. Tim Layden, "Why Jim Brown Matters," *Sports Illustrated*, October 6, 2015, https://www.si.com/mmqb/2015/09/28/jim-brown-cleveland-browns-hall-of-fame -nfl-greatness.

5. "Jim Brown," Syracuse University Basketball Player Index, http://www .orangehoops.org/jbrown.htm.

Chapter 5

1. "Michael Phelps," Swim Swam, https://swimswam.com/bio/michael-phelps.

2. Ibid.

3. Ibid.

Chapter 6

1. Max Mann, "Deion Sanders: Best Corner Ever? What about Best Player Ever?" Bleacher Report, April 15, 2008, http://bleacherreport.com/articles/17936 -deion-sanders-best-corner-ever-what-about-best-player-ever.

2. "Deion Sanders," Baseball Reference, https://www.baseball-reference.com/ players/s/sandede02.shtml.

3. "Deion Sanders—Biography," Deion-Sanders.com, http://www.deion-sanders .com/bio.html.

4. "Deion Sanders," Pro Football Reference, https://www.pro-football-reference .com/players/S/SandDe00.htm.

Chapter 8

1. "Jackie Joyner-Kersee," Sports Reference: Olympic Sports, https://www .sports-reference.com/olympics/athletes/jo/jackie-joyner-kersee-1.html.

2. "Kersee, Jackie Joyner," Learning to Give, https://www.learningtogive.org/ resources/kersee-jackie-joyner.

3. Joe Morgenstern, "Worldbeater: Olympic Athlete Jackie Joyner-Kersee," *New York Times*, July 31, 1988, http://www.nytimes.com/1988/07/31/magazine/ worldbeater-olympic-athlete-jackie-joyner-kersee.html.

4. "Jackie Joyner-Kersee," USA Track and Field, https://www.usatf.org/HallOf Fame/TF/showBio.asp?HOFIDs=201.

Chapter 9

1. John Krich and Mike Chinoy, "The Most Unusual Friendship in Olympic History," OZY, August 5, 2016, http://www.ozy.com/flashback/the-most-unusual-friendship-in-olympic-history/70663.

2. "Rafer Johnson," Sports Reference: Olympic Sports, https://www.sports-reference.com/olympics/athletes/jo/rafer-johnson-1.html.

3. "Rafer Johnson—Standout Athlete," JRank.org, http://sports.jrank.org/pages/2339/Johnson-Rafer-Standout-Athlete.html.

Chapter 10

1. "Muhammad Ali, American (1942–2016)," RoGallery, http://rogallery.com/Ali_Muhammad/ali_bio.htm.

2. Norman Mailer, "Ego," *Life*, March 19, 1971, https://books.google.com/books?id=iVMEAAAAMBAJ&pg=PA19-IA15#v=onepage&q&f=false.

3. "Muhammad Ali," Boxing Record, http://boxrec.com/en/boxer/180.

Chapter 11

1. John Saccoman, "Willie Mays," Society for American Baseball Research, https://sabr.org/bioproj/person/64f5dfa2.

2. "Willie Mays," Baseball Reference, https://www.baseball-reference.com/players/m/mayswi01.shtml.

3. "Alex Rodriguez Speaks about His Regrets (a Few) and Willie Mays (the Greatest Ever)," *New York Times*, May 2, 2015, https://www.nytimes.com/2015/05/02/sports/baseball/alex-rodriguez-speaks-of-his-regrets-a-few-and-willie-mays-the-greatest-ever.html.

4. Craig Muder, "Mays Honored as Top Player of 1960s by *Sporting News*," Baseball Hall of Fame, https://baseballhall.org/discover/inside-pitch/mays-honored-as-top-player-of-1960s.

Chapter 12

1. "Babe Ruth," Baseball Reference, https://www.baseball-reference.com/players/r/ruthba01.shtml.

2. Allan Wood, "Babe Ruth," Society of Baseball Research, http://sabr.org/bioproj/person/9dcdd01c.

3. "Babe Ruth," Baseball Reference.

4. Ibid.

Chapter 13

1. Kevin Max, "The Story of Ashton Eaton, the World's Greatest Athlete," *1859 Oregon's Magazine*, April 2, 2015, https://1859oregonmagazine.com/think-oregon/art-culture/oregon-olympic-athlete-ashton-eaton.

2. "Ashton Eaton," Sports Reference: Olympic Sports, https://www.sports-reference.com/olympics/athletes/ea/ashton-eaton-1.html.

3. Max, "The Story of Ashton Eaton."

4. "Ashton Eaton," Sports Reference: Olympic Sports.

5. Max, "The Story of Ashton Eaton."

Chapter 14

1. Larry Schwartz, "Didrikson Was a Woman Ahead of Her Time," ESPN Classic, https://www.espn.com/sportscentury/features/00014147.html.

2. "Babe Didrikson," Sports Reference: Olympic Sports, https://www.sports-reference.com/olympics/athletes/di/babe-didrikson-1.html.

Chapter 15

1. Steve Smith, "Greatness Revisited: Why Wilt Chamberlain Was the Greatest NBA Player Ever," Bleacher Report, February 26, 2009, http://bleacherreport.com/articles/130817-greatness-revisited-why-wilt-chamberlain-is-the-greatest-nba-player-ever.

2. "Wilt Chamberlain," Basketball Reference, https://www.basketball-reference.com/players/c/chambwi01.html.

3. "Chamberlain's Dominance over Russell: A Head-to-Head Statistical Analysis," NBA Stats Lab, September 30, 2017, http://nbastatslab.com/index.php/2017/09/30/chamberlain-russell-player-comparison.

4. "Wilt Chamberlain Bio," NBA Encyclopedia, http://www.nba.com/history/players/chamberlain_bio.html.

5. Bryn Swartz, "The Greatest NBA Player of All-Time: Michael Jordan or Wilt Chamberlain?" Bleacher Report, October 13, 2008, http://bleacherreport.com/articles/68568.

Chapter 16

1. "Jackie Robinson," Baseball Reference, https://www.baseball-reference.com/players/r/robinja02.shtml.

2. "Biography," Jackie Robinson—The Official Licensing Website of Jackie Robinson, https://www.jackierobinson.com/biography.

3. Neil Paine, "Advanced Stats Love Jackie Robinson," FiveThirtyEight, April 16, 2014. https://fivethirtyeight.com/features/advanced-stats-love-jackie-robinson.

4. "Jackie Robinson," Baseball Reference.

Chapter 17

1. "Rickey Henderson," Baseball Reference, https://www.baseball-reference.com/players/h/henderi01.shtml.

2. Joseph Wancho, "Rickey Henderson," Society for American Baseball Research, https://sabr.org/bioproj/person/957d4da0.

3. "Rickey Henderson," Baseball Reference.

Chapter 18

1. "Bo Jackson," Pro Football Reference, https://www.pro-football-reference.com/players/J/JackBo00.htm.

2. "Bo Jackson," Baseball Reference, https://www.baseball-reference.com/players/split.fcgi?id=jacksbo01&year=Career&t=b.

3. Ron Flatter, "Bo Knows Stardom and Disappointment," ESPN Classic, http://www.espn.com/classic/jackson_bo.html.

4. Chad Scott, "Bo Jackson's Game-by-Game Auburn Football Stats," Gridiron Now, June 22, 2015, http://gridironnow.com/bo-jacksons-game-by-game-auburn-football-stats.

Chapter 19

1. "The Legendary Jesse Owens," Big Ten, February 1, 2009, http://www.bigten.org/genrel/013007aai.html.

2. Frank Litsky, "On This Day: Jesse Owens Dies of Cancer at 66; Hero of the 1936 Berlin Olympics," *New York Times*, April 1, 1980, http://www.nytimes.com/learning/general/onthisday/bday/0912.html.

Chapter 20

1. Jen Christensen, "Besting Ruth, Beating Hate: How Hank Aaron Made Baseball History," CNN, http://www.cnn.com/interactive/2014/04/us/hank-aaron-anniversary.

2. "Hank Aaron," Baseball Reference, https://www.baseball-reference.com/players/a/aaronha01.shtml.

3. "Hank Aaron Biography," ESPN, http://www.espn.com/mlb/player/bio/_/id/17499/hank-aaron.

4. "Hank Aaron," Baseball Reference.

5. Ibid.

Chapter 21

1. 2017 Super Bowl Play-by-Play, ESPN, http://www.espn.com/nfl/playbyplay?gameId=400927752.

2. Rich Cimini, "Story of a Boy Named Tom Brady," *New York Daily News*, January 25, 2008, http://www.nydailynews.com/sports/football/giants/story-boy-named-tom-brady-article-1.341686.

3. "Tom Brady," Pro Football Reference, https://www.pro-football-reference.com/players/B/BradTo00.htm.

4. Ibid.

Chapter 22

1. "Lawrence Taylor," Pro Football Reference, https://www.pro-football -reference.com/players/T/TaylLa00.htm.
2. David Whitley, "LT. Was Reckless, Magnificent," ESPN, https://www.espn .com/sportscentury/features/00016487.html.
3. "Lawrence Taylor," Pro Football Hall of Fame, http://www.profootballhof .com/players/lawrence-taylor/biography.

Chapter 23

1. "Carl Lewis Wins Dramatic Long Jump—1996 Atlanta Olympics," YouTube, March 1, 2010, https://www.youtube.com/watch?v=JuD1OdoXe9Q.
2. "Carl Lewis," Sports Reference: Olympic Sports, https://www.sports -reference.com/olympics/athletes/le/carl-lewis-1.html.
3. Sarah Pileggi, "Going to Great Lengths," *Sports Illustrated*, June 1, 1981, https://www.si.com/vault/1981/06/01/825675/going-to-great-lengths-long-jumping -is-a-family-affair-for-carl-lewis-the-world-indoor-record-holder-and-sister-carol -who-has-the-us-girls-junior-mark.
4. "Carl Lewis," Houston Cougars, http://www.uhcougars.com/sports/c-track/ mtt/carl_lewis_866793.html.
5. "Carl Lewis," Sports Reference: Olympic Sports.

Chapter 24

1. "Reggie White," Pro Football Reference, https://www.pro-football-reference .com/players/W/WhitRe00.htm.
2. "Reggie White Biography," JRank.org, http://biography.jrank.org/pages/2548/ White-Reggie.html.
3. Ibid.
4. "Reggie White," Pro Football Reference.
5. Robert Mays, "The Signature Moves of the NFL's Best Pass Rushers," The Ringer, August 25, 2017, https://www.theringer.com/nfl/2017/8/25/16202270/ pass-rushing-signature-moves.
6. "Reggie White," Pro Football Reference.

Chapter 25

1. "Bruce Jenner," Sports Reference: Olympic Sports, https://www.sports -reference.com/olympics/athletes/je/bruce-jenner-1.html.
2. Sean Dooley, Margaret Dawson, Lana Zak, Christina Ng, Lauren Effron, and Meghan Keneally, "Bruce Jenner's Journey through the Years," ABC News, April 24, 2015, http://abcnews.go.com/Entertainment/bruce-jenners-journey -years/story?id=30571195.
3. "Bruce Jenner," Sports Reference: Olympic Sports.

Chapter 26

1. "Ray Robinson," Boxing Record, http://boxrec.com/en/boxer/9625.
2. Ron Flatter, "The Sugar in the Sweet Science," ESPN, https://www.espn.com/sportscentury/features/00016439.html.
3. Lee Wylie, "The Technical Breakdown: Sugar Ray Robinson," The Sweet Science, October 30, 2012, http://www.thesweetscience.com/feature-articles/15497-the-technical-breakdown-sugar-ray-robinson.
4. Ibid.

Chapter 27

1. "Don Hutson," Pro Football Reference, https://www.pro-football-reference.com/players/H/HutsDo00.htm.
2. "Don Hutson," Daily Dose, December 2, 2016, http://dailydsports.com/don-hutson.
3. "Don Hutson," Pro Football Reference.
4. Bryn Swartz, "Why Jerry Rice Is NOT the Greatest Wide Receiver in NFL History," Bleacher Report, March 24, 2009, http://bleacherreport.com/articles/143974-why-jerry-rice-is-not-the-greatest-wide-receiver-in-nfl-history.
5. "Don Hutson," Daily Dose.

Chapter 28

1. Frank Litsky, "Bob Hayes, Stellar Sprinter and Receiver, Is Dead at 59," *New York Times*, September 20, 2002, http://www.nytimes.com/2002/09/20/sports/bob-hayes-stellar-sprinter-and-receiver-is-dead-at-59.html.
2. Ibid.
3. "Bob Hayes," Pro Football Reference, https://www.pro-football-reference.com/players/H/HayeBo00.htm.
4. Litsky, "Bob Hayes."

Chapter 29

1. "Bill Russell," Basketball Reference, https://www.basketball-reference.com/players/r/russebi01.html.
2. "Bill Russell Bio," NBA.com, http://www.nba.com/history/players/russell_bio.html.

Chapter 30

1. Chris Young, "The 'Fearsome Foursome' of the Los Angeles Rams," Bleacher Report, July 25, 2010, http://bleacherreport.com/articles/424715-the-fearsome-foursome-of-the-los-angeles-rams.

2. Keith Thursby, "David 'Deacon' Jones Dies at 74; Fearsome L.A. Rams Lineman," *Los Angeles Times*, June 3, 2013, http://www.latimes.com/local/obituaries/la-me-0604-deacon-jones-20130604-story.html.

3. Ibid.

4. Ibid.

Chapter 31

1. "Sandy Koufax," Baseball Reference, https://www.baseball-reference.com/players/k/koufasa01.shtml.

2. Marc Z. Aaron, "Sandy Koufax," Society for American Baseball Research, http://sabr.org/bioproj/person/e463317c.

3. Gregory Orfalea, "The Incomparable Career of Sandy Koufax," *Atlantic*, October 6, 2016, https://www.theatlantic.com/entertainment/archive/2016/10/sandy-koufax/503036.

4. "Sandy Koufax," Baseball Reference.

Chapter 32

1. James Lincoln Ray, "Mickey Mantle," Society for American Baseball Research, https://sabr.org/bioproj/person/61e4590a.

2. "Mickey Mantle," Baseball Reference, https://www.baseball-reference.com/players/m/mantlmi01.shtml.

3. Ray, "Mickey Mantle."

4. "Mickey Mantle," Baseball Reference.

Chapter 33

1. Andrew Heisel, "The Plot to Kill the Slam Dunk," Vice Sports, February 12, 2015, https://sports.vice.com/en_us/article/xyj9gk/the-plot-to-kill-the-slam-dunk.

2. "Kareem Abdul-Jabbar," Pro Basketball Reference, https://www.basketball-reference.com/players/a/abdulka01.html.

3. "Kareem Abdul-Jabbar Bio," NBA.com, http://www.nba.com/history/players/abduljabbar_bio.html.

4. "Kareem Abdul-Jabbar," Pro Basketball Reference.

5. Ibid.

Chapter 34

1. "Lou Gehrig," Baseball Reference, https://www.baseball-reference.com/players/g/gehrilo01.shtml.

2. James Lincoln Ray, "Lou Gehrig," Society for American Baseball Research, https://sabr.org/bioproj/person/ccdffd4c.

Chapter 35

1. "Emlen Tunnell Bio," Pro Football Hall of Fame, http://www.profootballhof.com/players/emlen-tunnell/biography.

2. Bob Carroll, "Emlen Tunnell: A Giant of Defense," *Coffin Corner* 16, no. 5 (1994), http://www.profootballresearchers.org/archives/Website_Files/Coffin_Corner/16–05–578.pdf.

3. Mark E. Dixon, "Emlen Tunnell: NFL Hall of Famer and All-Around Nice Guy," January 2010, *MainLine Today*, http://www.mainlinetoday.com/Main-Line-Today/January-2012/Emlen-Tunnell-NFL-Hall-of-Famer-and-All-Around-Nice-Guy.

4. Carroll, "Emlen Tunnell."

Chapter 36

1. "Jerry West," NBA Encyclopedia, http://www.nba.com/history/players/west_bio.html.

2. "Jerry West," Basketball Reference, https://www.basketball-reference.com/players/w/westje01.html.

3. "Jerry West," NBA Encyclopedia.

4. stephanieg, post #1, "Jerry West Was More Athletic than Kobe Bryant?" Inside Hoops message board, http://www.insidehoops.com/forum/showthread.php?t=108115.

5. "Jerry West," Basketball Reference.

Chapter 37

1. "Anthony Munoz," Pro Football Reference, https://www.pro-football-reference.com/players/M/MunoAn00.htm.

2. "Anthony Munoz," USC Legends, https://web.archive.org/web/20060629053637/http://www.usclegends.org/anthony-munoz.php.

3. "Anthony Munoz: 1958," JRank.org, http://biography.jrank.org/pages/3408/Munoz-Anthony-1958-Former-Professional-Football-Player-Young-Athlete.html.

4. Jay Greenberg, "The King of the Block," *Sports Illustrated*, September 10, 1990, https://www.si.com/vault/1990/09/10/122617/the-king-of-the-block-anthony-munoz-sets-a-standard-for-linemen-on-and-off-the-field.

5. "Anthony Munoz," Pro Football Hall of Fame, http://www.profootballhof.com/players/anthony-munoz/biography.

Chapter 38

1. Paul Dickson, "The Importance of Oscar Charleston," The National Pastime Museum, July 20, 2014, https://www.thenationalpastimemuseum.com/article/importance-oscar-charleston.

2. "Oscar Charleston," Baseball Reference, https://www.baseball-reference.com/register/player.fcgi?id=charle001osc.

3. Dickson, "The Importance of Oscar Charleston."

4. John Schulian, "Was Ty Cobb the White Oscar Charleston?" Daily Beast, April 6, 2015, https://www.thedailybeast.com/was-ty-cobb-the-white-oscar-charleston.

5. Dickson, "The Importance of Oscar Charleston."

Chapter 39

1. "Top 10 Finals Moments: Magic Johnson Steps in at Center in 1980," NBA.com, May 17, 2017, http://www.nba.com/top-nba-finals-moments-magic-johnson-center-game-6-1980-finals.

2. "Magic Johnson," Basketball Reference, https://www.basketball-reference.com/players/j/johnsma02.html.

3. "Magic Johnson Bio," NBA.com, http://www.nba.com/history/players/johnsonm_bio.html.

4. "Magic Johnson," Basketball Reference.

5. Ibid.

Chapter 40

1. Deane McGowen, "Joe Louis, 66, Heavyweight King Who Reigned 12 Years, Is Dead," *New York Times*, April 13, 1981, http://www.nytimes.com/learning/general/onthisday/bday/0513.html.

2. "Biography: Joe Louis," CMG Worldwide, https://www.cmgww.com/sports/louis/biography.

3. "Joe Louis," Boxing Record, http://boxrec.com/en/boxer/9027.

Chapter 41

1. "Kobe Bryant," Basketball Reference, https://www.basketball-reference.com/players/b/bryanko01.html.

2. "Kobe Bryant Bio," NBA.com, https://web.archive.org/web/20100306020711/http://www.nba.com/playerfile/kobe_bryant/bio.html.

3. Hadarii Jones, "Kobe Bryant vs. LeBron James: The Difference between Skill and Ability," Bleacher Report, October 27, 2011, http://bleacherreport.com/articles/912726-kobe-bryant-vs-lebron-james-the-difference-between-skill-and-ability.

Chapter 42

1. "Serena Williams," WTA Tennis, http://www.wtatennis.com/players/player/230234/TITLE/SERENA-WILLIAMs.

2. "Serena Williams Biography and Detailed Game Analysis," Online Tennis Instruction, http://www.onlinetennisinstruction.com/serenawilliamsbiography.html.

3. Ibid.

4. "Serena Williams," WTA Tennis.

5. Ibid.

Chapter 43

1. Ben Tracy, "Rare Honus Wagner Baseball Card Found in Attic," CBS News, July 11, 2012, https://www.cbsnews.com/news/rare-honus-wagner-baseball-card-found-in-attic.

2. "Honus Wagner," Baseball Reference, https://www.baseball-reference.com/players/w/wagneho01.shtml.

3. Ibid.

4. Jan Finkel, "Honus Wagner," Society for American Baseball Research, http://sabr.org/bioproj/person/30b27632.

5. "Honus Wagner," Baseball Reference.

Chapter 44

1. Patrick Redford, "36 Years Ago Today, Dr. J Scored the Coolest Basket in NBA History," Deadspin, May 11, 2016, https://deadspin.com/36-years-ago-today-dr-j-scored-the-coolest-basket-in-1776166859.

2. "Julius Erving," Basketball Reference, https://www.basketball-reference.com/players/e/ervinju01.html.

3. "Julius Erving," Academy of Achievement, http://www.achievement.org/achiever/julius-erving.

Chapter 45

1. "Gale Sayers," Pro Football Reference, https://www.sports-reference.com/cfb/players/gale-sayers-1.html.

2. "Brian's Song," Home of Heroes, http://www.homeofheroes.com/DG/07d_brian.html.

3. M. B. Roberts, "Fame Couldn't Wait for Sayers," ESPN, https://www.espn.com/sportscentury/features/00016460.html.

Chapter 46

1. "U.S. Star Wambach Breaks Hamm's World Scoring Record," CNN, June 21, 2013, https://edition.cnn.com/2013/06/21/sport/football/abby-wambach-hamm-record-football/index.html.

2. Bryan Armen Graham, "Abby Wambach, World's All-Time Leading Goalscorer, Announces Retirement," *Guardian* [UK], October 27, 2015, https://www.theguardian.com/football/2015/oct/27/abby-wambach-worlds-all-time-leading-goalscorer-announces-retirement.

3. "Abby Wambach," Biography, https://www.biography.com/people/abby-wambach-21331043.

4. "Bracket Challenge Round 2: Babe Didrikson Zaharias or Abby Wambach?" ESPNW, http://www.espn.com/espnw/news-commentary/debate/13506647/babe-didrikson-zaharias-abby-wambach.

5. Ibid.

Chapter 47

1. "Jerry Rice," Pro Football Reference, https://www.pro-football-reference.com/players/R/RiceJe00.htm; "Jerry Rice Game Log," Pro Football Reference, https://www.pro-football-reference.com/players/R/RiceJe00/gamelog/post.

2. Sam Gardner, "Jerry Rice, Mississippi Valley Lit Up Scoreboards 30 Years Ago," Fox Sports, October 21, 2014, https://www.foxsports.com/college-football/story/jerry-rice-mississippi-valley-lit-up-scoreboards-30-years-ago-102114.

3. Ibid.

4. "Jerry Rice," Pro Football Reference.

5. Mike Sando, "The Case for Rice as the Greatest Ever," ESPN, February 4, 2010, http://www.espn.com/blog/nfcwest/post/_/id/13874/the-case-for-rice-as-the-greatest-ever.

6. "Jerry Rice Game Log," Pro Football Reference.

Chapter 48

1. Vince Barr, "Pete Sampras: Best of All Time?" Tennis Server, http://www.tennisserver.com/wildcards/wildcards_03_11.html.

2. "Pete Sampras Biography," Online Tennis Instruction, http://www.onlinetennisinstruction.com/petesamprasbiography.html.

3. "Pete Sampras Bio," ATP World Tour, http://www.atpworldtour.com/en/players/pete-sampras/s402/bio.

4. Barr, "Pete Sampras."

Chapter 49

1. "Eric Heiden," Sports Reference: Olympic Sports, https://www.sports-reference.com/olympics/athletes/he/eric-heiden-1.html.

2. Larry Schwartz," Eric Heiden Was a Reluctant Hero," ESPN, https://www.espn.com/sportscentury/features/00014225.html.

Chapter 50

1. "Shaun White," ESPN: XGames, http://xgames.espn.com/xgames/athletes/3014000/shaun-white.

2. "Shaun White Pulls Armadillo in Portland Dew Tour," YouTube, August 15, 2010, https://www.youtube.com/watch?v=PssQ-ZAbeU8.

3. Graham Bell, "Shaun White, the Man Who Made Snowboarding Cool," *Telegraph* [UK], November 23, 2016, http://www.telegraph.co.uk/travel/ski/interviews/graham-bell-interviews-snowboard-legend-shaun-white.

4. Yi-Ywn Yen, "Double Ripper," *Sports Illustrated*, July 7, 2003, https://www.si.com/vault/2003/07/07/345870/double-ripper-at-16-shaun-white-rules-snowboarding-now-the-red-hot-redhead-is-launching-himself-into-big-time-skateboarding-too.

Chapter 51

1. "Simone Biles," Olympic.org, https://www.olympic.org/simone-biles.

2. "Simone Biles," USA Gymnastics, https://usagym.org/pages/athletes/athleteListDetail.html?id=164887.

3. Ibid.

4. Julia Grassie, "Who Is . . . Simone Biles," NBC, http://www.nbcolympics.com/news/who-simone-biles.

Chapter 52

1. "Stan Musial," Baseball Reference, https://www.baseball-reference.com/players/m/musiast01.shtml.

2. Jan Finkel, "Stan Musial," Society for American Baseball Research, https://sabr.org/bioproj/person/2142e2e5.

3. "Stan Musial," Baseball Reference.

Chapter 53

1. "Willie Pep," *Guardian* [UK], December 2, 2006, https://www.theguardian.com/news/2006/dec/02/guardianobituaries.boxing.

2. "Willie Pep," Boxing Record, http://boxrec.com/en/boxer/43.

3. "Willie Pep," *Telegraph* [UK], November 30, 2006, http://www.telegraph.co.uk/news/obituaries/1535533/Willie-Pep.html.

4. Jeremiah Preisser, "Part One: The Greatest Defensive Fighters Ever—Willie Pep," Grueling Truth, July 8, 2016, http://thegruelingtruth.net/boxing/greatest-defensive-fighters-ever-part-one-willie-pep.

Chapter 54

1. "Walter Payton," Pro Football Reference, https://www.pro-football-reference.com/players/P/PaytWa00.htm.

2. Ron Taylor, "Walter Payton, Bears RB, 1975–1987," Chicago Bears History, 2002, http://www.bearshistory.com/lore/walterpayton.aspx.

3. "Walter Payton," Pro Football Reference.

4. Ibid.

Chapter 55

1. Eoghan Macguire, "Althea Gibson: The 'She-ro' Who Inspired Tennis to Change," CNN, September 2, 2014, http://edition.cnn.com/2014/09/02/sport/tennis/us-open-althea-gibson-tennis/index.html.

2. Fritz Knapp, *Althea Gibson: Perseverance* (Chicago: Price World, 2012).

3. Macguire, "Althea Gibson."

Chapter 56

1. "Henry Armstrong," Boxing Record, http://boxrec.com/en/boxer/9018.

2. Larry Schwartz, "He Was 'Homicide Hank' for a Reason," ESPN, https://www.espn.com/sportscentury/features/00014077.html.

3. Ibid.

4. John Heinis, "Manny Pacquiao vs. Henry Armstrong: The Fantasy Tale of the Tape," Bleacher Report, February 2, 2011, http://bleacherreport.com/articles/594397-manny-pacquiao-vs-henry-armstrong-the-fantasy-tale-of-the-tape.

Chapter 57

1. "Joe Montana," Pro Football Reference, https://www.pro-football-reference.com/players/M/MontJo01.htm.

2. Larry Schwartz, "No Ordinary Joe," ESPN, http://www.espn.com/classic/montana_joe.html.

3. "Joe Montana," Pro Football Reference.

Chapter 58

1. Andrew Eisele, "Mike Tyson: Fight-by-Fight Record," ThoughtCo, https://www.thoughtco.com/mike-tyson-career-record-424338.

2. Jabber Head, "Mike Tyson: His Childhood and Early Boxing Years," Bleacher Report, November 21, 2010, http://bleacherreport.com/articles/523260-boxing-mike-tyson-and-the-early-years.

3. "Mike Tyson—Six Degrees of Devastation," My Boxing Coach, August 28, 2012, https://www.myboxingcoach.com/mike-tyson.

Chapter 59

1. Larry Schwartz, "Butkus Was One Mean Bear," ESPN, https://www.espn.com/sportscentury/features/00014131.html.

2. Dan Jenkins, "A Special Kind of Brute with a Love of Violence," *Sports Illustrated*, October 12, 1984, http://www.si.com/vault/1964/10/12/612597/a-special-kind-of-brute-with-a-love-of-violence.

3. Schwartz, "Butkus Was One Mean Bear."

Chapter 60

1. Tracy Caulkins," Sports Reference: Olympic Sports, https://www.sports-reference.com/olympics/athletes/ca/tracy-caulkins-1.html.

2. "Tracy Caulkins Biography," JRank.org, http://sports.jrank.org/pages/850/Caulkins-Tracy.html.

3. Braden Keith, "Legends of the Pool," Swim Swam, August 10, 2010, https://swimswam.com/legends-of-the-pool-tracy-caulkins-the-most-underrated-swimmer-ever.

Chapter 61

1. Liam Boylan-Pett, "20 Years Ago, Michael Johnson Set a New Gold Standard for Speed," SB Nation, July 20, 2016, https://www.sbnation.com/2016/7/20/12212298/michael-johnson-200-meter-record-gold-cleats-olympics-usa.

2. "Michael Johnson," USA Track and Field, http://www.usatf.org/athletes/bios/TrackAndFieldArchive/2001/Johnson_Michael.asp.

3. Helena de Bertodano, "Michael Johnson: 'For Eight Years, I Was a Five-Time Gold Medalist. Then It Was Four-Time. It's Not the Same,'" *Telegraph* [UK], July 9, 2012, http://www.telegraph.co.uk/sport/olympics/athletics/9378922/Michael-Johnson-For-eight-years-I-was-a-five-time-gold-medallist.-Then-it-was-four-time.-Its-not-the-same.html.

4. Dr. Liam Hennessy, "Physical Characteristics of Sprinters and Runners," Setanta College, https://www.setantacollege.com/physical-characteristics-sprinters-runners.

Chapter 62

1. "Bob Beamon's World Record long Jump—1968 Olympics," YouTube, January 21, 2010, https://www.youtube.com/watch?v=DEt_Xgg8dzc.

2. Larry Schwartz, "Beamon Made Sport's Greatest Leap," ESPN, https://www.espn.com/sportscentury/features/00014092.html.

3. Ibid.

Chapter 63

1. Bill Simmons, "The Legacy of Oscar Robertson," Grantland, March 15, 2012, http://grantland.com/features/the-big-o-had-plenty-game-plenty-chips-shoulder.

2. "Oscar Robertson Bio," NBA.com, http://www.nba.com/history/players/robertson_bio.html.

3. "Oscar Robertson," Basketball Reference, https://www.basketball-reference.com/players/r/roberos01.html.

4. Simmons, "The Legacy of Oscar Robertson."

Chapter 64

1. "Mike Schmidt," Baseball Reference, https://www.baseball-reference.com/players/s/schmimi01.shtml.

2. "Mike Schmidt: From Unremarkable to Exceptional," JRank.org, http://sports.jrank.org/pages/4285/Schmidt-Mike-From-Unremarkable-Exceptional.html.

3. "Mike Schmidt," Baseball Reference.

Chapter 65

1. "Larry Bird," Basketball Reference, https://www.basketball-reference.com/players/b/birdla01.html.

2. Marty Gitlin, *Powerful Moments in Sports: The Most Significant Sporting Events in American History* (Lanham, MD: Rowman and Littlefield, 2017), chap. 18

3. Ira Berkow, "Bird Does the Best He Can," *New York Times*, April 25, 1982, http://www.nytimes.com/1982/04/25/sports/bird-does-the-best-he-can.html.

Chapter 66

1. "Lindsey Vonn," Team USA, https://www.teamusa.org/us-ski-and-snowboard/athletes/Lindsey-Vonn.

2. Lindsey Vonn and Marc Myers, "Skier Lindsey Vonn: Before Alpine Peaks, a Cozy Basement," *Wall Street Journal*, October 4, 2016, https://www.wsj.com/articles/skier-lindsey-vonn-before-alpine-peaks-a-cozy-basement-1475594406.

3. Gordy Megroz, "Lindsey Vonn Needs a Nap, but First She Is Going to Become the Best Ski Racer of All Time," *Ski*, December 21, 2016, https://www.skimag.com/ski-performance/vonn-needs-nap.

Chapter 67

1. "Karl Malone," Basketball Reference, https://www.basketball-reference.com/players/m/malonka01.html.

2. "Karl Malone," Hollywood Politics, http://www.hollywoodpolitics.us/karl-malone.html.

3. Charley Rosen, "Who's Mr. Clutch?" ESPN, http://www.espn.com/page2/s/rosen/030501.html.

Chapter 68

1. "Mike Trout," Baseball Reference, https://www.baseball-reference.com/players/t/troutmi01.shtml.

2. Tom Verducci, "Kid Dynamite," *Sports Illustrated*, August 27, 2012, https://www.si.com/vault/2012/08/27/106225913/kid-dynamite.

3. Alden Gonzalez, "N.J. Hometown Maintains Love Affair with Trout," MLB.com, January 30, 2013, https://www.mlb.com/news/c-41253024.

4. "Mike Trout," Baseball Reference.

Chapter 69

1. Curry Kirkpatrick, "Lights! Camera! Cheryl!" *Sports Illustrated*, November 20, 1985, https://www.si.com/vault/1985/11/20/638247/lights-camera-cheryl.

2. "Cheryl Miller," Sports Reference, https://www.sports-reference.com/olympics/athletes/mi/cheryl-miller-1.html.

3. "Cheryl Miller," Riverside Sports Hall of Fame, https://www.riverside sporthalloffame.com/cheryl-miller.

4. David Woods, "Who Is the Greatest Women's Basketball Player Ever?" *USA Today*, July 16, 2014, https://www.usatoday.com/story/sports/basketball/2014/07/16/tamika-catchings-lisa-leslie-ann-meyers-diana-taurasi-cheryl-miller-greatest-women-players/12756509.

5. Kirkpatrick, "Lights! Camera! Cheryl!"

Chapter 70

1. "Mark Spitz," Sports Reference: Olympic Sports, https://www.sports-reference.com/olympics/athletes/sp/mark-spitz-1.html.

2. M. B. Roberts, "Spitz Lived Up to Enormous Expectations," ESPN, https://www.espn.com/sportscentury/features/00016480.html.

Chapter 71

1. Elena Dockterman, "Tony Hawk Wants Skateboarding to Be Part of the Olympics," *Time*, September 30, 2015, http://time.com/4056689/tony-hawk-skateboarding-2020-tokyo-olympics.

2. Official Tony Hawk, http://www.tonyhawk.com.

3. Ibid.

4. Tim Layden, "What Is This Man Doing on a Skateboard? Making Millions," *Sports Illustrated*, September 2, 2015, https://www.si.com/edge/2015/09/02/si-vault-tony-hawk-tim-layden-skateboarding.

Chapter 72

1. "Williams vs. DiMaggio," Tyler's Think Tank, June 15, 2014, http://tylers thinktank.blogspot.com/2014/06/williams-vs-dimaggio.html.

2. "Joe DiMaggio," Baseball Reference, https://www.baseball-reference.com/players/d/dimagjo01.shtml.

3. Lawrence Baldassaro, "Joe DiMaggio," Society for American Baseball Research, http://sabr.org/bioproj/person/a48f1830.

4. "Joe DiMaggio," Baseball Reference.

5. "Williams vs. DiMaggio," Tyler's Think Tank.

6. "Joe DiMaggio," Baseball Reference.

Chapter 73

1. Jane Johnson Lewis, "Peggy Fleming: Olympic Gold Medal Figure Skater," ThoughtCo, May 15, 2017, https://www.thoughtco.com/peggy-fleming-3529087.

2. "Peggy Fleming: Thrown into the Spotlight," JRank.org, http://sports.jrank.org/pages/1483/Fleming-Peggy-Thrown-into-Spotlight.html.

3. Peggy Fleming," Sports Reference: Olympic Sports, https://www.sports-reference.com/olympics/athletes/fl/peggy-fleming-1.html.

4. Lewis, "Peggy Fleming."

5. Lloyd Garrison, "The Ballerina on Skates," *New York Times*, February 10, 1968, http://www.nytimes.com/packages/html/sports/year_in_sports/02.10.html.

Chapter 74

1. "Walter Johnson," Baseball Reference, https://www.baseball-reference.com/players/j/johnswa01.shtml.

2. Charles Carey, "Walter Johnson," Society for American Baseball Research, http://sabr.org/bioproj/person/0e5ca45c.

3. Ibid.

Chapter 75

1. "Barry Sanders," Pro Football Reference, https://www.pro-football-reference.com/players/S/SandBa00.htm.

2. "Barry Sanders Biography," JRank.org, http://biography.jrank.org/pages/2822/Sanders-Barry.html.

Chapter 76

1. Daniel Ginsburg, "Ty Cobb," Society for American Baseball Research, http://sabr.org/bioproj/person/7551754a.

2. "Ty Cobb," Baseball Reference, https://www.baseball-reference.com/players/c/cobbty01.shtml.

3. Daniel Ginsburg, "Ty Cobb."

4. Ibid.

Chapter 77

1. "Bonnie Blair," Sports Reference: Olympic Sports, https://www.sports-reference.com/olympics/athletes/bl/bonnie-blair-1.html.

2. "Bonnie Blair—The Winter Olympian of the Century," Olympics 30, http://www.olympics30.com/30greatest/bonnie-blair-speed-skating.asp.

3. Ibid.

Chapter 78

1. Marty Gitlin, *Powerful Moments in Sports* (Lanham, MD: Rowman and Littlefield, 2017), 159.

2. "Secretariat," National Museum of Racing and Hall of Fame, https://www.racingmuseum.org/hall-of-fame/secretariat.

3. Ibid.

Chapter 79

1. "Rocky Marciano," Boxing Record, http://boxrec.com/en/boxer/9032.

2. Ed Fitzgerald, "Rocky Marciano—The Blockbuster from Brockton," *Sport*, January 1953, https://web.archive.org/web/20090502012324/http://www.thesportgallery.com/rockymarciano2.html.

3. Monte D. Cox, "Rocky Marciano: Is He a Top 5 All Time Heavyweight?" Cox's Corner, http://coxscorner.tripod.com/rocky.html.

4. Ibid.

Chapter 80

1. "Classic Tailback: Red Grange Illinois Highlights," YouTube, October 5, 2016, https://www.youtube.com/watch?v=0ieIbClaB84.

2. "Why Every Football Fan Should Know Red Grange," *Daily Herald*, September 4, 2008, http://prev.dailyherald.com/story/?id=231974.

3. "About Harold 'Red' Grange," Red Grange Collection, Wheaton College Archives and Special Collections, https://web.archive.org/web/20071008023624/http://www.wheaton.edu/learnres/ARCSC/collects/sc20/bio.htm.

Chapter 81

1. Kevin Allen, "Chris Chelios: 100 Greatest Hockey Players," NHL.com, January 1, 2017, https://www.nhl.com/news/chris-chelios-100-greatest-nhl-hockey-players/c-285364680.

2. "Chris Chelios," Hockey Reference, https://www.hockey-reference.com/players/c/chelich01.html.

3. Allen, "Chris Chelios."

4. "Chris Chelios Biography," Legends of Hockey, http://www.legendsofhockey.net/LegendsOfHockey/jsp/LegendsMember.jsp?mem=p201301&page=bio.

5. Jason Kay, "Top 10 American Players of All Time—From Brett Hull to Jeremy Roenick," *Hockey News*, July 4, 2014, http://www.thehockeynews.com/news/article/top-10-american-players-of-all-time-from-brett-hull-to-jeremy-roenick.

Chapter 82

1. "Chris Evert Bio," International Tennis Hall of Fame, https://www.tennisfame.com/hall-of-famers/inductees/chris-evert.
2. Ibid.

Chapter 83

1. Frank Litsky, "Al Oerter, Olympic Discus Champion, Is Dead at 71," *New York Times*, October 2, 2007, http://www.nytimes.com/2007/10/02/sports/othersports/02oerter.html.
2. "Al Oerter," Sports Reference: Olympic Sports, https://www.sports-reference.com/olympics/athletes/oe/al-oerter-1.html.
3. Litsky, "Al Oerter, Olympic Discus Champion, Is Dead at 71."
4. "Throwing Events," Talk Athletics, http://www.talk-athletics.co.uk/guides/athletics_throwing_events.html.

Chapter 84

1. "Mary T. Meagher," Sports Reference: Olympic Sports, https://www.sports-reference.com/olympics/athletes/me/mary-t-meagher-1.html.
2. Meredith Hargis, "Catching Up with 1984 Olympic Gold Medalist Mary T. Meagher," *Louisville*, July 12, 2016, https://www.louisville.com/content/catching-1984-olympic-gold-medalist-mary-plant.
3. "Mary T. Meagher," Sports Reference: Olympic Sports.
4. Frank Litsky, "Mary T. Meagher's Subtle Imperfections," *New York Times*, July 1, 1984, http://www.nytimes.com/1984/07/01/sports/mary-t-meagher-s-subtle-imperfections.html.

Chapter 85

1. "Lisa Leslie—First Women's Dunk," YouTube, September 14, 2007, https://www.youtube.com/watch?v=-xjMFRfX4MY.
2. "Lisa Leslie," Sports Reference: Olympic Sports, https://www.sports-reference.com/olympics/athletes/le/lisa-leslie-1.html.
3. "Lisa Leslie," Basketball Reference, https://www.basketball-reference.com/wnba/players/l/leslili01w.html.
4. Connor Ennis, "Athlete Bio: Lisa Leslie," *New York Times*, July 26, 2008, http://www.nytimes.com/2008/07/26/sports/olympics/bioleslie.html.

5. Lonnie White, "Morningside's Leslie Scores 101 in One Half: Girls' Basketball; She Is Initially Credited with Record-Tying 105, but Game Officially Ends When Opponents Refuse to Play," *Los Angeles Times*, February 8, 1990, http://articles.latimes.com/1990–02–08/sports/sp-572_1_scoring-record.

Chapter 86

1. "O. J. Simpson," Pro Football Reference, https://www.pro-football-reference.com/players/S/SimpO.00.htm.
2. Larry Schwartz, "Before Trial, Simpson Charmed America," ESPN, http://www.espn.com/sportscentury/features/00016472.html.
3. "O. J. Simpson," Pro Football Reference.
4. Joe Marshall, "Now You See Him, Now You Don't," *Sports Illustrated*, October 29, 1973, https://www.si.com/vault/1973/10/29/618411/now-you-see-him-now-you-dont.
5. Mal Florence, "The USC 440-Relay Team That Secured a Place in History: 20 Years Ago Today, Trojans Burned Track," *Los Angeles Times*, June 17, 1987, http://articles.latimes.com/1987–06–17/sports/sp-4512_1_years-ago-today.

Chapter 87

1. "Billie Jean King," Tennis Hall of Fame, https://www.tennisfame.com/hall-of-famers/inductees/billie-jean-king.
2. Marty Gitlin, *Billie Jean King: Tennis Star and Social Activist* (North Mankato, MN: ABDO, 2011), 17–19.
3. Ibid, 17–19.

Chapter 88

1. "Wilma Rudolph, 1940–1994: 'The Fastest woman in the World,'" ManyThings.org, http://www.manythings.org/voa/people/Wilma_Rudolph.html.
2. Miranda Bain, "Biography: Wilma Rudolph—Athlete," The Heroine Collective, March 17, 2016, http://www.theheroinecollective.com/wilma-rudolph.

Chapter 89

1. "Things You Probably Didn't Know about Kelly Slater," SurferToday, https://www.surfertoday.com/surfing/13035-things-you-probably-didnt-know-about-kelly-slater.
2. Hillard Grossman, "Brevard's Own Kelly Slater: Surfing Superman, Regular Guy," *Florida Today*, May 25, 2002, https://web.archive.org/web/20060701070402/http://www.floridatoday.com/%21NEWSROOM/special/surfing/localcoverage/052902slaterprofile.htm.

3. "Surfers = Athletes?" Surf Strength Coach, https://surfstrengthcoach.com/surfers-athletes.

Chapter 90

1. "Johnny Unitas," Pro Football Reference, https://www.pro-football-reference.com/players/U/UnitJo00.htm.

2. David Ginsburg, "Unitas: Grits, Guts, and Surprising Athletic Ability," Louisville Athletics, September 11, 2002, http://gocards.com/news/2002/9/11/Johnny_Unitas_Dead_At_69.aspx.

3. Frank Litsky, "Johnny Unitas, NFL's Genius of the Huddle, Dies at 69," *New York Times*, September 12, 2002, http://www.nytimes.com/2002/09/12/sports/johnny-unitas-nfl-s-genius-of-the-huddle-dies-at-69.html.

4. "Johnny Unitas," Pro Football Reference.

5. Ginsburg, "Unitas."

Chapter 91

1. John F. Paciorek, *The Principle of Baseball: All There Is to Know about Hitting and More* (Bloomington, IN: Balboa Press, 2012), 150.

2. "Ted Williams," Baseball Reference, https://www.baseball-reference.com/players/w/willite01.shtml.

3. "Ted Williams Bio," ESPN, http://www.espn.com/mlb/player/bio/_/id/28096/ted-williams.

4. Ibid.

5. "Ted Williams," Baseball Reference.

6. Ibid.

Chapter 92

1. Bill Plaschke, "Greg Louganis Remembers the 1988 Dive That Made History," *Los Angeles Times*, September 12, 2013, http://articles.latimes.com/2013/sep/12/sports/la-sp-plaschke-louganis-20130913.

2. "Greg Louganis," Sports Reference: Olympic Sports, https://www.sports-reference.com/olympics/athletes/lo/greg-louganis-1.html.

3. "Greg Louganis," IMDB, http://www.imdb.com/name/nm0005163/bio.

4. "Which Sport Requires the Most Athleticism?" Examined Existence, https://examinedexistence.com/which-sport-requires-the-most-athleticism.

Chapter 93

1. Glenn DuPaul, "Josh Gibson: A Legend in Every Sense of the Word," SB Nation, March 29, 2012, https://www.beyondtheboxscore.com/2012/3/29/2909312/josh-gibson-legend.

2. Bill Johnson, "Josh Gibson," Society for American Baseball Research, https://sabr.org/bioproj/person/df02083c.

3. "Josh Gibson," Baseball Hall of Fame, https://baseballhall.org/hall-of-famers/gibson-josh.

Chapter 94

1. Associated Press, "Moses' Streak Is Ended at 122," *New York Times*, June 5, 1987, http://www.nytimes.com/1987/06/05/sports/moses-streak-is-ended-at-122.html.

2. "Edwin Moses," Sports Reference: Olympic Sports, https://www.sports-reference.com/olympics/athletes/mo/edwin-moses-1.html.

3. Oliver Irish, "Do You Remember When . . . Ed Moses Was Almost Invincible," *Guardian* [UK], May 31, 2003, https://www.theguardian.com/sport/2003/jun/01/athletics.features2.

4. Curry Kirkpatrick, "The Man Who Never Loses," *Sports Illustrated*, July 30, 1984, https://www.si.com/vault/1984/07/30/620185/the-man-who-never-loses.

Chapter 95

1. "Jack Nicklaus," World Golf Hall of Fame, http://www.worldgolfhalloffame.org/jack-nicklaus.

2. Ibid.

3. Ibid.

4. "Jack Nicklaus Biography," The Famous People, https://www.thefamouspeople.com/profiles/jack-nicklaus-3466.php.

Chapter 96

1. "Rogers Hornsby," Baseball Reference, https://www.baseball-reference.com/players/h/hornsro01.shtml.

2. C. Paul Rogers III, "Rogers Hornsby," Society for American Baseball Research, https://sabr.org/bioproj/person/b5854fe4.

3. Ibid.

4. "Rogers Hornsby," Baseball Reference.

Chapter 97

1. "Florence Griffith Joyner," Sports Reference: Olympic Sports, https://www.sports-reference.com/olympics/athletes/gr/florence-griffith-joyner-1.html.

2. Jere Longman, "Florence Griffith Joyner, 38, Champion Sprinter, Is Dead," *New York Times*, September 22, 1998, http://www.nytimes.com/1998/09/22/sports/florence-griffith-joyner-38-champion-sprinter-is-dead.html.

3. "Florence Griffith Joyner: Fastest Woman on Earth," Legacy.com, http://www.legacy.com/news/celebrity-deaths/article/florence-griffith-joyner-fastest-woman-on-earth.

4. Longman, "Florence Griffith Joyner, 38, Champion Sprinter, Is Dead."

Chapter 98

1. Mark Emmert, "Assist from Sister Sends Gabby Douglas to London," *USA Today*, July 2, 2012, https://usatoday30.usatoday.com/sports/olympics/london/gymnastics/story/2012–07–02/Gabby-Douglas-Olympics-gymnastics-London/55988698/1.

2. "Gabby Douglas," Sports Reference: Olympic Sports, https://www.sports-reference.com/olympics/athletes/do/gabby-douglas-1.html.

3. Juliet Macur, "A Very Long Journey Was Very Swift," *New York Times*, August 2, 2012, http://www.nytimes.com/2012/08/03/sports/olympics/gabby-douglas-of-united-states-wins-gymnastics-all-around.html.

4. Liz Clarke, "Olympic Gymnastics: Has Athleticism Overtaken Artistry and Joy?" *Washington Post*, August 1, 2012, https://www.washingtonpost.com/sports/olympics/olympic-gymnastics-has-athleticism-overtaken-artistry-and-joy/2012/08/01/gJQAIQxPQX_story.html.

Chapter 99

1. "The Most Important Basketball Player You've Never Heard Of," Fountain City Frequency, December 18, 2017, http://fountaincityfrequency.com/archiver podcast/2017/12/18/the-most-important-basketball-player-youve-never-heard-of.

2. "Lynette Woodard," Kansas Historical Society, https://www.kshs.org/kansapedia/lynette-woodard/12244.

3. "Lynette Woodard," Sports Reference: Olympic Sports, https://www.sports-reference.com/olympics/athletes/wo/lynette-woodard-1.html.

4. "The Most Important Basketball Player You've Never Heard Of," Fountain City Frequency.

5. "Games of the XXIIIrd Olympiad—1984," USA Basketball, December 21, 2011, https://www.usab.com/history/national-team-womens/games-of-the-xxiiird-olympiad-1984.aspx.

6. Ibid.

Chapter 100

1. "Tiger Woods Tournament Results," ESPN, http://www.espn.com/golf/player/results/_/id/462/tiger-woods.

2. "Tiger Woods," Official World Golf Ranking, http://www.owgr.com/en/Ranking/PlayerProfile.aspx?playerID=5321.

3. "Which Sport Requires the Most Athleticism?" Examined Existence, https://examinedexistence.com/which-sport-requires-the-most-athleticism.

INDEX

ABOUT THE AUTHOR

Martin Gitlin is a sports and pop culture book author based in Cleveland. He has won more than forty-five writing awards as a newspaper sportswriter, including first place for general excellence from the Associated Press in 1996 for his coverage of the 1995 World Series. That organization also selected him as one of the top four feature writers (sports or otherwise) in Ohio in 2001. Gitlin turned his attention to freelance writing in 2002 and has had about 140 books published since 2006, including *The Greatest Sitcoms of All Time* (Scarecrow Press, 2013), *The Greatest College Rivalries of All Time* (Rowman & Littlefield, 2014), and the highly acclaimed *Powerful Moments in Sports: The Most Significant Sporting Events in American History* (Rowman & Littlefield, 2017).